The Extent of the Literal

Metaphor, Polysemy and Theories of Concepts

Marina Rakova

著作权合同登记　图字：01-2004-0798
图书在版编目(CIP)数据

字面意义的疆域：隐喻、一词多义以及概念理论／(英)拉科娃(Rakova, M.)著.—影印本.—北京：北京大学出版社，2004.9
(西方语言学原版影印系列丛书·2)
ISBN 7-301-06878-6

Ⅰ.字… Ⅱ.拉… Ⅲ.字面意义-研究-英文 Ⅳ.H030

中国版本图书馆 CIP 数据核字(2004)第 072128 号

Reprinted by permission of Palgrave Publishers Ltd ©2003

书　　　名：	The Extent of the Literal: Metaphor, Polysemy and Theories of Concepts
	字面意义的疆域：隐喻、一词多义以及概念理论
著作责任者：	〔英〕Marina Rakova 著
责 任 编 辑：	李　颖
标 准 书 号：	ISBN 7-301-06878-6/H·0957
出 版 发 行：	北京大学出版社
地　　　址：	北京市海淀区成府路 205 号　100871
网　　　址：	http://cbs.pku.edu.cn
电　　　话：	邮购部 62752015　发行部 62750672　编辑部 62767347
电 子 信 箱：	zbing@pup.pku.edu.cn
印 刷 者：	北京飞达印刷有限责任公司
经 销 者：	新华书店
	890 毫米×1240 毫米　A5　8.25 印张　290 千字
	2004 年 9 月第 1 版　2006 年 12 月第 3 次印刷
定　　　价：	20.00 元

未经许可，不得以任何方式复制或抄袭本书之部分或全部内容。
版权所有，翻版必究

总 序

胡壮麟

"西方语言学原版影印系列丛书"是北京大学出版社外语编辑部建立以来的一个新产品，具有重大意义。随着国内高等教育的发展，这几年来本科生、硕士生和博士生的招生名额都扩大了，教材建设再次提上了日程。除组织国内老师自行编写外，从国外直接引进仍不失为一个有效途径。语言学是一门领先科学，因此本丛书的有些内容对其他专业的老师和学生、研究者，甚至业余学习者也有很高参考价值。例如，像有关语料库、认知语言学的著作除外语老师外，计算科学、统计学、认知科学、词典编辑等专业的研究人员和师生也有一读之必要。

北大版"西方语言学原版影印系列丛书"的问世是意料中的事。早在 2002 年 1 月北京大学出版社已出版过"西方语言学丛书"，从剑桥大学出版社引进了六卷本《英语语言史》，Robert D. van Valin 和 Randy J. Lapolla 的《句法：结构、意义与功能》，Andres Radford 的《最简方案：句法理论与英语结构》……共七种，在外语界独树一帜。经过两三年的摸索，经验更丰富了，视野更扩大了。这表现在选题方面语言学和应用语言学并重，这更符合研究生专业目录中有关"语言学和应用语言学"的基本要求。我们的学生既要有理论知识，也要有如何运用有关理论的知识，只有这样，才能将所学的专业知识更好地为国家建设服务。

另一点值得我们考虑的是，全面掌握语言学和应用语言学的专业知识固然是保证教学质量的一个方面，我们还要让高等学校的学生经常站在本学科的前沿，接触本学科的最新成果，掌握本学科的最新动向。这也是保证教材质量，从而保证所培养学生质量的一个重要方面。因此，本丛书既引进有关学科在各时期的经典著作，更注意引进 21 世纪的新著。长江后浪推前浪，许多经典著作最初也是以新著的形式问世的，其作者的年龄往往属于新生代。因此，时代意识是本系列丛书的一大特征。

为了实现这一目标，本丛书采取灵活的出版发行方式，既可系统成套出版，也可成熟一本，出版一本。这样，只要国外有好的新著出版，北京大学出版社根据该书的质量和国内的需要，及时引进。这在信息爆炸的今天，尤为重要。我们还认为，这套丛书的建设与广大读者的监督和支持是分不开的。我们欢迎读者对本丛书不足之处提出宝贵意见，我们更欢迎读者和业内行家向我们推荐有引进价值的著作！

2004 年 5 月
北京大学蓝旗营

导　读※

　　李　杰

一、概　述

　　一词多义(polysemy)在任何语言中都是很普遍的现象。一个形式所具有的多种意义间的关系一直吸引众多语言学家的关注。Bolinger认为："语言的自然状况应是一个词形一种意义，一种意义一个词形"(转引自Hopper and Traugott 1995:71)。根据这种观点，最理想的语言应该是每一个词的意义都非常明显，毫无歧义。然而，这样的语言是不可能存在的，也是行不通的，因为一个人的大脑要记住这么多意义的每一个词形似乎是不可能的。虽然任何一个词在刚产生的时候总是用来指称某一特定的事物或现象，然而随着社会的发展，如果每一个事物或现象都用特定的词汇来指代，给每一个义项都设立一个独立的词项，就会非常困难。过多的词汇既不利于记忆，也不利于交流。因此，不可避免地出现了一词多义的现象。

　　一词多义的现象一直是语言学家研究的重要课题。传统意义上的语义学的研究对象主要局限在词的层面上。因此在从语义学这门学科建立之始，学者们就已经注意到了对一词多义现象的研究。有语义学创始人之称的 M.Bréal 认为，多义词是语言经济的结果，要想给每一个义

　　※　承蒙姜望琪教授阅读本文，先生对行文和结构方面提出了宝贵的意见。谨表衷心感谢！

　　本书作者 Marina Rakova 现为 St. Petersburg 大学的讲师，主要教授英文和哲学。先后在英国爱丁堡大学取得语言学硕士和博士学位，后来又去墨西哥的 Universidad Nacional Autónoma de México 从事博士后研究。此书是在其博士论文的基础上发展而成的。

项都设立一个独立的词项是不可能的（转引自龚放 1998）。Katz & Fodor（1963）认为，语义应由与句法结构有别的语言形式描述层面来表达，用作句子分析的叫"语义表征"（semantic representation）或"语义结构"（semantic structure），用于词项分析的叫做"语义特征"（semantic feature）。这一语言结构层面通过投射规则与句法结构联系起来，即每一句法规则都有一语义规则与之相对应（Jackendoff 1983:10，转引自章宜华 2002:150—151）。该理论还基于词组间的类似性，试图解释大量潜在的意义对照。Katz & Postal（1964:13）指出，对词义的完全分析必须包括将意义分解成最基本的成分（转引自王寅 2001：111）。他们在分析词语的"语义"时，常常把这些词语的语义分解成"语义成分"进行比较。比如，可以用"语义成分"来衡量某一个短语是否有意义或是否可以接受；只要分析构成某个短语的各个单词的"语义成分"就可"推知"这个短语的意义。然而这种语法规则还不足以揭示自然语言的语义（章宜华 2002:150—151）。

　　语义学研究领域的一个重要成果便是语义场理论(Theory of Semantic Field)。该理论是20世纪30年代由德国语言学家 J. Trier 等人受到 Saussure 结构主义语言学的影响所创立的理论模式。语义场理论主要系统论述了各种涵义关系（sense relations），在理论上和方法上都是对传统语义学的重大突破（王寅 2001:17）。根据 Trier 的观点，语义场指的是由一组有共同义素的语言单位构成的结构系统，代表着相同的范畴概念，即"场"（章宜华 2002：51）。Trier 还认为语言词汇中的词在语义上是互相联系的，它们共同构成一个完整的词汇系统，不应该孤立地研究单个词的语义变化，应通过分析、比较词与词之间的语义关系，确定一个词的真正涵义。词只有作为"整体中的一部分"才有它自己的"词义"，词只有在"语义场"中才有意义。语义场理论把一词多义现象看成多义结构，认为多义场是历时演变为共时的语义网络。其扩充和结构受制于语言的普遍规律和个别规律，特别是词义的演变规则。这个多义结构是以一个核心义位（本义或基本义）为中心，含有一个或几个共同义素的，带有整体性的语义聚合体（张志毅、张庆云 2001：95）。另外，由于各个"语义场"是分开研究的，而且，对各个语义场之间的语义联系未能作直接的解释；再者，语义场理论的核心是探讨上位词统辖下的下位词间或类概念统辖下的种概念间的关系（张志毅、张庆云 2001:81）。显然，一词多义现象在语义场理论中不可能得到很好的解释。

　　认知语言学提出应结合人们的基本认知能力来系统地研究语言。Langacker(1987,1991)认为：一个词语的若干意义或义项构成了一个有层次的语义结构或网络。王寅认为我们不仅可以通过研究这些微系统来逐步了解语言大系统，而且还可以了解人类的认知过程（2001:212）。Johnson(1987)认为语义理论除了研究句子的真值条件外，还应研究范畴化问题、图式、隐喻、转喻等等。认知语义学家们也试图将原型理论和范畴理论的主要观点用于词汇的一词多义的分析和解释。Taylor 在《语言的范畴化:语言学理论中的类典型》一书中对一些常用的英语词汇的语义范畴的一词多义现象有不少令人称道的精辟分析。他指出，大多数的语言范畴呈现出的不是单一的中心结构(mono-centric structure)，而是多中心的结构(polycentric structure)。它们通常表现出多个原型，这些原型通过家族相似性互相连接(Taylor 1995:99)。Taylor 赞成 Wittgenstein 提出的"家族相似性原理"，并将这一原理通过隐喻等方式使原型子范畴发生联系，形成了意义链(meaning chain)而构建起来家族相似性范畴(family resemblance category)。Taylor 还认为，从认知语言学的角度出发，多义词的词义范畴的特征是它拥有一个共同的"意义核心"(meaning core)，使得不同的多义项附属在同一个词汇上。认知语言学强调人的认知对概念形成的作用，认为多义现象是一个词语有多种具有互相联系意义的语言现象，其研究表明多义现象是通过人类认知手段(如隐喻、换喻)由一个词的中心意义或基本意义向其他意义延伸的过程，是人类认知范畴和概念化的结果(赵艳芳 2000:36)。隐喻已在很大程度上构成了人们的概念系统，决定着人们语言的运用，并成为多义词的丰富来源。从同一单词的不同意义之间的相关性可以得出结论：多义词不仅仅是语言经济原则的结果，更是隐喻认知的产物；换言之，隐喻认知对多义词的形成起着无可替代的作用。正如 Sweetser(1990:8)所归纳的那样，

"大多数的多义词是由于隐喻使用的结果。"

在《字面意义的疆域：隐喻、一词多义以及概念理论》一书中，作者 Marina Rakova 对"经典的"隐喻研究持怀疑态度，并认为认知语言学对隐喻的研究也没有解决多少问题。本书的开篇便直截了当地向区分"字面意义—隐喻意义"的设想提出质疑。作者把这种设想叫做"标准设想"(Standard Assumption)。标准设想认为多义词仅有一个意义是字面的或基本的。大多隐喻研究都赞同标准设想的观点，认为多义形容词只有一个意义是字面性的，其余都是隐喻意义。Rakova 认为，以往的隐喻理论大多主张从常规性、扩展的相同性或不依赖语境等方面来理解字面意义；但实际上这种主张不知不觉地预设了概念首要性（conceptual primacy）的观点。这种首要意义的概念在很大程度上依赖于某种概念首要的假设。如果说这种假设在传统的隐喻研究中比较含蓄的话，在认知语义学所提倡的概念隐喻理论中则被发挥得淋漓尽致了。所以，Rakova 认为认知语义学在很多方面也不是全新的东西，而是传统理论的一种自然延续。大多传统隐喻理论都赞成多义词只有一个意义属于字面意义的观点；在 Lakoff 和 Johnson 看来，概念是隐喻性地建构的，其结构是从最接近我们形象化体验中的一套非隐喻性概念派生而来的。因此认知语义学同样属于传统理论的一个翻版：承认多义词的首要意义，认为多义词的其他意义均属于隐喻意义或派生意义。Rakova 还指出了经验主义哲学的一些问题。经验主义者把着眼点放在了概念隐喻方面，而他们没有一个研究意义的理论（p.27）。这也就是为什么他们的观点并没有在认知科学领域，特别是哲学领域更为广泛地流行的原因（cf. Gibbs 1994:437）。经验主义者声称，"意义总是人类理解的问题"(Johnson 1987:174)，"意义基于经验的理解"(Lakoff 1988:150)，甚至说"我们体验意义"(Johnson & Lakoff 2002)。Marina Rakova 认为，这样的说法是不能算作意义理论的。尽管说概念同经验有明显的关系，但我们也不能说我们"体验"概念，更不能说"体验"意义。任何意义理论都必须提供规范性的概念（notion of normativity）(Marconi 1997)。因而在 Marina Rakova 看来，除了反复地说意义是被具体化的，抽象概念是通过概念隐喻来理解的,似乎经验主义者并没有告诉我们任何其他东西(p.28)。

但 Rakova 声明,本书的目的并非与隐喻研究作对,也不是想同任何理论为敌,而只是想对词汇、意义以及它们之间的关系作一些尝试性的探讨。她由此而提出了概念结构的非多义性的观点。非多义性观点的一个重要部分就是反对把意义和概念重合(conflate)起来。她认为,进一步的研究有可能证明或者推翻她所提出的这种观点,但任何研究必须要有一个全局的眼光:应该考虑到本书中涉及的神经学、神经语言学、心理学、心理物理学、心理语言学,以及有关跨语言的、儿童发育研究等方面的成果,甚至包括更广、更宽的研究领域。

二、内容介绍

该书探索了一条研究隐喻、一词多义现象及其与概念结构的关系的崭新之路。作者向认知语言学、词汇语义学及分析哲学理论框架范围内的有关隐喻研究提出了挑战,呼吁要对标准设想的有关字面意义的观点及其概念结构关系进行再思考。尽管作者的看法和他人大相径庭,但本书的内容并不空洞,阐述也不武断,作者运用了大量的神经生理学和心理学方面的实验数据来支撑自己的观点。作者文风质朴、娓娓道来,令人大有先睹为快之感。全书共有十一个章节,下面将作一一介绍:

第一章 引言:"字面意义—隐喻意义"区分的性质

作者在本章中概述了一些"经典的"隐喻理论,讨论了有关"字面意义—隐喻意义"区分的几种流行的观点,其目的是要给读者展示好多通常看来似乎不同的隐喻理论实际上存在很大的相似性,它们对隐喻的处理有表面化的倾向。如 I. A. Richards 在隐喻研究中有一种倾向,认为所有的语言都是"非常隐喻性的"。Richards 认为一个词的字面意义仅仅是用于表达一定的"经验次序"(orders of experience),而当意义和载体属于不同的经验次序的时候,我们就用隐喻了。Monroe Beardsley 提出了一种隐喻的"内涵理论"(intensional theory),指通过词汇标准意义的转换可以获得附加的隐喻意义。所有词汇都具有决定其适用域的标准意义,但任何词汇都可能成为一个句子或更大语言单位的"隐喻成分"。与 Beardsley 不同,Goodman 的隐喻理论是一种"外延理论"(extensional theory);隐喻在意义中产生一种变化,也就是说隐喻涉及"域的改变"(change of realm)。当词汇从常用的域转到新的域时就产生了隐喻。他也认为,由隐喻引起的词义转移获得了一种新的扩展。而 Donald Davidson 对隐喻意义持基本否定的态度;他认为,在严格意义上来讲,不存在隐喻意义的说法;语言是受制于规则的,而对隐喻的理解很少与规则有关,这就是为什么通常很难决定一个特定的隐喻的内容究竟是什么。他认为,隐喻不具有发话人想传达的"一个明确的认知内容"。隐喻使用者所说的并没有超出他所使用的字面意义。隐喻并不涉及意义而是使用(p.10)。

作者要阐明的是,我们谈论字面意义和隐喻意义的方式,特别是针对形容词的一词多义现象,被严重误导了!作者认为,不仅仅是我们的直觉能告诉我们,就是心理学方面的研究也确认了在我们思维中多义词词义之间的相关性,多义形容词只有一个首要意义的说法是站不住脚的(p.3)。

第二章 认知语言学中的隐喻

作者认为,尽管有许多重要的发现,包括具体化概念引入到一词多义现象和概念结构的讨论之中,概念隐喻的理论是不尽人意的。作者首先指出当今的很多隐喻研究都是在认知语言学的理论框架内进行的。Lakoff 和 Johnson 的理论是革命性的,他们的理论把众多的概念减少到通过隐喻来涵盖人类整个认知域的经验型基本概念(primitive concepts)。正如 Lakoff(1993)所言,那些被看成是经典的隐喻理论错在它们试图找到语言中控制隐喻使用的一般规律。隐喻语言的源头存在于思维中,在概念系统的组织结构中。隐喻被认为是基本的认知过程,是人们将经验和外部世界概念化的基本图式(basic schema)(Gibbs 1994:1)。概念隐喻的哲学基础是经验主义。不像许多其他概念理论,经验主义非常重视人类身体和感觉运动经验在认知和语言方面的作用。思维和语言不可能脱离我们人类本身而存在。感觉运动能力(sensorimotor capacity)构建了我们的经验,意象图式是我们在外部世界中身体运作的基本原则(如感知、空间运动、对物体的控制)。经验主义试图通过我们的具体化的体验对概念隐喻现象作出解释，但这两种东西是明显有区别的。也就难怪对 Lakoff 和 Johnson 的理论出现了许多不同的反应：一些语言学家几乎全般接受，而许多心理学家和哲学家却持怀疑的态度。

作者还指出了经验主义哲学的一些问题。隐喻性地建构概念的观点已经广泛地受到许多心理学家、语言学家和哲学家的批评；其中 Murphy 的批评最为激烈。Murphy（1996）认为，隐喻表述（隐喻结构概念的假设）的观点在心理学上是不可行的。隐喻体现的观点意味着我们会对隐喻结构域做出许多不正确的推论。对于 Lakoff & Johnson（1999）的神经形象化(neural embodiment) 的概念，Rakova 认为尽管她本人对形象化的概念持肯定态度，但问题是这一概念并不支持他们的概念隐喻的结构性。在解释神经形象化概念时，Lakoff & Johnson（1999）引用了 Christopher Johnson 的域重合理论（theory of domain conflation）(1997a,b)；该理论试图通过儿童早期发育的经验的相关性来解释一词多义现象。根据该理论，儿童对困难的概念化可以被缩影为他们对"大"物体的概念化。但并没有理由相信困难一开始就被概念化为大体积的东西。然而，儿童发育时期的域重合和域差异（domain conflation and domain differentiation）两个假设也没有能在儿童发育阶段对多义形容词的理解方面找到合适的证据。儿童至少在三岁时差别是存在的，他们排斥物质形容词的心理意义；稍后当他们理解了两种意义的时候，也仍然认为两种意义是独立的；而域重合阶段或能发现相似形阶段至少是在十岁左右了（p.30）。而且，研究还发现儿童对心理意义的获得并不依赖于对物质意义的获得（Asch and Nerlove，1960: Chapter 5）。

第三章 多义词 "Hot"

本章涉及形容词 "hot" 的多义性问题。在英语中这个词既用作表示"热感"也用作表示"味感"。作者采用神经生理学的研究成果来解释为什么我们会认为一些食物 "hot"，并说明我们对温度的感知和味觉的辛辣刺激都是以相同的机制为中介的。本章首先讨论了神经生理学同语义学的关系问题。作者引用的证据是 Brent Berlin & Paul Kay (1969) 对基本色彩词的研究成果。Eleanor Rosch （1974,1978; et al.)后来的研究也证明了Berlin & Kay的研究成果的正确性；Rosch 的结论是，色彩空间是一个表明知觉—认知因素对语言产生影响的很好例子。人类语言的色彩词不是任意划分光谱的，而是普遍受制于我们的视觉系统。语言发展时期对色彩词的习得阶段同我们的色彩分辨系统的形成阶段相吻合。有关色彩分辨问题最为广泛接受的理论是Hering (1920)的"对向肌理论"（the opponent theory）。该理论认为，在我们的视觉系统中，有两组神经元对不同光波的波长做出反应。不同语言中的基本颜色词，以及语言中表达这些词的方式，要受到我们视觉系统的神经生理方面的限制（Kay & Mcdaniel 1978; Boynton & Olson 1987）。在这个意义上，基本颜色词，甚至基本色彩范畴或概念，具有普遍性的特点，都是由我们的神经网络结构决定的。因此，我们的语言和概念结构同神经生理网络结构是有必然联系的。

第四章 交叉感知模式

本章讨论了联觉感知类形容词。人类们能够进行交叉感知联想（associations between different modalities），而且在解读联觉感知类形容词方面是惊人的相似。然而标准设想的理论却无法解释为什么人们对联觉感知类形容词的理解并不遵循刺激关联的模式。作者主张概念结构的非多义性的观点（no-polysemy view）。也就是说，联觉感知类多义形容词所有的意义都映射在同一心理基本概念（psychologically primitive concept）上。作者还强调非多义性的观点比标准设想更能很好地解释"物质性—物质性"（physical-physical）的多义词的情况。作者通过 Marks 等人的研究成果向读者展示：人们在把视觉感官刺激同听觉感官刺激相关联方面没有任何问题，同样的关联模式也存在于联觉感知与非联觉感知之间（Marks 1978）；很小的儿童在判断视觉刺激与听觉刺激的相似性方面是一致的，这说明交叉感知的相同性具有普遍意义，而且很可能是一种天生的感知属性（Marks & Bornstein 1987:62）；有些联觉感知隐喻出现在儿童发育早期，而另一些则来源于经验（p.55）。Wilkins 和 Wakefield 的进一步研究表明，人类，包括儿童在内，都能形成跨感官体（amodal）特征表述，而其他灵长类动物则不能。在此基础上 Wilkins 和 Wakefield 认为人类认知能力一个显著的特点便是具有跨情景概括出抽象属性的能力。在他们看来，这种能力很可能就是语言词汇化（lexicalization）的基础（p.71）。Wilkins 和 Wakefield 的另一个贡献是认为语言发生于表述能力和概念化能力的变化，而并非产生于不断增加的交际需要（p.72）。用 Derek Bickerton（1990:102）的话来说，"语言是一种表述外部世界的非常复杂的方式。"那么人类认知结构的建立是同知觉信息处理过程的重组相吻合的，其结果很可能就是使人类具有了抽象和表述感官输入的具体特征的能力。如果这样的假设成立的话，其结果便是针对概念的产生不只是同单个的感官体有关。联觉感知类形容词也许正是反映了我们概念结构的这种特点。

第五章 双功能形容词

基于跨语言的证据，作者表明把双功能形容词的生理意义看成隐喻意义是完全错误的。概念结构的非多义性的观点可以为联觉感知类形容词和双功能形容词提供一致的解释。Solomon Asch 在对双功能形容词的研究中发现大量的这类形容词可以同时用来表达物质的和心理的特征。在他 1955 年的研究中，他对一些在词源上和地域上毫无联系的语言中的双功能形容词进行了比较，如古希伯来语、汉语、泰语、马来语等（1955:31）。他的研究目的是想发现这些语言是否也使用同样的形容词来描述物质的和心理的特征，以及在不同的语言中双功能形容词的心理意义是否一致。其研究结果表明，所有这些语言中都有一些形容词既可表示物质意义也可表达心理意义；换言之，在不同的语言中这些形容词所表达的心理意义之间存在不可辩驳的相似性（p.76）。Asch 还就双功能形容词的问题在儿童身上作了一系列的实验，结果显示：双功能形容词的心理意义是独立习得的，同其所表示物质性意义没有联系（p.78）。

作者认为，联觉感知类形容词和双功能多义形容词映射在相应的心理基本概念上，而形容词本身并非是多义性的，如在 "deep water"、"deep grief" 中的 "deep" 一词就是映射在 DEEP 的心理基本概念上。我们暂且可以把心理基本概念看成组织有关我们的经验特征的信息的先天的模式(innate patterns)。作者认为，完全不同于标准设想的观点，概念结构的非多义性理论把多义形容词的心理意义同样看做非隐喻意义，而且这一说法已在跨语言的研究中找到了充足的证据。

第六章 再论双功能形容词

在本章中作者继续着同一话题。她首先从心理语言学实验中寻找证据。在作者看来，Williams的实验（1992）可以被借用来支持概念结构的非多义性的观点，因为Williams的实验结果强有力地表明多义形容词的各种意义之间既有相互关联性又有独立性。此外，目前一些涉及左右脑半球对意义处理的研究结果并不支持标准设想，而恰恰支持的是概念结构非多义性的观点（p.98）。现在神经生理学家们普遍承认，许多认知方面的任务都需要两个脑半球的参与。一些涉及语言的工作不仅依赖于左脑半球的功能，同时还涉及右脑半球。许多研究表明，右脑半球损伤会导致一些认知能力的丧失，而这样的认知能力正是组成语言交际的重要部分，包括幽默的产生与理解、情感、间接言语行为、将输入的话语组织成连贯的语篇的能力，等等（Burgess & Chiarello 1996; Paradis 1998）。

有一些研究结果显示（Tompkins 1990; Brownell, et al. 1984, 1990），右脑损伤的病人对不同意义的自动处理不受影响，同常人无异，只是速度不同而已(p.102)。Giora及同事们的研究并没有表明右脑损伤的人有理解隐喻方面的缺陷（Giora, et al. 1997），而恰恰相反的是，左脑损伤的人对理解隐喻性短语有一些困难（Zaidel 2002; Chobor & Schweiger 1998）。

Rakova的态度是，既然我们还没有找到充分的实验证据来支持，而又要下结论说词汇的某些意义会选择性地由右脑半球来表达（或者说当右脑半球受损后那种表达能力就被破坏了）就是极其荒唐的。换言之，既然还不能证明"字面意义—隐喻意义"的区别是否属于不同大脑半球的语义表达，我们就不能断言一词多义形容词仅有一个字面意义，而其他意义都是隐喻性地派生出来的。

第七章 词汇与概念

本章很短，仅仅作为一个联系实证研究和理论探索的纽带。作者勾画出了多义形容词及其概念之间可能存在的种种关系，并提出了一种现实的概念理论。概念是遇到一组声音或字母后被激活的心理实体，而一组组的声音或字母正是构成语言中意义单位的东西。也可以说概念是用来连接我们和外部世界的心理实体，而词汇是概念的名称，概念构成词汇的意义。

第八章 回到认知语义学

作者认为 Sweetser 的"以身喻心"的隐喻（mind-as-body metaphor）仍然不能令人满意，因为该理论并不能解释联觉感知类和双功能形容词的概念体现情况。Sweetser(1990)提出了通过隐喻映射连接内部感觉和外部感觉的"以身喻心"的概念隐喻。Sweetser坚持认为，语义演变是以相同的方式进行的——语义演变总是从具体的（物质性的和社会性的）意义到抽象的（情感的和心理的）意义，而且只有认知语义学能解释这种现象。但在Rakova看来，Sweetser的理论依据主要是语义演变的单向性以及在内部自我域和外部自我域之间（between the domains of external and internal self）存在大量的语义映射。

作者表示自己对"以身喻心"的概念隐喻持怀疑态度的原因在于，从词源学的角度来解释共时语义学的效度问题。而且，认知语义学坚持认为，"概念系统产生于日常经验"（Sweetser 1990:1）。Rakova反驳说，那么不清楚是什么因素让认知语义学家们确定一个人的内部世界或者说他/她的人际、社会关系不是其日常经验的一部分呢？实际上，一个人的日常经验也应该包括情感因素（cf. Damasio 1999），以及内省，而这些因素对好多概念都有直接的影响（cf. Barasalou 1999）。Sweetser（1990）认为，从物质意义到心理意义的映射也是单向性的。但作者的观点是，尽管在语法化的研究中大多承认单向性的存在，然而语义演变的情况同隐喻的情况是不同的。

认知语义学对语言中的联觉感知现象的解释是，"从更易理解"（accessible）的概念到不易理解的概念的语义映射似乎比其他任何解释要更加"自然"（Shen, Y. 1997）；Shen认为概念的易理解性（accessibility）主要由两个因素决定：一是感知与被感知实体之间的接触的直接性；二是是否存在特殊的感官体(p.113)。但问题是，Shen

并没有解释为什么某些听觉词汇比另一些听觉词汇更易于映射在视觉刺激上，为什么某些视觉词汇比另一些视觉词汇更易于映射在听觉刺激上（Marks et al 1987；参见 Chapter 4）。"易于理解性"的概念也是值得怀疑的：视觉如何就能比听觉更易于理解？

第九章　词汇语义学中的一词多义现象

在本章中，作者讨论了 Ray Jackendoff 和 James Pustejovsky，以及 Jerry Fodor 之间的争论。Jackendoff 在其《语义与认知》（*Semantics and Cognition*, 1983:18）一书中明确表示，语义理论必须对语法事实和认知心理负责。在 Jackendoff 看来，概念结构的成分要素就是语义的原始体现，这样的体现会跨越所有的概念域，而且能根据具体情景中多义词的不同使用产生复杂的体现。在本书的开始部分，Jackendoff 还以实例（如"keep"等词）阐述了采用概念结构来解释语义概括（semantic generalization）的理由。他的这一方法叫做"主题关系假说"（Thematic Relations Hypothesis），其优点是，允许通过单一范畴等手段进行跨越语义场范围的概括。在 Jackendoff 的《心智的语言》（1992）一书中又以更加简洁的方式再现了这一观点。但却遭到 Jerry Fodor 的猛烈攻击（1998a: 49—56）；Jerry 根本不相信结构概念这一说。如果把 Jerry 反对 Jackendoff 的理由放大来看的话，Rakova 认为 Jackendoff 的分解理论的问题根源在于没有假定足够的体现层面 (p.123)。Pustejovsky（1995: 55—57）提出了生成词库（generative lexicon）的概念，他认为对词汇在新语境中的理解不仅依赖背景知识，还有赖于词汇知识，即对词汇意义的了解。因此，要限制对词汇在一定语境下的意义理解，词汇体现中就得引进较大的内部结构。以多义词 BOOK 为例，它既指一个物质性的客体，也指书的内容。于是 Pustejovsky 还提出了比表达词汇条目的更为丰富的语义体现的主张，允许不同的词汇涵义重合在单一的元词条（meta-entry）中或词汇概念范畴中。正如 Pustejovsky（1998:291）所言，"由于语义特征（意义）随语境变化而变化，我们用同样的体现方式便可以适用于众多的目的。"

然而，尽管 Pustejovsky 和 Jackendoff 都似乎认为不能采用形式语义的方法来分析形容词的一词多义问题（p.128），但在他们看来，首要意义（primary meanings）毕竟是存在的(p.130)。 实际上，字面意义与隐喻意义的区别原原本本地保留在 Pustejovsky 的语义学理论中（p.131）。

第十章　非多义性的观点：内容界定

本章详尽地阐述了概念结构的非多义性的观点。作者指出，在前面的讨论中我们已看到"物质性—物质性"的一词多义属于不同感官体之间的表述转移（transfer of predicate），而这种表述转移不只是依赖于知觉联系，而有赖于我们的知觉运作。同样的机制既要负责检测热温感（hot）还要负责检测辛辣味感（hot），但我们能够将二者区分，并将差异概念化。这已有实验为证；即使是年龄较小的儿童也能够进行跨感官体的表述转移，这种转移既不以语义为中介，也不受制于刺激强度的相似性。Gerald Winner（2001）及其同事的最新研究成果进一步表明，人们对跨感官区域的表述转移的理解并非隐喻性的，而是汇合性的（syncretic）。Rakova 指出， 种种迹象表明，标准设想的概念结构的观点难以令人置信。至今还没有人讲得清楚为什么理解"sharp sound"中的 SHARP 是在理解"sharp knife"中的 SHARP 之后。"sharp sound"和"sharp knife" 同我们熟悉的隐喻的情况是不可相提并论的；如在"My job is a jail"中，我们能发现主题（topic）和喻体(vehicle)之间的共性。同认知语义学家冠以概念隐喻的那些一词多义的动词的情况也不一样（如"take a paragraph out of the text"）。

根据概念结构的非多义性的观点，诸如 BRIGHT, SHARP, COLD 等等这些概念都是横跨（spanning）所有感官经验域的心理基本概念（psychologically primitive concept）。它们的内容不能够进一步分解成更原始、更基本的（primitive）特征。我们可以把这些心理基本概念想像成针对一系列刺激的反应性的神经元结构。尽管心理概念结构和感知运作关系密切，其内容却不能被它详尽地加以表述。它们仅仅是表述系统中最基本的东西，是进一步处理来自不同感官体的刺激的内在机制。非多义性观点的一个重要部分便是不主张把意义和概念重合（conflate）。比方说，HOT 属于一个心理基本概念并不意味着我们就对"hot"的各种意义不加以区分。尽管说一个词的不同意义与不同的真实世界的特征相关联，但语言使用者毫无疑问可以将他们加以区分。非多义性的观点便可以说明我们具体是怎么操作的(p.149)。

非多义性的观点同外延语义学（denotational semantics）的观点有相似之处。我们既可以承认 BRIGHT 是一个心理基本概念，同时也承认"bright"一词在"bright sound"与在"bright light"中的意义是不同的，因为"brightness"的特征在视觉感官体和听觉感官体有不同的体现。BRIGHT 概念是一个横跨视觉和听觉感官体的超级原子概念（supramodal atomic concept）。无论在理解"bright light"或理解"bright sound"时，BRIGHT 概念就被激活。表程度的形容词（degree adjectives）也有类似的情况。我们可以说"a big mouse"和"a big elephant"；但很明显，我们是就"老鼠"范畴而言来理解某个老鼠"大"，而不是在"象"的范畴去理解老鼠的大小。因此，在某种程度上，我们要讨论的不是"BIG"的意义，而是 "big X"的意义。我们所具有的是心理基本概念 BIG；我们将这个概念同具有"being big"的特征相联系。进入表达"big"的具体形式是 [BIG (X)]，其中 X 是一缺省值，表示"就 X 本类而言"。BRIGHT 概念就属于这样的情况，它是通过语义体现 [BRIGHT（X）]映射在 BRIGHT 的概念上。概念的层面就是指那种我们所讨论的形象化（embodiment）或者感知刺激；而意义的层面则是语义表达的层面（p.153）。

而根据非多义性的观点，句子是可以有隐喻意义的，其原因是句子可以用来表达命题（propositions）。然而一个隐喻表达的不只是惟一的命题，即使说这个命题与发话的情景有关，而是一系列不确定的命题。类似于句子中没有明言的成分，隐喻对命题内容的表述在很大程度上不同于发话人试图表达的意思。在这个意义上，即使说隐喻可以表达命题，但所表达的并非有真值的命题。

第十一章 结 语

作者坦言，本书的主要目的是想探讨词汇、意义、概念以及它们之间的关系，要阐明的是语言中的字面意义或非隐喻意义要比人们传统上假定的要多；作者主要是以联觉感知类和双功能性形容词为例，试图说明它们不应该算作隐喻。作者认为,概念并非意义,非多义性观点尤其不容许把二者混为一谈。概念是连接我们和外部世界的心理实体,具体体现为知觉的和形象化的系统性组合(schematism)。概念结构的非多义性的观点算是把不同的有关意义理论进行了综合:因为哲学家所关心的是意义的真值与指称问题,语言学家关心的是语义表达的问题,而心理学家关心的是意义在记忆中的存储问题。跨学科的研究非常重要,因为我们理解中的一些盲区可以由此而暴露,从而使我们具有新颖的洞察力。作者还指出,通过新理论对研究数据进行再解释也是科学往前迈进的一种方式。正是基于这种方式,本书便尝试性地对隐喻、一词多义现象以及概念结构等方面的问题进行了探讨。

三、初步评析

隐喻研究源远流长,从亚里士多德到现在已有 2000 多年的历史了。传统的隐喻研究一般将隐喻视为一种修辞手段。而从 20 世纪 80 年代,自 G. Lakoff 等人的 *Metaphors We Live By* 和 *Women, Fire and Dangerous Things* 问世以来,隐喻研究被纳入了认知研究的领域,隐喻被认为是人类赖以生存的基础;语言中处处充满隐喻性的表达。于是隐喻研究的热情之火更是越烧越旺。当今世界范围内似乎已经掀起了一场"隐喻革命";Johnson 将这种现象称为"隐喻狂热"(metaphormania)(王寅 2001:302)。而 Marina Rakova 博士的大作《字面意义的疆域:隐喻、一词多义以及概念理论》可算是隐喻革命浪潮中最不可忽略的另一种声音。归纳起来,该书有如下主要特点:

1. 观点新颖

Marina Rakova 一开始便针对隐喻研究中存在的一些问题进行了解剖。尽管她没有从亚里士多德谈起,但她对 20 世纪一些具有代表性的隐喻理论作了一个概述, 如 Monroe Beardsley 的内涵理论(intensional theory),Eva Kittay 和 Josef Stern 的隐喻语义理论等。她想给大家展示的是:好多通常看来似乎不同的隐喻理论实际上存在很大的相似性,都没有超出标准设想的理论范畴。这表现在它们大多认为词汇只具有一个字面意义的观点,而且认为字面意义是首要的、基本的,其余的意义是隐喻性的,隐喻意义是从字面意义派生而来的。

Rakova 认为这些理论对隐喻的处理有表面化的倾向。她也承认，认知语言学为修正传统隐喻理论的不足提供了基础，但她认为认知语言学的隐喻理论同样属于传统隐喻理论的一个翻版：承认多义词的首要意义，认为多义词的其他意义均属于隐喻意义或派生意义；因此，认知语言学解释一词多义现象的方法仍然不尽人意。认知语言学家一般认为，概念化就是概念形成的过程，也是一个认知过程。概念是概念化的结果，因此语义实际上也就等于概念。Jackendoff (1988)就主张概念和语义合二为一。Langacker (1987,1991)认为语义等于象征结构（symbolic structure）(王寅 2001:82—183)。但 Rakova 不同意这样的观点，并声称一个概念理论并不一定同时也可以作为意义或语义体现的理论（chapter10）；她所推崇的非多义性观点的一个重要部分便是反对把意义和概念重合起来。

2. 视角独特

如果只在一个语言系统内部论证某一现象，必然导致循环论证。要摆脱这种循环论证，必须到语言外部去寻找依据（石毓智 2000:3）。沈家煊先生也提倡到语言外部去寻找解释语言结构的理由（1999:20）。其实这也是功能语言学和认知语言学的共同主张。在本书中 Marina Rakova 并没有只是在语言研究领域思辨性地去论证想要说明的问题，而是通过大量的神经生理学和心理学等方面的实验数据来支撑自己的观点。比如，通过 Brent Berlin & Paul Kay (1969) 对基本色彩词的研究成果，以及 Eleanor Rosch （1974, 1978；et al.）后来的研究对 Berlin 和 Kay 的成果的正确性的肯定；Rakova 想说明的是，生理学和语义学之间有着的密切关系，我们的语言和概念结构同神经生理网络结构是有必然联系的。作者还通过展示 David Julius 等人的实验成果，说明在英语中 spicy 一词可以用 hot 来作同义词，其根据是由"辣味食品"（spicy food）和"较高的温度"所引起的感觉效应具有相同的分子结构机制（the same molecular mechanisms）(p.38)；同一痛觉机制（pain-detecting mechanism）可以既被辣椒素的刺激激活，也被热度的刺激激活。很显然，Rakova 想要告诉我们的是，从生理学的角度把 "chili pepper"理解为 "hot" 是很有道理的（p.31），而并非像大多隐喻理论所认为的英语词汇"hot"仅有表示"热感"的意义才是字面性的，而表示"味感"的意义便是隐喻性的了。

3. 问题与不足

尽管在很多方面，该书不愧为一本"新书"，但也有一些不足之处。作者一方面承认 Lakoff 和 Johnson 等人的理论的革命性，而另一方面又认为认知语言学框架内的隐喻研究仅仅是传统隐喻理论的一种自然延续，认为它们的共性在于对待一词多义现象的方式：一个词只有一个字面意义，即首要意义，其余的为隐喻意义或派生意义。但实际上传统的隐喻研究同认知语言学的隐喻研究存在本质的区别。可以说认知理论框架内的隐喻研究是划分传统隐喻研究理论和当代隐喻理论的分水岭（王寅 2001:309）。传统的语言理论把隐喻看做修辞手段，是文学作品中装饰性的语言标志。而认知语言学把隐喻看做一种重要的认知方式；隐喻无处不在，人类的思维过程充满了隐喻。以往语义学理论认为一词多义现象是一个单一的语言形式具有两种或两种以上密切相关意义的聚合(Taylor 1995:99)。可以说传统的语义理论并没有把握多义现象的本质，未能对此现象做出充分的解释。认知理论认为多义现象的形成是人类通过认知手段(如隐喻、换喻)由一个词的中心意义或基本意义向其他意义延伸的过程，是人类认知范畴和概念化的结果。Langacker(1991)认为：多义词的多种意义之间的联系不是任意的，而是通过特定的语义引申机制从典型发展而成，各个值之间的每一种联系都是有理据的（王寅 2001:230）。

此外，Marina Rakova 认为她对概念隐喻持怀疑态度的原因在于从词源学角度来解释共时语义学的效度问题。她觉得，尽管在语法化的研究中大多承认单向性的存在，然而语义演变的情况同隐喻的情况是不同的。Rakova 不同意"作为语义演变中的主要机制的隐喻很快扩展成了概念演变的主要机制"的说法，但她并没有对此作进一步的论证或阐述。接着作者还比较"主观"地推测说"况且也不大可能说'早期'的词汇表只包括用来描述物质实体和事件的词汇"，"再说，OED 的词条中在给多义形容词释义时也并没有划分出其首要意义和派生意义"(pp.110—117)。尽管通过少量的词源对比，作者的确发现在某些词条中似乎典型意义（prototypical meaning）出现的时间比隐喻意义还要晚一些；比如 "cold"一词意为"(of soil) slow to absorb heat"出现的时间为 1398 年,而"cold"用作"void of ardour, warmth or intensity of feeling"的时间是从 1175 年才开始,但仅仅用如此少量的例证来说明一个大问题,似乎显得论据不够充分。

参考文献[*]：

Hopper, P. J. and E. C. Traugott. *Grammaticalization*. Beijing: Foreign Language Teaching & Research Press, 2001.

Lakoff, G. and M. Johnson. *Metaphors We Live By*. Chicago: Chicago University Press, 1980.

Lakoff, G. *Women, Fire and Dangerous Things: What Categories Reveal about the Mind*. Chicago: Chicago University Press, 1987.

Sweetser, E. F. *From Etymology to Pragmatics: Metaphorical and Cultural Aspects of Semantic Structure*. Beijing: Peking University Press, 2002.

Taylor, J. R. *Linguistic Categorization: Prototypes in Linguistic Theory*. Beijing: Foreign Language Teaching & Research Press, 2001.

Ungerer, F. and H. J. Schmid. *An Introduction to Cognitive Linguistics*. Beijing: Foreign Language Teaching & Research Press, 2001.

龚放:"论英语同形异义词与多义词的识别——与曹务堂先生商榷",《外语教学》,1998 年第 2 期。

沈家煊:《不对称和标记论》,南昌:江西教育出版社,1999。

石毓智:《语法的认知语义基础》,南昌:江西教育出版社,2000。

束定芳:《隐喻学研究》,上海:上海外语教育出版社,2000。

王寅:《语义理论与语言教学》,上海:上海外语教育出版社,2001。

张志毅、张庆云:《词汇语义学》,北京:商务印书馆,2001。

章宜华:《语义学与词典释义》,上海:上海辞书出版社,2002。

赵艳芳:《认知语言学概论》,上海:上海外语教育出版社,2001。

---

[*] 内容介绍部分的参考文献请见书后的参考书目。

*To the memory of my mother
Svetlana Rakova
and
to my father
Boris Rakov*

Contents

Preface   1

1 Introduction: On the Nature of the Literal–Metaphorical Distinction   1

2 Metaphor in Cognitive Linguistics   18
2.1 The cognitive linguistics revolution   18
2.2 Experientialism and conceptual organization   19
2.3 Reasons to take experientialism seriously   21
2.4 Cognitive semantics and the literal–metaphorical distinction   22
2.5 Some problems for the philosophy of experientialism   23
2.6 Adjectival polysemy in the experientialist framework   28

3 The 'Hot' Polysemy   34
3.1 Why neurophysiology matters to semantics   34
3.2 The capsaicin receptor   36
3.3 Are hot peppers 'hot' for everyone?   38
3.4 The pain pathway   40
3.5 The standard assumption and the 'hot' polysemy   43

4 Across Sensory Modalities   48
4.1 Bright sounds and loud lights   48
4.2 Seeing sounds and tasting shapes   51
4.3 How different are synaesthetes and non-synaesthetes?   54
4.4 Cross-modal associations and synaesthetic metaphors   58
4.5 Synaesthetic adjectives and the standard assumption   64
4.6 The no-polysemy view of conceptual structure   67
4.7 How could have psychologically primitive concepts come about?   69

5 Double-Function Terms   74
5.1 A puzzle   74
5.2 Asch on double-function adjectives   75
5.3 Discussing Asch's research: cross-linguistic study   79
5.4 Conceptual atomism   82
5.5 Discussing Asch's research: language acquisition study   85

6	**Double-Function Terms Again**	90
6.1	Adjectival polysemy in psycholinguistic research	90
6.2	Discussing Williams' results	94
6.3	The processing of alternative meanings by cerebral hemispheres: the beginnings	98
6.4	The processing of alternative meanings by cerebral hemispheres: later studies	100
7	**Words and Concepts**	105
8	**Back to Cognitive Semantics**	109
8.1	Sweetser's mind-as-body metaphor	109
8.2	Enter criticisms	110
9	**Polysemy in Lexical Semantics**	118
9.1	Semantics and conceptual structure: the beginnings	118
9.2	Polysemy and conceptual structure	119
9.3	The generative lexicon	124
9.4	The disquotational lexicon and the problem of polysemy	131
10	**The No-Polysemy View: What It Is and What It Is Not**	139
10.1	The one literal meaning assumption	139
10.2	The no-polysemy view	141
10.3	Words, meanings, concepts, and more	151
10.4	Metaphors forever	165
11	**A Very Short Conclusion**	172
	Notes	174
	References	206
	Index	227

Preface

I don't like prefaces where the author goes on and on about his/her sufferings in writing the book. I am sure you do not want to hear anything about this. Still, I think that there is a very important function that prefaces serve. It is to acknowledge one's debt to those without whom the whole thing would not have been what it is.

This book is an expanded, modified and generally improved version of the doctoral dissertation that I wrote at the University of Edinburgh under the supervision of Professor James R. Hurford and Professor Timothy Williamson. Working under their supervision felt like being supervised by Beethoven and Chopin at the same time. But things have worked out surprisingly well and I owe them both a lot in intellectual terms. Besides, without Jim's active interference this book would not have been at all, and without Tim's 'after-sales service' it would have been a lot worse. I also wish to thank another person from Edinburgh times, Professor James Miller, for his comments on Chapter 9 and for trying to divert my mind in many useful directions, not all of which are fully explored in this book.

Converting a dissertation into a book does take some time and effort. I had a wonderful opportunity to work on this book during my Postdoctoral Fellowship at the Instituto de Investigaciones Filosóficas, UNAM. The Instituto provided me with an excellent research environment and facilities to make this work a much more pleasant experience than it might have been otherwise. I would like to say a special thank you to Dr Maite Ezcurdia Olavarrieta and Dr Atocha Aliseda Llera for getting me involved into things and thus, somewhat inadvertently, making the content of this book take its final form. I also wish to thank Dr Andrei M. Tune of St Petersburg State University for a kind permission to extend my research leave at the Instituto to complete the work on the book.

The Instituto has an excellent philosophy library but I needed more than that. So I wish to thank Sr Miguel A. Sánchez, Sra MariCarmen Saldaña Nicolas and Sr Pedro Espinosa Ruiz for tracing innumerable books and articles necessary for my work. I am also grateful to Ms Lorna Cheyne of the Edinburgh University Library for her help with the bibliographical material.

I also wish to thank my editor Jill Lake who pushed me into doing more than I ever thought I could. But this is what good editors are for. And I owe a special thank you to the reviewers for Palgrave Macmillan for their thoughtful comments. I am infinitely grateful to Pr Noel Burton-Roberts for his comments on Chapter 9 and his inspiring suggestions that resulted in the extended Chapter 1. And I am hugely indebted to Dr Robyn Carston for the title of the book and the detailed comments on Chapter 10.

I wish to thank my partner Denis Gladkov for bearing with me through the entire period of writing this book, but also for helping me to sharpen the ideas that went into it and to prepare the final script.

Now, for the very final standard disclaimer. All good ideas in this book can ultimately be traced to their source in the people mentioned above. All mistakes and misrepresentations are entirely mine.

Acknowledgement

I wish to thank Mouton de Gruyter for a kind permission to reproduce here as part of Chapter 2 a modified version of my article 'The Philosophy of Embodied Realism: A High Price to Pay' which appeared in *Cognitive Linguistics* 13–3 (2002) 215–44. I also wish to thank *Cognitive Linguistics*' editor, Pr Arie Verhagen, for his help with arranging for the permission and his comments on the issues discussed in the aforementioned article.

MARINA RAKOVA

1
Introduction: On the Nature of the Literal–Metaphorical Distinction

Do you like talking to people who smile at you coldly and give you sharp replies? Or do you prefer people who greet you warmly and are sweet with you? What kind of strong things do you value: strong relationships, strong governments, strong tastes? What kind of soft things do you appreciate: soft pillows, soft colours, soft voices? Deep people intrigue us and provoke admiration, while deep grief is sometimes too much to bear. Bright light may be blinding, but bright music sets us into a cheerful mood, and bright children with bright eyes are a delight to every parent. Connoisseurs may have a penchant for dry wine, but people with a dry sense of humour often put off their collocutors . . . .

Put together in one paragraph, all these examples appear a bit odd: what do soft pillows have in common with soft voices? And what properties do bright music and bright eyes share? However, any of them used on its own in our everyday speech would not even attract our attention. Nor would it cause comprehension difficulty. When we read in Agatha Christie 'A warm sweet feeling of intoxication ran through her veins' or 'She spoke with ready enthusiasm, but inwardly she was conscious of a sudden chill' (*Death on the Nile*, p. 20 and p. 19, HarperCollins) we do not pause to calculate the meaning of 'warm', or 'sweet', or 'chill'. We do not wonder whether feelings can indeed be 'warm' or 'sweet', or whether it is possible to be chilly from inside rather than outside.

The kind of people who do pause and wonder about such things are linguists, philosophers, psychologists and cognitive scientists. The reason one may be impelled to pause is that, on the one hand, the ways which help us decide whether a pillow is soft or hard are different from the ways which help us decide whether a voice is soft or harsh. Philosophers call these ways of deciding whether something is A or B 'truth-conditions': ascertaining that 'this pillow is soft' is true is based

2 The Extent of the Literal

on different procedures from ascertaining that 'this voice is soft' is true. A conclusion that is made frequently is that 'soft' plays different roles in 'soft pillow' and 'soft voice', or that there are two different 'soft': 'soft$_1$' and 'soft$_2$', as it were (in more familiar parlance, that there are two different meanings of 'soft').

On the other hand, our intuition tells us that somehow in our thought all the different meanings of 'soft' are related, perhaps related more tightly and in a qualitatively different way than the meanings of 'cat' and 'dog', or even 'mother' and 'father'. For instance, in interpreting novel utterances. If we know what 'cat' means, we shall not be able to guess what 'cat and dog' means unless we also know what 'dog' means. But if we know what 'soft' means, we know what it means both in 'soft pillow' and 'soft voice'. Or rather, if we know what 'soft$_1$' (as in 'soft pillow') means, we can guess what 'soft$_2$' (as in 'soft voice') means, and guess correctly. Even when we hear 'soft'-phrases which are completely novel for us, we do not twist our minds in an effort to understand them, we just understand them. To notice how widespread such cross-sensory uses of words are one only has to watch television: 'Why wear cotton, if you can wear silk?' could have been about clothes, but it was about Galaxy chocolates, and it worked. Silk is softer and smoother than cotton, tastes also have degrees of softness and smoothness. When we watch this advert, we may want to try a Galaxy, but we do not wonder whether it is appropriate to call tastes 'soft', as we call 'soft' those objects that give us tactile sensations of softness. The kind of people who wonder about such things also wonder why this is so.

Adjectives such as 'soft', 'sharp', 'dry', 'cold', 'deep', 'bright', and others are called polysemous adjectives because they can be used with nouns of different kinds and their meaning depends on the nouns they modify. People who are professionally interested in language tend to think of such adjectives as either having a number of different unrelated meanings, or as having one major meaning, called 'literal meaning'. They consider all other meanings of these adjectives as metaphorical, that is derived from the literal meaning and thus related to it. (Or else, sometimes they think of such adjectives as presently having several literal meanings, but etymologically only one primary literal meaning.) Thus, they believe that 'soft' is something that can be properly or literally said only about clothes or materials. It follows that when we call voices 'soft', we are not speaking properly or literally. We are speaking metaphorically. To call voices 'soft' is to use a synaesthetic metaphor. Correspondingly, to call people 'soft' (in character, not to the touch) is also to use a metaphor. Adjectives which can be used both in physical and psychological contexts are sometimes labelled 'double-function' adjectives.

Synaesthetic and double-function adjectives form the central topic of this book. I am going to argue that the way we talk about the literal and the metaphorical, especially with respect to polysemous adjectives, is badly misguided. Consider the following examples. Metaphor is traditionally defined as a transfer of predicates from one domain where they properly belong to some other domain where they do not belong, but where they can be transferred if there is a certain similarity between what is being transferred and where it is being transferred to. If I call my cat a 'dog', it is a metaphor: I know for sure that my cat is a cat, and that an animal cannot be both a cat and a dog. But I can call him a 'dog' if he exhibits behaviour typical of dogs and not typical of cats (he wags his tail and carries my bag in his mouth). If I call my cat an 'ayatollah', it is also a metaphor: as far as we know, cats do not have religious beliefs. But I can call him an 'ayatollah' because he is Persian and usually behaves as if he were the spiritual leader of my household.

However, this is not the case with 'soft', or 'sharp', or 'dry'. My cat walks softly, and is soft tempered but this is not so because he is fluffy or soft to the touch. You remember 'on the one hand' and 'on the other hand'? I am going to argue that people who think that the meanings of polysemous adjectives are unrelated are wrong: not only our intuitions, but psychological research confirms that they are interconnected in our thinking. Likewise, I am going to argue that people who think that polysemous adjectives have only one primary meaning are also wrong because there are no grounds for an explicit comparison and transfer between various kinds of softness or sharpness, and because this view also contradicts the data we have. Finally, I am going to argue that some of our assumptions about language and thought have to be reconsidered if we want to give a coherent account of the nature of adjectival polysemy.

The main aim of this book is to bring into serious doubt a widespread assumption concerning the literal–metaphorical distinction. The assumption is that, for a large number of words (in particular, for polysemous adjectives), only one meaning has to be considered as literal or basic, and all the other meanings have to be treated as its metaphorical extensions. I label it 'the standard assumption'.

Let me now present a brief historical overview of how the standard assumption has surfaced in different theories of metaphor. Two remarks have to be made before I begin. First, note that metaphor research has often been concerned with a different kind of examples, which are copulated statements of the form 'NP is NP', such as 'Juliet is the sun', 'Man is a wolf', 'My job is a jail', 'Poverty is a crime', and so on. Second, I do not propose to give a full coverage of theories of metaphor. For this reason, the overview does not begin with Aristotle, but starts at the twentieth century. Neither do I propose to analyse particular theories in detail: the purpose of this overview is to show that there exists some curious similarity between various theories of metaphor which are often taken to be in opposition to each other. What makes them all similar is precisely how they approach the literal–metaphorical distinction, in particular with respect to synaesthetic and double-function adjectives.

I.A. Richards

There is a trend within metaphor research which claims that all language is 'vitally metaphorical' and which began with I.A. Richards' *The Philosophy of Rhetoric* (1936; similar views are found in Cassirer, 1946, and Ricoeur, 1975). Richards's book was a reaction against numerous *Manuals of Rhetoric* which pedantically taught proper usage and considered metaphor as a mere ornament or embellishment. In his book, Richards resists the desire of rhetoricians to impose inappropriate rigidity on ordinary discourse and particularly the discourse of poetry, labelling it the 'Proper Meaning Superstition' or the 'One and Only One True Meaning Superstition'. Instead, he proposes the 'context theorem of meaning', according to which all discourse has multiplicity of meaning, so that meanings of sentences can shift, and with them meanings of individual words. As Richards says, words do not possess their senses as people possess their names: what a word means in a sentence is determined by its neighbour words.

Since words interanimate each other, one can see why it is difficult to decide whether a word is used literally or metaphorically, and why the boundary between 'literal and metaphoric uses is not quite fixed or constant' (p. 118). Thus metaphor can indeed be 'the omnipresent principle of language', its constitutive form. However, taken at its face value, the claim that all language is vitally metaphorical seems to undercut itself, for it casts doubt on the very distinction it presupposes. Where is the contradiction? I suspect that the feeling of something having gone wrong arises only if we interpret Richards as saying that there are no clearly defined literal meanings. But a more careful reading reveals that this is not the case. In fact, it seems to be perfectly clear to Richards what the literal meaning of a word is: words apply literally only to certain 'orders of experience', and we have a metaphor when the tenor and the vehicle belong to different orders (p. 124). For this reason, only babies and hunters crawl literally (p. 120); for this reason, lights are only metaphorically strong (p. 101), and rivers, but not minds, can be literally deep (p. 121). Language is vitally metaphorical only because words apply literally to a very limited range of objects, properties or actions. And this is what the standard assumption says.

Max Black

Some researchers hold that the distinction between the literal and the metaphorical is self-evident and does not need to be spelled out explicitly. This is the view that we find in the writings of Max Black (1962, 1993; see also Cohen, 1997) which were greatly inspired by the ideas of I.A. Richards. Black follows Richards in claiming that metaphors cannot be paraphrased literally without a significant loss to the cognitive content of metaphor. And he is also sympathetic to the view that metaphors should not be considered as 'some kind of deviation or aberration from proper usage' (1993, p. 22). However, according to Black, the difference between literal and metaphorical interpretations is not problematic, the distinction itself is 'common-sense' (ibid.). Literal meaning is that which we find included in dictionary definitions and which allows us to recognize paradigm cases of application. Because we tacitly know literal meanings of words, we recognize metaphor by a feeling of tension it creates when two different things are put together. For this reason, instances of catachresis or filling in gaps in the vocabulary, such as 'falling in love', should not be considered as good instances of metaphor.

Monroe Beardsley

Monroe Beardsley (1962, 1978) proposed an intensional theory of metaphor, according to which words can acquire additional metaphoric senses through a transformation of their standard senses. In Beardsley's theory, an intension is a set of properties, such that each distinguishable intension produces a distinguishable sense of a word. All words have standard senses which determine their proper domain of application. Thus, words are used literally if they possess some defining properties which '*must* be present if the word is to be correctly applied to an object' (1962, p. 306).

However, any word can potentially become a 'metaphorical segment' (1978, p. 4) of a sentence or a larger linguistic unit if it is predicated of something that does not possess the properties which are in that word's standard intension. According to Beardsley, there exist 'credence-properties' that we associate with words, something that is salient in our thinking about objects denoted by them. Thus, when words are used metaphorically, credence-properties become transformed into metaphorical intensions. For example, 'difficulty of changing' is a property that we associate with iron things, but it is not a property in the standard intension of 'iron'; in the expression 'iron will' this property is transformed into the metaphorical sense of 'iron' (1978, p. 8). It is easy to see that in the case of polysemous adjectives such as 'warm' (1962, p. 304), only one meaning will be considered as literal, or possessing all the necessary properties, whereas other meanings will be treated as metaphorical because some defining conditions for application will have to be excluded. Once upon a time someone may have been looking for a word that would metaphorically describe people and hit upon the word 'warm' among whose connotations are approachable, pleasurable-in-acquaintance, inviting.

Nelson Goodman

Unlike Beardsley's, Nelson Goodman's (1968) theory of metaphor is an extensional theory. Metaphor produces a change in denotation, and consideration of belief-properties is not present in his account. Thus according to Goodman, metaphor involves a 'change of realm' (p. 72): we have a metaphor when a set of labels is transferred from a realm 'to which it is customarily applied' to some new domain. Which is to say that all mental labels have their proper home realms. Predicates apply literally only within the realm where they belong. 'Sad' applies literally only to sentient beings, and all its other applications, as for instance in 'sad picture', are metaphorical. We know that we have a metaphor if the application of a term is somehow 'contra-indicated' (p. 69).

Whether a term is used literally or metaphorically depends, for Goodman, on its prior denotation, and 'what is literal is set by present practice' (p. 77). Our practice determines that 'sad' applies literally only to sentient beings; pictures are not in the extension of sentient beings; the denotation of 'sad' is fixed prior to the application of 'sad' to non-sentient beings; therefore, 'sad' cannot literally apply to pictures. And this is what distinguishes metaphor from euphemism: euphemism 'substitutes proper for improper labels', whereas metaphor 'applies labels for proper things to improper things' (p. 81). As one can see, this is the standard assumption in full swing again: only one meaning of a polyseme can be properly considered as its literal meaning.[1]

Goodman also says that labels transferred by a metaphor acquire a new extension. This is the process by which metaphors eventually become more literal 'as their novelty vanishes': 'cold colour' (p. 68) is one such expression. Literal uses of terms precede and inform their metaphorical uses, but with the passage of time a metaphor may 'evaporate', so that instead of metaphor we have ambiguity, or two literal uses. It would seem that the standard assumption is thus avoided, for Goodman admits that two meanings of a polyseme can be its literal meanings. However, admitting this is hardly consistent with his view of the literal as having no prior denotation. Besides, the standard assumption says that only one meaning of a polyseme can be its literal *or* basic meaning. Theories, according to which a polyseme (presently) has two literal meanings, but one of them is in some sense more basic than the other, fall within its province.

Eva Kittay

Eva Kittay's (1987) theory of metaphor is a semantic theory, according to which it is possible to establish what the metaphoric meaning of an expression is. Kittay's theory of metaphor is known as the semantic fields theory: every word in a language belongs to its proper semantic field ('cat' belongs to the semantic field of animals, 'sun' belongs to the semantic field of celestial objects, and so on). A term's literal meaning is determined by a set of semantic features and semantic combination rules within a field where it belongs (p. 53). As Kittay says, the distinction between the literal and the metaphorical must be intuitively clear: normally we have no difficulty making it (p. 40). We know metaphor by the way it 'breaks certain rules of language, rules governing the literal and conventional senses of terms' (p. 24). Which is to say that metaphor violates boundaries between semantic fields and creates literal incongruity. Thus, the semantic fields theory is a very clear manifestation of the standard assumption (see, for instance, p. 54): a polyseme can belong only to its proper field; when the field is changed, its meaning is a metaphoric meaning.

Josef Stern

Josef Stern's (2000) theory of metaphor is also a semantic theory of metaphoric meaning. And the way the literal–metaphorical distinction is drawn there is also guided by the standard assumption. Thus, the literal meaning of a word or expression is its semantic interpretation, which minimally contains its extension or referent (p. 23). Stern distinguishes two classes of metaphor. In one class, the literal meaning of an expression is extended, so that at least one condition in the literal meaning is eliminated, but the metaphorical interpretation still contains the literal interpretation (as in the expression 'to demolish an argument'). In the other, metaphor effectuates a complete change of extension, so that the domain of application for the resulting expression is disjoint from the original domain (p. 27).

The literal meaning of a word is that which can be assigned to it independently of context, and the speaker knows the literal meaning of a word if he knows under which conditions a word does or does not apply (p. 318). On this view, dead metaphors are not particularly interesting, or even particularly metaphorical (since the speaker may know the precise conditions of application, p. 310). However, besides the sameness of extension, being literal presupposes a certain historical priority (cf. 'metaphors are frequently used to express content for which no literal expression is available at the time of utterance', p. 266). And this, in conjunction with the notion of transfer across domains, shows that the assumption of primary meanings for polysemes is still there. Indeed, even though synaesthetic and double-function metaphors have long been dead and are 'only debatedly metaphors' (p. 310), Stern thinks that 'cold music' has to be interpreted metaphorically, by exploiting the features commonly associated with the literal meaning of 'cold' (p. 109, see also p. 51).

Other semantic and pragmatic theories of metaphor

Above I said that it is not the purpose of this overview to discuss all theories of metaphor. The preceding paragraphs were a selection of views on metaphor which seem to illustrate particularly well one common assumption concerning the literal–metaphorical distinction. I have labelled it 'the standard assumption', and it says that only one meaning of a polyseme (in particular, of a synaesthetic or double-function adjective) can be its literal or basic meaning, whereas all its other meanings have to be considered as metaphorical derivations.

I have briefly discussed two semantic theories of metaphor – Eva Kittay's and Josef Stern's. There is another semantic theory of metaphor that appeared earlier, the feature-cancellation theory (Levin, 1977; J. Cohen, 1993). According to the feature-cancellation theory, a word's literal meaning is its lexical meaning, or a set of component features which constitute that word's lexical description. The metaphoric meaning of a word is produced by deleting certain features of the literal meaning, and in this sense, metaphoric meaning is contained within literal meaning. It is not difficult to see that the standard assumption is also in operation in the feature-cancellation theory: various meanings of a polyseme are derived from its primary meaning by deleting some of its determining features (for example, the domain of application).

Not all theories of metaphor are semantic. Perhaps a greater number of them are pragmatic (see, for instance, Fogelin, 1988; Sadock, 1993; Searle, 1993). Pragmatic theories distinguish between sentence meaning (literal meaning) and speaker's meaning. Metaphor does not belong to semantics, or the study of word or sentence meaning; metaphoric meaning is speaker's meaning. A sentence containing a 'metaphorical segment' says nothing beyond what it says literally, but its meaning goes beyond its literal meaning. To understand a sentence's metaphoric meaning the hearer must identify the speaker's intentions in using a sentence that is either obviously false ('Juliet is the sun') or blatantly true ('No man is an island'). Here is not the place to discuss pragmatic theories of metaphor, but it has to be remarked that with respect to the literal-metaphorical distinction there is no significant difference between the two kinds of theories: pragmatic theories of metaphor also presuppose the notion of literal meaning which is given in terms of extensions or truth-conditions (see Searle, 1993).

Donald Davidson

If I had been diligently sticking to the temporal order in which various theories of metaphor were proposed, Donald Davidson's famous 1978 essay 'What metaphors mean' (Davidson, 1978/1984a) should have been mentioned before the theories of Kittay and Stern. However, the temporal order was violated so that semantic theories could be mentioned first. The theories of Kittay and Stern were in some ways a reaction against a highly negative position on metaphoric meaning taken by Davidson (see also Cooper, 1986; Rorty, 1987). Since Davidson's essay had been very influential, and since I believe that its negative claim has been given a lot more attention (for instance, in Stern, 2000) than its few positive claims, I propose to spend some time here discussing it in a slightly different way than is usually done.

Davidson's negative claim consists in denying meaning to metaphor in any 'strict sense of meaning'. Literal language is rule-governed, but understanding metaphor 'is little guided by rules' (p. 245), which is why it is often so hard to decide what the content of a particular metaphor is. If you think that setting out the content of a metaphor does not present a big difficulty, consider the following example. When you read 'Poverty is a crime', can you assign a specific content to this sentence such that a vast majority of language speakers would agree with you on what that content is? Can you be sure that the content you assign to it will be univocal across speakers as it is in the case of 'Murder is a crime' or 'In such and such country, poverty is a crime'?

Perhaps we can arrive at the content of a metaphor by taking into account the speaker's intentions in uttering it. However, according to Davidson, metaphor does not possess 'a definite cognitive content that its author wishes to convey' (p. 262). What the maker of a metaphor says does not go beyond the literal meaning of a sentence he uses: 'metaphors mean what the words, in their most literal interpretation, mean, and nothing more' (p. 245). There is all difference in the world between what words mean and what they are used to do: metaphor is not about meaning, but about use. Although Davidson does not explicitly say anywhere why the maker of a metaphor cannot intend it to be understood with a particular cognitive content, he presumably thinks that if the maker of a metaphor wanted to convey some idea, he could have done so without any recourse to metaphor.

In any case, Davidson should not be understood as saying that metaphor does not 'have a point'. In using a metaphor, the speaker 'makes us attend to some likeness' or 'appreciate some fact' (pp. 247, 262). A metaphor may provoke thoughts, but according to Davidson, it would be a mistake to confuse the content of the thoughts that a metaphor provokes in us with the content of that metaphor itself. The speaker chooses to use a metaphor when he or she intends us to wonder about certain things. Or else, what he or she intends us to notice is similarly non-propositional for him as well. Which is why metaphors cannot be paraphrased, for 'there is nothing there to paraphrase' and 'there is no limit to what a metaphor calls to our attention' (pp. 246, 263). These are the negative claims of Davidson's essay which often come under the critique of those theorists who believe that there must be an account of metaphoric meaning. But let us now address the question of literal meaning as understood by Davidson. This will help us get clearer on what may be wrong with the very notion of metaphoric meaning.

For Davidson, a metaphor means 'what the words, in their most literal interpretation, mean, and nothing more'. Consider the following sentence: 'Tolstoy was a great moralizing infant'. True, Tolstoy was once an infant, as everyone else was, but Tolstoy referred to in the sentence is the adult writer. What all infants have in common is that the predicate 'infant' applies to them. And the literal meaning of 'infant' is the extension that includes all infants in virtue of their 'exhibiting the property of infanthood' (p. 247). If someone wants to say that the word 'infant' acquires an additional metaphoric meaning in this sentence, he or she will have to say what property all infants and the adult Tolstoy have in common. But it is doubtful that one can find a property that would justify postulating the existence of the extension 'all infants and the adult Tolstoy'. (An intensional account of metaphoric meaning is equally problematic, for it would require one to multiply senses *ad infinitum*: besides the property of infanthood, one would need to postulate a sense in which all infants and the adult Tolstoy all share some other specific property). Thus, literal meaning is understood in terms of extension. And the accounts of metaphoric meaning which say that the literal meaning of a word used metaphorically is extended to include a new class of entities make all sense of metaphor evaporate. If the adult Tolstoy is placed in the extension of infants, to say that the adult Tolstoy was an infant will no longer be a metaphor.

As Davidson says, to think of metaphoric meaning as extended meaning, or 'to think of words in metaphors as directly going about their business of applying to what they properly apply to' (p. 248), is to eliminate all difference between metaphor and the introduction of new terms into the vocabulary. The reason why metaphor is different is that it depends on 'the primary or original meanings of words' (p. 249). Since Davidson disagrees with Goodman that a word once used metaphorically may become merely ambiguous (as in Goodman's 'cold colours'; Davidson, 1978/1984a, p. 249f.), we can take it that only one meaning of a polysemous adjective has to be considered as its literal meaning. And this is the way of thinking that the standard assumption prescribes. There is one correction that has to be made now. According to Davidson, when metaphors are dead, they are dead forever. One such example is 'mouth' which can refer to animal apertures, entrances to rivers and openings of bottles. As Davidson says, once upon a time bottles did not literally have mouths, and the word 'mouth' applied to them metaphorically. However, now 'mouth' applies to bottles literally. Hence, 'mouth' is merely ambiguous. But, presumably, not 'cold' or 'strong'. And this account is somewhat contradictory, especially if one considers that for Davidson novelty does not play any important role in taking a sentence as literal or metaphorical. As he says, 'a word may easily be appreciated in a new literal role on a first encounter' (p. 252).

Cards on the table
One could think that the main distinguishing feature of literal meaning is context-independence: literal meanings can be assigned to words out-

side particular contexts of use. However, as you may have noticed, the central idea running through the various accounts of metaphor outlined above is that to be used *literally* is to be used *properly*; we have a metaphor when words are not used as they should. When a word is used properly, it is used within its proper domain or semantic field; to be used within a proper domain is to exhibit sameness of extension in all instances of application. So far so good. But the story does not end here because words are said to be used properly when they are used with their primary or basic meanings, their literal meanings.

What does saying that literal meanings are basic meanings amount to? Let me illustrate this on an example from I.A. Richards, 'strong light'. Polysemous adjectives are called that because they have more than one meaning. If context-independence had indeed been the criterion of literalness on which various authors relied either implicitly or explicitly, the question of 'strong light' being metaphorical would not have arisen. We would have said that 'strong' is polysemous, and thus that it has different meanings in 'strong boy' and 'strong light'. This, however, is not the line of reasoning that would generally characterize, for instance, Davidson's account of such polysemes. According to the theories outlined above, 'strong' in 'strong light' is used metaphorically because 'strong' applies literally only to animate beings.

At this point we could ask a somewhat naive question: what are one's grounds for deciding that 'strong' applies literally to animate beings, and not to lights or smells? Or generally, how does one know which of the meanings of a polysemous adjective is its literal or primary meaning? There are three possible answers to this question. One may be found in I.A. Richards, and it says that literal meanings are descriptions of 'physical happenings' which are historically transformed by metaphor into new and more abstract senses (1936, p. 91). So, the first answer is that literal or primary meanings of words are those which denote physical entities or properties of physical entities. However, lights and smells are physical phenomena with physical properties. And thus the answer has to be modified to suggest a gradation in the relative primacy or importance of properties. This kind of modified answer is given by cognitive linguistics (see next chapter), and one of the central tasks of this book is to show that the notion of literal meaning (particularly, as concerns polysemous adjectives) cannot be cashed out in terms of either physical primacy or proper domain application.

The other two answers are, in my opinion, weaker than the first one. The second answer says that literal meanings appear first in the historical order, and that all the other meanings of a polyseme are derivational or metaphorical in the sense of having appeared later. There are two objections to this view. One is that many authors who subscribe to the standard assumption often emphasize that historical considerations are irrelevant to the study of what and how words mean presently. Which meanings are literal meanings is determined by our current practice (Goodman, 1968, p. 77), and the literal–metaphorical distinction can be drawn only with respect to a language's current state (Kittay, 1987, p. 22). The second objection is that words can change their meanings with the course of time, and thus etymological considerations often conflict with, rather than support, one's idea of what is literal that is proposed on the basis of some other considerations (see section 8.2).

Finally, the third answer is a normative one. What is literal is determined, in a way, arbitrarily (frequency considerations are not usually mentioned in philosophical analyses). Thus, we can decide that 'strong' applies literally only to animate beings. This way we establish a norm for using the word 'strong', because semantic normativity affects individual words (cf. Marconi, 1997, p. 124). All the other uses of 'strong' will thus be automatically excluded from the range of its literal application. Since other uses of 'strong' cannot be considered its literal uses, we are forced to say that they are its metaphorical uses, whatever that means besides saying that they are not its literal uses.

The main motivation behind the semantic normativity answer is the desire to preserve the sameness of extension for a word in all its uses. This principle is known as full-blown or strict compositionality. For instance, when one wants to give the truth-conditions of the sentence 'The cat is on the mat' (to say in what circumstances this sentence is true), one assumes that the word 'cat' always denotes a specific class of animals, and that the word 'mat' always denotes a specific class of objects, such that all cats literally have something in common, and all mats are called 'mats' because they share some specific property (the property of being mats). This way, a limitless number of sentences containing 'cats' and 'mats' can be evaluated relative to the context of utterance solely on the basis of their semantics (given that there is one salient cat and one mat in the domain of evaluation). Thus, the rigorous notion of compositionality presupposes a finite vocabulary.

Now imagine that 'cat' sometimes refers to animals known to us as 'cats', sometimes to spiteful women ('She's a real cat'), and sometimes to pimps (as it does in a variety of Russian slang). Imagine that 'mat' sometimes refers to objects that are used for covering the floor, sometimes to beds (with a scorn), and sometimes to people who cannot stand up for themselves ('She's a door-mat'). This would make evaluating 'The cat is on the mat' almost impossible. In order to understand what makes sentences true and false, one discards the metaphorical uses of 'cat' and 'mat'. The same principle is supposed to work for polysemous adjectives as well. However, as I argue in this book, if we want to understand something about natural languages, this approach will not do, for the various uses of 'strong' are not related in the same way as the various uses of 'cat'. (And if one considers polysemous adjectives as merely ambiguous, not metaphorical, one completely eliminates the intuition that all their meanings are related in some unarbitrary way).[2]

The last sentence says that the meanings of a polysemous adjective are related in an unarbitrary way. As you remember, Davidson rejects Goodman's idea that after a metaphor lost its novelty, the word becomes merely ambiguous ('cold light'). According to Davidson, the difference between metaphor and ambiguity is that metaphor depends on the primary meanings of words, whereas ambiguity does not: 'primary or original meanings of words *remain active* in their metaphorical setting' (1978/1984a, p. 249). And in Goodman we read that '[w]hen one use of a term precedes and *informs* another, the second is the metaphorical one' (1968, p. 71; my italics in both quotations).

I have already said why historical precedence cannot determine which meaning of a polyseme has to be considered as its primary meaning. I have also said why determining what the literal meaning of a polyseme is from the point of view of semantic normativity is completely arbitrary. Thus, even Goodman and Davidson (who talk about words being used properly or improperly, which is the normativity talk) must have something else in mind. Primary meanings are those that 'remain active' and 'inform' other meanings, and this is the question of conceptual primacy. One of the central tasks of this book is to argue that the claims about one meaning (literal or primary) of a polysemous adjective 'informing' its other meanings, on analysis, turn out to be empty. Or, in other words, it is to argue that the standard assumption cannot find support in the notion of conceptual primacy.

Let me give you some indication of what I think is wrong with the criterion of meaning dependence for distinguishing between metaphor and ambiguity. 'Strong light' is said to be metaphorical. Thus, the meaning that 'strong' has in 'strong boy' should remain active in your understanding of 'strong light'. But how does it remain active? Davidson would probably reply that on encountering 'strong light' our imagination supplies us with images of animate beings that are properly called 'strong' (elephants? body-builders?; cf. Davidson, 1978/1984a, p. 253). I do not think that this is a good answer. Moreover, research shows that imagery does not play an important cognitive role in language (Pylyshin, 1981; Rousset, 2000). And some people never see images. But they can understand metaphors (cf. Gibbs, 1994, p. 134).

Another example from Davidson is 'the mouth of a bottle'. The word 'mouth' in 'the mouth of a bottle' is not used metaphorically; 'mouth' is ambiguous. It is not metaphorical, according to Davidson, because we no longer notice a likeness between mouths as animal apertures and mouths as bottle openings. However, as several researchers have noticed (Cooper, 1986; Stern, 2000), dead metaphors can easily be brought to life again. As in the following feminist joke: 'What do men and bottles have in common?' – 'They are both empty above the mouth.' (Would Davidson still say no jokes are unfunny?; cf. 1978/1984a, p. 245). One meaning of 'mouth' is activated in its other meaning, and our attention is drawn to the likeness between them. Noticing likeness is not a good criterion for distinguishing between metaphor and ambiguity.

Still, there is something in Davidson's essay that I take to be its positive claim. Davidson says that 'a word may easily be appreciated in a new literal role on a first encounter' (p. 252).[3] And this expresses one of the main arguments of this book. For I am going to argue that the standard assumption is wrong. I am going to argue that there is much more literalness in language than has traditionally been supposed, or in other words, that all meanings of synaesthetic and double-function adjectives may well be their literal meanings. This explains the choice of the title – *The Extent of the Literal*. For I believe that the restrictive notion of literal meaning that underlies most discussions of metaphor and polysemy is not the notion of literal meaning that could help us understand why language is the way it is.

The cards have been laid on the table. I have disclosed the main objectives of this book. Let me now tell you briefly how we are going to proceed.

As we have seen, the notion of literal meaning that is presupposed by all theories of metaphor mentioned in this chapter, turns out to depend not on context-invariance or even sameness of extension, but the assumption that words possess primary or basic meanings in virtue of some conceptual necessity.

This view became explicitly formulated in cognitive linguistics theory of conceptual metaphor which I discuss in Chapter 2. I am going to argue that despite many of its important insights, including the introduction of the notion of embodiment into the discussion of polysemy and conceptual structure, the theory of conceptual metaphor is largely unsatisfactory. In particular, this concerns the explanation of adjectival polysemy within the theory of conflation which cannot lend support to the idea of metaphorically structured concepts.

Chapter 3 is about the polysemy of the adjective 'hot' which is used in English to denote thermal and gustatory sensations. As it turns out, there are good physiological reasons for perceiving chilli peppers as hot, and that is why the taste meaning of 'hot' cannot be derived metaphorically from its temperature meaning. Other considerations also speak against the standard assumption explanations.

Chapter 4 discusses synaesthetic adjectives. From an early age people are capable of cross-modal associations and are strikingly uniform in their interpretations of synaesthetic adjectives. However, neither direct perceptual similarity nor standard assumption theories can explain why the interpretation of synaesthetic adjectives does not follow patterns of stimuli correlation. It is there that I introduce the no-polysemy view of conceptual structure, according to which all meanings of a synaesthetically polysemous adjective map onto the same psychologically primitive concept.

In Chapter 4 I argue that the no-polysemy view can provide a better explanation for cases of physical–physical polysemy than the standard view. But can it explain double-function adjectives which seem to be good candidates for being metaphors? This is why in Chapter 5, on the basis of cross-linguistic and developmental evidence, I try to show that there are no serious reasons to consider the psychological meanings of double-function terms as their metaphoric meanings. The no-polysemy view is consistent with the evidence and, besides, proposes a uniform explanation for both synaesthetic and double-function adjectives.

Chapter 6 continues on the same issue. I argue that some assumptions about the literal–metaphorical distinction are not as well-grounded as they may appear. Psycholinguistic experiments do not lend support to the view that physical meanings are primary meanings of double-function terms. Similarly, a more careful consideration of research on brain-damaged populations does not support the assumption that literal and metaphoric meanings can be distinguished by their hemispheric distribution.

Chapter 7 is a short chapter that serves as a bridge between the discussions of empirical and theoretical questions. I outline possible relations between polysemous adjectives and corresponding concepts, and argue for a realistic theory of concepts.

Chapter 8 is about cognitive linguistics again. I consider Eve Sweetser's mind-as-body metaphor theory and a number of related accounts which offer a different explanation of synaesthetic and double-function polysemy than the theory of domain conflation. I argue that the mind-as-body metaphor theory is also unsatisfactory as a theory of conceptual structure able to support these two types of adjectival polysemy.

Chapter 9 is about polysemy from the perspective of lexical semantics. I discuss a number of issues from the debate between Ray Jackendoff and James Pustejovsky, on the one hand, and Jerry Fodor, on the other hand. I argue that the Thematic Relations Hypothesis cannot preserve concept univocality, and that the generative lexicon theory encounters a number of problems in dealing not only with metaphorical but also non-metaphorical adjectival polysemy. However, the disquotational lexicon suffers from similar problems and is even less able to accommodate synaesthetic and double-function polysemy.

Chapter 10 develops the no-polysemy view of conceptual structure in more detail. According to the no-polysemy view, all meanings of a synaesthetic or double-function adjective map onto the same psychologically primitive concept. For this reason, all their meanings are their literal meanings. I argue that the causal theory of reference that can be invoked against the no-polysemy view in fact supports it. I further argue that conceptual necessity has to be distinguished from metaphysical necessity, and that a theory of concepts does not have to be at the same time a theory of meaning or semantic representation. I also outline the position of the no-polysemy view with respect to a number of issues in the semantics–pragmatics debate, and place it into a broader perspective of metaphor and polysemy research. Finally, in a very short Chapter 11 I summarize the main arguments of this book.

Since the no-polysemy view diverges radically from the standard view, and since it takes about two hundred pages to explain the motivation and the need for it, as well as to develop its proposals in more detail, it is hard to fully express it in the contents outline. If you think that outrageous ideas may have a chance of being true, you should keep on reading. The exposition in this book could remind you of a crime fiction story. This is the way I intended it. In a good detective story, there is a problem in the beginning and a number of clues all the way through. The clues seem to be pointing in one particular direction. However, when they are all considered together, they suggest that we should look for a solution somewhere else. I believe that in my solution to the puzzle all bits and pieces fit, although perhaps they do not as yet stick closely. To make them stick we need the glue of future research (and this, by the way, is a trite metaphor).

2
Metaphor in Cognitive Linguistics

2.1 The cognitive linguistics revolution

Today many metaphor researchers work in the framework of cognitive linguistics. The cognitive linguistics revolution began in 1980 with the publication of George Lakoff and Mark Johnson's *Metaphors We Live By*. In their book, Lakoff and Johnson amassed an amazing number of examples showing that the way we talk about abstract domains appears to be systematically structured by the way we talk about certain more concrete domains. Thus, we talk about theories and arguments as if they were buildings: theories can have support and arguments can be demolished. These observations gave rise to the theory of conceptual metaphor which moved metaphor out of language into our conceptual organization. According to Lakoff and Johnson, linguistic expressions such as 'to demolish a theory' or 'the foundation of a theory' are not isolated expressions but parts of the conceptual metaphor THEORIES ARE BUILDINGS.

Besides analysing the way we talk into conceptual metaphors, Lakoff and Johnson argued for a new theory of human conceptual organization which received the name of 'experientialism'.[1] Unlike many other theories of concepts, experientialism does not ignore the role of human body and sensorimotor experience in shaping human cognition and language. We are not just minds floating in the air, but beings whose successful operation in the world depends on being able to manipulate the environment. Thought and language cannot be independent of our embodiment.

In Chapter 1, I showed that 'classical' theories of metaphor presuppose the notion of literal (primary) meaning which turns out to depend not on context-invariance or sameness of extension, but rather on some conceptual primacy. However, these theories (with the exception of Richards') are never explicit about what conceptual primacy is. The theory of Lakoff and Johnson is revolutionary in the sense that it brings the notion of conceptual primacy to the fore. It reduces a large number of concepts to experiential primitives which are extended via metaphor to cover the whole domain of human understanding. And thus, the notion of metaphor becomes reconsidered as well. As Lakoff says in 'The contemporary theory of metaphor' (Lakoff, 1993), the classical theory was wrong in trying to find generalizations governing the use of metaphoric expressions in language. The source of metaphoric language is in thought, in the organization of our conceptual system. In this new theory, metaphor is considered as a fundamental cognitive process, as a basic schema 'by which people conceptualize their experience and the external world' (Gibbs, 1994, p.1).

In this chapter we shall have a look at some experientialist ideas. It has to be emphasized, though, that Lakoff and Johnson's theory is only one particular strand within a much broader area of cognitive linguistics, and that not all cognitive linguists share their philosophical views. However, since what interests us here are questions of conceptual organization, we shall not discuss either the theory of 'cognitive grammar' which seeks semantic motivation for grammatical constructions (Langacker, 1987, 1990) or the theory of 'conceptual blending' which concentrates on novel individual expressions rather than on systematic projections between conceptual domains (Fauconnier and Turner, 1996, 1998). Moreover, the impact of experientialism was felt by scholars in other traditions of research (Edelman, 1992; Glenberg, 1997; Glenberg and Robertson, 2000), and we shall presently see why.

2.2 Experientialism and conceptual organization

As I said above, Lakoff and Johnson proposed a new theory of metaphor which is based on a philosophical position called 'experientialism'. The essence of the experientialist explanation consists in the answer it provides to the old question of how experience relates to the genesis of concepts and the organization of conceptual structure.

Experientialism emphasizes the role of the human body in the formation of concepts, and one of its central notions is the notion of 'embodiment', which means that thought and understanding are characterized in terms of our having our particular kind of bodies. For an experientialist, there are two types of concepts that are directly meaningful because of the role they play in bodily experience. These are basic-level concepts and kinaesthetic image schemas. Basic-level concepts are sometimes described as concepts for middle-sized objects, and at this level objects are most easily grouped together because of their perceptual salience. Thus, CAT is a basic-level concept because all cats are more or less perceptually similar; whereas ANIMAL is a superordinate concept because animals can differ greatly in their looks (see Lakoff, 1988, p. 133).

The second type of directly meaningful concepts are image schemas, which include simple schemas such as CONTAINERS, PATHS, FORCES, and schemas for orientations and relations such as UP-DOWN or CENTRE-PERIPHERY. Our experience is structured by our sensorimotor capacities, and image schemas are basic principles of our bodily operation in the world (perception, movement through space, and physical manipulation of objects). Image schemas are pre-conceptual, non-propositional and nonfinatary because they exist prior to and independently of our conceptualizations of the world. In fact, they determine how the world is conceptualized, but an explanation of their operation in our experience cannot be given with the help of finatary representations (Johnson, 1987, p. 23). That is, we have the concept of containment, because CONTAINMENT is an image schema that structures our perception and manipulation of objects, but its content cannot be given in the form of a statement 'Containment is . . .'. According to experientialism, the concept of containment cannot be understood without taking into account its embodied character.

These two types of concepts – basic-level concepts and image schemas – are directly meaningful and universal because they are directly experienced by everybody in identical ways. The universal character of kinaesthetic structuring comes from the 'gross patterns' of our experience such as 'our vertical orientation, the nature of our bodies as containers and as wholes with parts' (Lakoff 1987, p. 303). However, we also think and talk about abstract entities. According to experientialism, abstract conceptual domains are understood with the help of directly meaningful concepts via so-called metaphorical projection. Thus, abstract concepts are not directly meaningful, but acquire their meaning from directly meaningful concepts. Image schemas which are our primary conceptualizations serve as the basis for 'the nonpropositional dimension of metaphorical processes of inference' (Johnson, 1988, pp. 28–9). According to experientialism, we can talk of purposes as physical goals ('to reach an objective') because our understanding of purposive acts is structured by the experience of physical movement towards a location. Thus, the meaning of 'reach' in such expressions as 'to reach the pick of one's career' is metaphorically derived from the physical meaning of 'reach' ('to reach a shelf'). PURPOSES ARE PHYSICAL GOALS is the representation of this understanding in conceptual structure.

Metaphor becomes redefined in the experientialist framework as a way of 'understanding and experiencing one kind of thing in terms of another' (Lakoff and Johnson 1980, p. 5) or as 'a cross-domain mapping in the conceptual system' (Lakoff 1993, p. 203). This way it loses its old status of a linguistic means of expressing 'similar' concepts, and is understood as a mechanism of concept formation which is very much alive and active in human cognition. Which means that conceptual metaphors are part and parcel of our thought, and that abstract (not directly meaningful) concepts are represented via metaphor.

2.3 Reasons to take experientialism seriously

Lakoff and Johnson's theory is also sometimes called 'cognitive semantics'. Cognitive semantics studies relations between concepts as represented via conceptual metaphor (PURPOSES ARE PHYSICAL GOALS, THEORIES ARE BUILDINGS), whereas experientialism is a philosophy behind it which attempts to give an explanation of the phenomenon of conceptual metaphor in terms of our embodied experience. One can see that the two are clearly separable. This is why reactions to Lakoff and Johnson's theory varied from almost complete acceptance on the part of some linguists and many literary theorists to scepticism on the part of many psychologists and philosophers.[2] In this section I mention some reasons to take cognitive semantics *and* the philosophy of experientialism seriously.

Thus, I believe that the theory of experientialism contains a number of important claims that will have to be retained by any alternative account of the relationship between language, conceptual structure, and our being in the world. They include:

(a) the claim that 'objectivist' accounts of meaning which treat meaning as 'a relation between symbolic representations and objective (mind-independent) reality' (Johnson, 1987, p. 18) are unsatisfactory because they ignore the fact that meanings exist only for human beings. A satisfactory theory of meaning should take into account our perceptual and motor experience.
(b) the claim that the correct understanding of what our conceptual structure is like can only be achieved through a consideration of our bodily organization and the mechanisms of perception. The emphasis on the kinaesthetic structuring of experience, and therefore

conceptual structure, is supported by independent evidence on the existence of important links between visual processing and motor systems (Milner and Goodale, 1995).

(c) finally, and most importantly, the claim that polysemy has to be explained in terms of conceptual structure rather than in linguistic terms alone. In the last section, we saw how cognitive semantics treats the polysemy of 'reach' ('reach' is polysemous because one of its meanings is about the processes of physically extending, say, an arm, and its other meaning is about the processes of achieving something in the social world). Cognitive semantics offers a systematic treatment of polysemy by relating various meanings of a polyseme via the mechanism of metaphorical projection. Besides, it gives an explanation of this relation by grounding conceptual structure in our bodily organization.[3]

2.4 Cognitive semantics and the literal–metaphorical distinction

Metaphor researchers working in the traditional framework immediately noticed that in Lakoff and Johnson's theory of conceptual metaphor the notion of the literal-metaphorical distinction is significantly reconsidered. Much of the language that most researchers would consider as literal is claimed to be metaphorical by cognitive semanticists (Kittay, 1987, p. 20; Mac Cormac, 1985, pp. 57–70).

In Lakoff and Johnson's theory, abstract conceptual domains are metaphorically structured on the model of directly meaningful domains. Linguistic expressions are 'surface realizations' of such cross-domain mappings from physical to abstract domains (Lakoff, 1993, p. 203). Thus, linguistic expressions from abstract domains are considered to be metaphorical because they reflect these domains' metaphoric structuring. Even if the expression 'to attack an argument' appears to be conventional (and thus literal), in Lakoff and Johnson's theory it is considered to be metaphorical, because it forms part of the conceptual metaphor ARGUMENT IS WAR (we understand the domain of arguments in terms of the domain of war).[4] The general position of cognitive semanticists on the literal-metaphorical distinction is well summarized by Andrew Goatly:

> The only difference between literal and metaphorical language is that, in literal use, we adhere to conventional criteria for classification,

whereas in metaphorical use, the similarities, the criteria for interpretation are relatively unconventional. . . . In fact, if literal language is simply conventional metaphor, then, far from being an anomaly, metaphor becomes basic. (1997, p. 3)

There is no denial here of literal language, but many conventional expressions belong to domains that are structured metaphorically, and are thus metaphorical in the sense of being conceptually secondary. As we have seen, classical theories of metaphor, which claim to be understanding literal meaning in terms of conventionality, sameness of extension or context-independence, in fact all tacitly presuppose the notion of conceptual primacy (for a critique of the notion of literal meaning see Gibbs, 1993, 1994, Gibbs et al., 1993[5]; see also Glucksberg, 2001). And thus, it appears that rather than completely reconsidering the literal–metaphorical distinction, cognitive semantics is, in many respects, a natural continuation of the old tradition. Of course, the theory of conceptual metaphor is different from classical metaphor theories because the distinction between the literal and the metaphorical has for the first time been explicitly formulated in terms of conceptual structure. Nonetheless, from the point of view of conceptual organization and conceptual primacy, cognitive semantics it is not a radically new theory, but rather a step forward.

Classical theories of metaphor all subscribe to the standard assumption which says that only one meaning of a polyseme can be its literal meaning. According to Lakoff and Johnson, most concepts are metaphorically structured and derive their structure from a basic set of non-metaphorical concepts that are closest to our embodied experience. So, it appears that despite its divergence from the classical view, cognitive semantics also endorses a version of the standard assumption: there are primary meanings, and all other meanings of a polyseme are derivative and metaphorical. There are many important insights in the theory of conceptual metaphor, particularly the insight that the correct understanding of metaphor and polysemy can only be achieved if we conduct our inquiry at the level of conceptual structure rather than words alone. However, the experientialist theory of metaphor, just as classical theories of metaphor, subscribes to the standard assumption.

2.5 Some problems for the philosophy of experientialism

In section 2.3 I gave three reasons to take experientialism seriously. The most important reason is that it places questions of metaphor and polysemy[6] in the broader perspective of human cognition and conceptual organization. Nonetheless, a number of experientialist claims are difficult to accept. Elsewhere (Rakova, 2002) I discuss these claims in detail and show that they are either philosophically inconsistent or contradicted by empirical evidence. In this section I briefly discuss some of these claims, and then, in the next section, I offer a more detailed consideration of one claim that is directly relevant to the main topic of this book.

The idea of metaphorically structured concepts has been extensively criticized by many psychologists, linguists, and philosophers who noted, among other things, that only those domains whose structure is already known to us can be restructured metaphorically (Dahl, 1989; Garnham, 1989; Honeck, 1989; Indurkhya, 1992; Indurkhya, 1994; Jackendoff and Aaron, 1991; Maratsos, 1989; Murphy, 1996; Murphy, 1997). The most detailed critique of metaphoric representation has been proposed by Gregory Murphy (1996) who argued that the 'strong view of metaphoric representation' (the postulation of metaphorically structured concepts) is not psychologically viable. Thus, for example, the strong view of metaphoric representation implies that we should draw a large number of incorrect inferences about the metaphorically structured domains. If our concept LOVE were structured by our understanding of journeys, we would draw very peculiar inferences about love relations. But this does not happen, and thus the strong view of metaphoric representation must be wrong.

In his reply to Murphy, Ray Gibbs (1996)[7] emphasized that the critique missed the point of the experientialist position because it ignored the role that human embodiment plays in laying the foundations of representational thought. However, the theory of embodiment does not invalidate Murphy's criticisms. On the contrary, when the theory of embodiment is taken into account, it appears that the theory of conceptual metaphor is even less viable than one might have thought. And the main problem is that the theory of conceptual metaphor is compatible only with an empiricist position.[8] But it is doubtful that any empiricist position will turn out to be correct.

It has to be emphasized that the experientialist notion of embodiment is not the same notion of embodiment that is generally found in the cognitive science literature. And even in the cognitive science literature it is sometimes understood differently. It can refer to a reduction of mental entities and processes to the underlying neural organization, the purely physical stuff (as in Churchland, 1991). It can also refer to the idea that all cognitive operations are grounded in neural transformations and that the same neural mechanisms and pathways can be used for both perception and cognition (as in Barsalou, 1999). Finally, it can refer to the idea that 'tightly coupled organism-environment interactions' (Clark, 2001) which make large use of bodily action and local problem-solving mechanisms are at the heart of human cognitive processes (Ballard, 1991; Ballard et al., 1997; Kelso, 1995). None of these notions is the experientialist notion of embodiment. What experientialists mean by embodiment is that our concepts are structured by image schemas which emerge from our everyday interactions with the environment through the body.

This understanding of embodiment is particularly prominent in Lakoff and Johnson's earlier writings (Johnson, 1987; Lakoff, 1987). Thus, we find it, for example, in Johnson's (1987) discussion of the container schema. As he says, this image schema arises from our experience of containment such as perceiving our bodies as containers into which we 'put' food and air, perceiving our surroundings as containers in and out of which we move (rooms, clothes), and so on (p. 21). Since in the experientialist story image schemas are directly meaningful conceptual structures which give rise to all other concepts, this account is clearly an empiricist account. But it cannot be true because it grossly contradicts developmental evidence.

As most developmental psychologists would agree, children's understanding of containment as related to their bodies appears quite late in development. Similarly, the understanding of object permanence takes time to develop (Piaget, 1961/1969; Smith et al., 1999). And the understanding of the permanence of matter (such as air going into human lungs in Johnson's example) is simply out of question at this early age. Besides, the ability to derive the concept of containment from the activity of putting something into oneself presupposes the ability to represent oneself as an agent. However this ability appears only around the age of three or four (Perner, 1991; Flavell 1988; Wellman, 1990). Equally problematic is Johnson's claim that the image schema of containment emerges from perceiving our surroundings as containers, since the understanding of the surroundings as containers requires that external reference points be already mastered at that stage. However, external frames of reference also take time to establish (Piaget 1961/1969, p. 334; Sutherland, 1992).

The point is that the schema (and thus the concept) of containment cannot be derived from instances of putting something into oneself, analysing the visual field into containers, and understanding oneself as being placed into a container by an individual who is not perceptually 'equipped' for these purposes. However, to say that the idea of containment is not something that children learn from experience, but the way the world is perceived automatically and unconsciously from an early age would undermine the experientialist account of the image-kinaesthetic conceptual basis.

The psychologist Jean Mandler (1988, 1992a, 1992b, 1994), who is generally in agreement with the experientialist theory, noticed that the agentive perception of containment as described by Johnson is rather problematic, and suggested instead that image schemas are derived by infants from their early visual experience. Mandler follows Johnson in claiming that image schemas must have an empirical origin (1994, p. 68), but, on her account, infants' perceptual input is re-described into the format of image schemas, and those form the basic concepts of an early conceptual system. But although Mandler's account is more realistic than Johnson's, it also encounters a number of problems. Most importantly, Mandler cannot retain the distinction that she wishes to draw between innate mechanisms of analysis and innately given content (1992b, p. 592). The reason for this is that the most plausible non-nativist explanation according to which infants have an innate predisposition to form image schemas of certain types already presupposes a nativist account of content (mapping visual experience onto innately given schemas). As many psychologists agree today, the mechanisms of perceptual analysis are innately constrained and biased with respect to certain features of stimuli (Eimas, 1994; Landau, 1994; for related criticisms of Mandler's account see Laurence and Margolis, 2002, pp. 52–3; see also Vandervert, 1997).[9] Generally, whereas no one would object to the presence of schematic structures in perception and cognition, there is no reason to think that image schemas, and therefore concepts, have the 'experientialist' origin.[10]

But even more serious problems accompany the experientialist account of abstract concepts. There follow some observations to this effect. According to experientialism, abstract concepts are derived from directly meaningful concepts via metaphorical projection. Initially, the idea was that there exists a clear dividing line between directly and indirectly meaningful concepts. The existence of directly meaningful concepts was explained through naturalness of certain experiences. Natural kinds of experience, and thus directly meaningful concepts, included the experience of physical orientations, objects, substances, seeing, journeys, war, madness (sic!), food, buildings, and so on, and these were supposed to lend their structure to all other concepts (Lakoff and Johnson, 1980, p. 118). Later this account was modified because it became evident that one cannot just postulate natural kinds of experience without any further justification for treating some experiences as more natural than others (for example, how can one say about the conceptual metaphor LOVE IS MADNESS that the experience of madness is more natural than the experience of love?).

Thus, in later writings we find the idea that directly meaningful concepts are 'closer' to pre-conceptual image schemas than all other concepts. For example, the concept of journey is directly meaningful not because the experience of journeys is a natural kind of experience, but because we understand journeys directly in terms of the path image schema (there is a starting point, movement in a direction, and a final point to which movement was directed). Abstract concepts are not directly meaningful because they have no 'preconceptual structure of their own' (Lakoff, 1987, p. 303) and thus have to be metaphorically understood through directly meaningful concepts. What immediately makes one wonder, and what has caught everyone's attention but cognitive semanticists' (Dahl, 1989; Honeck, 1989; Indurkhya, 1992; Indurkhya, 1994; Jackendoff and Aaron, 1991; Maratsos, 1989; Murphy, 1996; Murphy, 1997) is that abstract concepts can be structured by preconceptual image schemas just as well as so-called directly meaningful concepts.

In this respect, the notion of conceptual metaphor is not needed to explain why sensorimotor schematisms may enter the understanding of abstract concepts. The theory of conceptual metaphor does not necessarily follow from the theory of cognitive embodiment. Experientialists have been running the two claims together without making it clear why the two positions cannot be separated. There are other theories of cognitive embodiment around, but none of them requires the existence of conceptual metaphors. Thus, although one certainly needs to give an explanation to the fact that there is 'the qualitative feel of sensorimotor experience to abstract concepts' (Lakoff and Johnson, 1999, p. 128), it does not follow that this explanation has to be formulated in terms of conceptual metaphor.[11]

It is also essential to remember that the content of abstract concepts cannot be reduced to sensorimotor or perceptual schematisms.[12] And because experientialists have concentrated all their efforts on trying to find more and more conceptual metaphors, they do not have a theory of meaning. This is also the reason why their views have not been very popular among the broader cognitive science community (cf. Gibbs, 1994, p. 437), and particularly among philosophers. Experientialists say that 'meaning is always a matter of human understanding' (Johnson, 1987, p. 174), that '[m]eaning is based on the understanding of experience' (Lakoff, 1988, p. 150), or even that we 'experience meaning' (Johnson and Lakoff, 2002). However, this kind of rhetoric cannot count a theory of meaning. If I ask you what 'Life has an end' means, you cannot reply that we understand life through the concept of journey, for it would be the same as to reply nothing at all. The point is that even though our concepts are clearly connected to our experience, we do not *experience* concepts. Even less do we *experience* meanings. Any theory of meaning has to accommodate the notion of normativity (Marconi, 1997). But it never makes its way into experientialist claims. Apart from reiterating that meaning is embodied and that abstract concepts are understood via conceptual metaphors, experientialists do not tell us anything else.

2.6 Adjectival polysemy in the experientialist framework

A detailed consideration of the theory of embodied realism is not our concern here. However, there is one issue that deserves particular attention. In addition to their old view on embodiment, Lakoff and Johnson (1999) introduce the notion of neural embodiment. The notion of neural embodiment can be employed in connection with colour concepts (the fact that humans have the colour concepts that they have largely depends on the neural circuitry of the visual system) or spatial-relations concepts (those would not be available to us without topographic maps and orientation-sensitive cells). But whereas this is the notion of embodiment that I am fully prepared to endorse, it does not support their views on metaphoric structuring of concepts.[13] I discuss one such example below which is especially interesting for us because it concerns adjectival polysemy.

In explaining the notion of neural embodiment, Lakoff and Johnson (1999) introduce Christopher Johnson's theory of domain conflation (1997a, b), which seeks to explain polysemy in terms of experiential correlations in early development. The term 'conflation' means that two conceptual domains are conflated in experience prior to the emergence of a conceptual metaphor. And the theory postulates two developmental stage: (1) the conflation stage, 'during which connections between coactive domains are established and the domains are not experienced as separate'; and (2) the differentiation stage, 'during which domains that were previously coactive are differentiated into metaphorical sources and targets' (Lakoff and Johnson 1999, p. 49).

Although the theory of domain conflation was proposed to explain the conceptual metaphor of knowing as seeing, it has been applied to other cases as well. Thus, Lakoff and Johnson discuss it in connection with the putative conflation of subjective experience with sensorimotor experience which are said to be undifferentiated in early childhood. According to the theory of domain conflation, early childhood associations between subjective and sensorimotor experience explain the existence of such expressions as 'a warm smile', 'a big problem' and 'a close friend'. It says, for instance, that since the experience of affection is regularly correlated in infancy with the feeling of being warm (being held), the association between the two domains becomes automatically 'built-in'. Later the domains become differentiated but the cross-domain mapping persists. The results of domain conflation are called 'primary metaphors' (Grady, Taub and Morgan, 1996; Grady, 1999). And the theory of domain conflation can be supplemented by the notion of neural embodiment (Narayanan, 1997). Thus, stable cross-domain associations of infancy and early childhood become realized neurally in permanent connections between the networks serving these conceptual domains, such that the activation of one domain results in the activation of the other domain. This way metaphorical thinking becomes built-in, automatic and unconscious.

But does the theory of domain conflation explain why there are such expressions as 'a big problem'? According to Grady (1999), the primary metaphors DIFFICULT IS HEAVY, PLEASING IS TASTY, and IMPORTANT IS BIG are the result of regular correlations in experience: lifting a heavy object produces an experience of strain, tasting a sweet object produces an experience of pleasure, and so on. Note that there is an important difference between the more traditional examples of verbal ('reach') and prepositional polysemy ('in') discussed by cognitive linguists and Grady's primary metaphors which concern adjectival polysemy. According to experientialism, abstract meanings of many verbs and prepositions are metaphorical because they share the same image-schematic structure with their physical meanings: every meaning of 'reach' is an instance of travelling along a path, and every meaning of 'in' is an instance of the container schema. Grady's primary metaphors are of a different kind: not everything that is difficult is heavy ('heavy music' is not necessarily music difficult to play or listen to; and 'heavy smell' is not necessarily a smell that is difficult to bear).[14] Besides, there is no clear unidirectionality in such examples: heaviness of an object can be conceptualized as an instance of encountering certain difficulty when dealing with it (grand-piano is certainly a heavy object, but it is also an object difficult to handle).

The claim that primary metaphors result from regular correlations in early experience such that the two domains are not experienced as separate is even more difficult to maintain. Consider the expression 'a big problem'. As follows from the theory of domain conflation, young children's conceptualization of difficulty can be reduced to their conceptualization of big physical objects. But do only big objects cause problems in childhood? Picking up a small object is a big, not a small problem for a young child. True, the conceptualization of difficulty (subjective experience) is most probably correlated with the conceptualization of physical size (sensorimotor experience). However, there are no reasons to believe that difficulty is initially conceptualized as large size. Besides, the postulated two stages in development – domain conflation and domain differentiation – do not fit developmental evidence on how children understand polysemous adjectives. They differentiate at least at the age of three, rejecting psychological meanings of 'physical' adjectives as unacceptable. Later they come to understand the two meanings but consider them independent, whereas the stage of 'conflation' or noticing similarities appears only by the age of ten. Moreover, the acquisition of psychological meanings was found not to depend on the acquisition of physical meanings (Asch and Nerlove, 1960; see Chapter 5).

Lakoff and Johnson (1999) say that when sensorimotor and subjective experiences are conflated, permanent neural connections between the networks serving the two domains become established. Primary metaphors appear as a result of simultaneous activation in the two networks. This way, thinking of problems as 'big' or friends as 'close' becomes automatic and unconscious in later experience. A question that immediately comes to mind is why one needs to postulate metaphoric connections, if subjective experience is present as early as sensorimotor experience (Ortony, 1988). Why cannot one say that the same predicates that are true of sensorimotor experience are true of subjective experience? As it happens, Lakoff and Johnson do not deny that we have 'literal' concepts of subjective experience (that we can be aware of our subjective experience). But they think that literal concepts have little 'flesh'. They do not allow us to make inferences, that is why they borrow inferences from the domain of sensorimotor experience with which they correlate (p. 58). And they can do so because there is a simultaneous activation of neural networks for the two domains which becomes established in early childhood on the basis of statistically reliable associations:

> The theory assumes that a sensorimotor neural system has more inferential connections, and therefore a greater inferential capacity, than a neural system characterizing subjective experience in itself. This is the source of asymmetry of primary conceptual metaphor. (ibid.)

This putative neural explanation is supposed to justify the existence of primary metaphors, but it cannot do the job. Neurological evidence shows that the site for subjective experience is the limbic system, the brain's mechanism for regulating cognitive and emotional processing (for recent data see Bush *et al.*, 2000; Liotti *et al.*, 2000). To claim that 'a neural system characterizing subjective experience in itself' is grounded in 'a sensorimotor neural system', Lakoff and Johnson should have bothered to present at least some evidence showing that in the human brain there are 'constitutive' neural projections from the one to the other, such that, for example, impairments of the latter lead to impaired functioning of the former. However, things are the other way round: the normal functioning of the motor system depends on the normal functioning of the limbic system. Thus, large dysfunction of the motor system such as in Parkinson's disease is associated with reduced limbic influence (Braak *et al.*, 2000). Connectionist assumptions to the contrary, brains do not support any kind of architecture one may care to impose on them.

One might object that Lakoff and Johnson (1999) are not talking of neural systems as such, but of neural systems as serving our conceptual structure. The objection does not hold, however, as we know very little about those: we do not know how concepts are distributed in the brain (cf. Caplan 1987, pp. 170–95). Neither do we know to what extent they are grounded in the sensorimotor system. Thus, although it is an established fact that cognitive tasks share some neural structures with sensorimotor tasks, certain structures are associated with either only cognitive or only sensorimotor tasks (Lowenthal, 1999).

Even if we grant that during the conflation period permanent neural connections develop between the domain of sensorimotor experience and the domain of subjective experience, we may still wonder how, in this case, domain differentiation is rendered neurologically possible. For instance, if conceptualizing quantity as verticality (the MORE IS UP conceptual metaphor) is a permanent connection established early in development, it follows that quantity qua verticality is the only concept available to us for thinking about quantities. And thus one may choose to call it metaphorical but, being the only concept we have, it is not metaphorical in any interesting sense.

Again, one might object that Lakoff and Johnson do not deny any independent content to the domain or concept of quantity, they only say that it is inferentially 'poor'. Neither do they assume that the connection between the domains is necessary ('[t]he neural connections between the domains, which constitute the metaphorical mapping, may or may not be activated', p. 56). But then, the neural story is not much help. We are back to the same old problem that has already been pointed out many times (Maratsos, 1989; Indurkhya, 1992, 1994; Murphy, 1996), namely that only those domains that have sufficient internal structure with relevant inferential potential can be metaphorically restructured through some other domain. Indeed, the neural story makes the very idea of metaphoric concepts problematic. If the connections become epigenetically wired, how can they be un-wired during the postulated differentiation stage (given that the environment does not change and still supports the associations made during the conflation stage)? So, it follows either that there is no concept of quantity other than quantity-qua-verticality (no concept of difficulty other than difficulty-qua-large-size, and so on) or that there is no such thing as primary metaphors. The latter option seems to be a lot more plausible one.[15]

Overall, while there is no doubt that experientialists have scored an important point in emphasizing the embodied character of human thought, some of their claims are difficult to accept. In particular this concerns the theory of conceptual metaphor. Still, despite my disagreement with their views, I propose, in a sense, to continue their line of reasoning. For I also believe that polysemy has to be explained in terms of conceptual structure. Thus, for example, I believe that an explanation in terms of conceptual structure is needed in order to understand why polysemy is so cognitively effective. (Think of the number of words you know, you could have easily learned another couple of thousands; languages with no polysemous terms but a large number of monosemous terms are logically possible). But for all that, I do not think that the cognitive semantics way is the right way of understanding polysemy in terms of conceptual structure. In this book I present a different story.

The examples I have selected for my story will also serve to further test the theory of conceptual metaphor. As I emphasized in this chapter, the major achievement of experientialism was to bring conceptual structure closer to perception and our bodily organization. Thus, one way to test its postulates is to consider a group of examples which are clearly about our experience of being in the world. The group of examples I mostly deal with in this book are adjectives expressing concepts for properties of objects of perceptual experience. Polysemous adjectives such as 'bright' or 'sharp' are interesting in the sense that they seem to be literal in descriptions of some domains of experience, but not of others. According to the view that I labelled 'the standard assumption', only one of the meanings of a polysemous adjective is its literal meaning, while all its other meanings are derivative and metaphorical. As we have seen, cognitive semanticists also subscribe to this assumption.

Therefore, if it is the case that some meanings of polysemous adjectives express concepts that are perceptually primary, while their other meanings can be derived from these primary meanings via metaphor, then the standard assumption is correct, and consequently, cognitive semantics claims are justified. If, however, it is the case that no such perceptual or conceptual primacy exists (for example, that 'bright' is not primarily or 'properly' the term for some property in the domain of vision) and metaphorical derivation of the supposedly metaphoric concepts is not feasible, then there is a good reason to doubt the standard assumption and the way the literal–metaphorical distinction has been drawn up to now.

3
The 'Hot' Polysemy

3.1 Why neurophysiology matters to semantics

Have you ever wondered why you call chilli peppers hot? Of course, you might say, because your mouth feels hot when you take a bite. Yes, but why does it feel hot? What makes you describe chillies as 'hot'? Why do use the same word as in 'hot stove' or 'hot day'?

This chapter is about the polysemy of the word 'hot'. We use it to describe the somewhat painful sensation produced on us by capsaicin (the pungent ingredient of capsicum peppers). And we use it to describe thermal sensations which at times can also be painful. The word 'hot' is polysemous between 'of noticeably high temperature' and 'spicy'. Recent work by David Julius and his colleagues (see Caterina *et al.*, 1997) shows that the connection between these two senses of 'hot' is not arbitrary; in fact, that there are good physiological reasons for calling chilli peppers hot.

But, you might say, why does it matter if we know that there is some physiological mechanism which is activated by both thermal stimuli and a certain chemical substance that peppers contain? What can it tell us about the word 'hot'? The answer is that this kind of knowledge matters a lot. The work of George Lakoff and his school, as well as the independent work of Lawrence Barsalou and other cognitive scientists, teaches us that our embodiment, our sensorimotor functioning in the world cannot be ignored. We do not have words and concepts just because it is nice for us to have them. Words and concepts are the devices that connect us to the external world. Without the body and the brain with its perceptual machinery we would not have the concepts that we have. For this reason, understanding the specifics of our perceptual mechanisms may shed light on the specifics of our conceptual system. But things work the other way round as well. Perception, cognition and language are inseparable. The study of linguistic patterns can tell us something about our cognition because language expresses thought. And our cognition would not be what it is were we not connected to the world through our senses.

The best-known example of how physiology and semantics can inform each other is found in the classical work of Brent Berlin and Paul Kay (1969) on basic colour terms. Although languages differ in the number of colour terms they have, colour vocabularies of different languages follow the same pattern. If there are only two basic colour terms in a language, they are always 'dark' and 'light'. The next comes 'red', then 'yellow' or 'green', then 'blue', and so on. Besides, regardless of the number of colour terms a language has, the best focal colours (the best red or the best green) are the same for people of different cultures all over the world.

The work of Eleanor Rosch (1974, 1978; Rosch Heider, 1972, 1973; Rosch Heider and Olivier, 1972) with the Dani people (from Western New Guinea) confirmed this. The Dani's language only has two colour terms. This does not mean that they see the world as we see it on the screen of a black-and-white TV. They have colour vision, and what they see is not different from what we see. The difference is in the number of words which our languages use to categorize colours. To have an idea of what it may feel like, compare your colour vocabulary with that of an interior decorator. In this comparison, your colour vocabulary seems impoverished. However, your perception of colours, and your communication about colours are not defective in any sense. You may never use the word 'honeyburst' to describe your colour experience, but this does not affect your life. The Dani use only two words to describe their colour experience, but that does not make their lives deprived of colour. Rosch found (with the help of coloured chips) that the Dani could easily learn names for colours, especially for focal colours. Moreover, memorization, recognition and recall of colour terms followed the pattern proposed by Berlin and Kay ('red' was the easiest to remember and recall). Thus, Rosch concluded that the colour space is a perfect example of the influence that perceptual–cognitive factors have on linguistic categories.

Colour terms of human languages do not arbitrarily divide the spectrum. They are universally constrained by our visual system. The stages of colour acquisition in the historical development of languages correspond to the system of colour discrimination that we share with higher primates. Up to date, the most commonly accepted account of colour discrimination is the opponent theory first developed by Hering (1920). According to the opponent theory, in our visual system there are paired sets of neurons which respond to light of different wavelengths. The evolutionarily oldest pair responds to the light/dark distinction; the next on the phylogenetic scale is the red/green pair, and so on. Basic colour terms that different languages have, and the way that languages come to express them are thus constrained by the neurophysiology of our visual system (Kay and McDaniel, 1978; Boynton and Olson, 1987). In this sense, basic colour terms, or rather basic colour categories or concepts, are universals which are determined by our specific neural makeup.[1]

In this and the following chapters I am going to pursue the same strategy as found in the work of Berlin and Kay: the way that languages are is not arbitrary; our linguistic and conceptual design is not independent from our neurophysiological design; learning something about the one can inform us about the other. The 'hot' polysemy is the beginning of this inquiry.

3.2 The capsaicin receptor

The work of David Julius and his colleagues that I discuss in this section belongs to the area of pain research. Prior to their work, it had been known for some time that the exposure to capsaicin leads to the excitation of sensory neurones and the subsequent perception of pain. Capsaicin is a natural product of capsicum peppers, 'the molecule that makes chilli peppers seem hot' (Clapham, 1997, p. 783).[2] It was thought that since capsaicin evokes the sensation of burning pain, the biological target of its action must play an important role in the detection of painful stimuli, and that the identification of 'capsaicin receptor' may illuminate fundamental mechanisms of pain production. As the result of their work, Julius and colleagues identified the DNA-encoded amino-acid sequence of the protein that comprises the receptor for both capsaicin and painful heat.

I now need to say a few words about how information is communicated in the nervous system. The words 'information' and 'communication' should not embarrass you. Nervous cells, or neurons, of the peripheral nervous system become activated ('excited') when they come into contact with different kinds of stimuli. Because neurons are connected into nets, they can send their activation to other neurons. This way, activation reaches different areas of the central nervous system (CNS hereafter), where decisions are taken on the basis of information received. Think of the example you probably know all too well: the reflex. When you touch a hot stove, you automatically withdraw your hand. The action itself may seem simple, but there is quite a lot going on in your nervous system. The signals from your hand are transmitted to the spinal cord, where the information is distributed to interneurons. Some of them send this information to the brain where the sensation of pain is registered, others send information to motor neurons. Motor neurons in turn send information to the muscles and thus make your hand move away from the source of pain.

Neurons consist of the cell body and two types of fibres: axons, or the output fibres, and dendrites, or input fibres. Neurons communicate by contact, not continuity. The point at which one neuron contacts another is called the 'synapse'. When neurons become active ('fire'), an electric current is produced and sent down the axon. At the synapse, certain chemical substances ('neurotransmitters') are released, and the other neuron also changes its activation state. Thus, neurons communicate by electro-chemical signals. Those neurons that send their fibres to the periphery (for example, the skin) are activated by contact with external stimuli through different types of receptors on their terminals.

Changes in the activation state of a neuron are possible because neurons are enveloped by a membrane, which separates the inside of the cell from its outside. The intracellular and extracellular environments differ in electric charge and chemical composition. The membrane is made of different proteins (transcribed segments of DNA) which comprise so-called 'channels' that are selectively permeable to different chemical substances. When a certain substance is released, a channel opens, and electrically charged particles penetrate into the cell. Changes in the chemical composition and electric charge inside the cell lead to that cell's firing and sending its own signal ('impulse' or 'action potential') to other neurons.

What Julius and colleagues discovered was the site of capsaicin action in nociceptors (sensory neurons involved in the detection of pain-producing stimuli). It is a 'nonselective plasma-membrane cation channel' (Julius and Basbaum, 2001, p. 205), which they called the 'capsaicin receptor', and which is known as vanilloid receptor subtype 1 (VR1).[3] Capsaicin activates sensory neurones by increasing the permeability of plasma membrane to cations (positively charged particles). When VR1 is activated, the channel opens, and positively charged extracellular calcium ions penetrate into the cell. The influx depolarizes the nerve fibres, and a nerve impulse is sent to the brain.

It had been suggested that capsaicin molecules act on a specific receptor within nociceptors. To achieve a more detailed understanding of capsaicin action, Julius and colleagues carried out a number of experiments by reconstituting capsaicin responsiveness in non-neuronal cells (VR1-clones). They discovered that the capsaicin receptor is an integral membrane protein which is found in small-diameter neurons within sensory ganglia (neuronal groups). They also discovered that different subjective ratings of hotness of pepper variants (ranging from *Habanero*, which has the highest vanilloid content, to *Poblano verde*, which has almost none) correlate with their rank order potencies as activators of VR1 (the hotter a variety of pepper, the more VR1 is activated).

Julius and colleagues made an ingenious suggestion that since vanilloid-induced pain has a 'burning' quality, 'vanilloids and heat may evoke painful responses through a common molecular pathway' (Caterina *et al.*, 1997, p. 821). Thus, one of their experiments was designed to test whether the increase in temperature from 22 °C to ≈ 45 °C (the noxious, or painful, range) had any effect on VR1's activity. They found that a large number of cells expressing VR1 'exhibited a pronounced increase in calcium levels within seconds of heat treatment' (ibid., p. 822). This indicated that VR1 is activated by noxious, but not innocuous (painless) thermal stimuli. The results of other temperature-related experiments showed that heat-evoked and vanilloid-evoked responses are probably mediated by the same entity. This allowed them to suggest that, apart from being a chemical transducer, VR1 may also act as a thermal transducer *in vivo* (that is, in living organisms), either by itself, or in conjunction with other cellular components. The suggestion received confirmation when it was found that even in a non-mammalian context VR1's heat sensitivity had the same temperature-response profile as that reported for thermal nociceptors.

Thus, the fact that 'spicy' has 'hot' as its synonym can be grounded in the fact that the same molecular mechanisms underlie the production of sensations caused by hot (spicy) foods and high temperatures. David Clapham, who described Caterina *et al.*'s article as a 'plausible molecular explanation for why we perceive foods that contain capsaicin as hot' (1997, p. 784), suggested that a better name for VR1, or the capsaicin receptor, might have been the HOT channel.[4]

3.3 Are hot peppers 'hot' for everyone?

In the last section we saw that the same pain-detecting mechanism, VR1, is activated by noxious chemical (capsaicin) and thermal (hot temperature) stimuli. We can thus suppose that it is not an accident that 'hot' can mean 'spicy'.

This other meaning of the word has existed in English for a long time. Kuhn and Reidy's *Middle English Dictionary* traces it back to 1390,[5] and gives the meaning of 'hōt' as 'biting' or 'peppery', something that is said of spices. The Oxford English Dictionary (OED hereafter) offers the following definition: 'hot ... [p]roducing an effect as of heat or burning, esp. on the nerves of taste or the mucous membrane; pungent, acrid, biting; corrosive; heating, ardent'. The first entry is dated 1548: 'The Englishemen ... dranke hote wynes in the hote wether, and did eate all the hote frutes ... that there fell sicke' (Edward Hall, *Chronicle*). Here are another two examples. 1596: 'The Mustard is too hot a little' (William Shakespeare, *The Taming of the Shrew*); 1806: 'The dish is ... too hot of pepper' (Alexander Hunter, *Culina Famulatrix Medicinae; or Receipts in Modern Cookery*).

But however physiologically justified the use of 'hot' to mean 'spicy' is, one could ask whether other languages follow the same pattern. Let us consider some examples.

Ancient Greek	hot (of taste) = δριμυs (the temperature term for 'hot' is θερμοs) δριμυs = I. piercing, sharp, keen II. said of things which affect the eyes or taste
Latin	hot (of flavours) = *feruidus* (the first temperature term for 'hot' is *calidus*) *feruidus* = (1) intensely hot, boiling, burning;.. (5) hot to the taste
Italian	hot (of food) = *piccante* (the temperature term for 'hot' is *caldo*) *piccante* = (a) spicy, hot (b) risqué, racy
Spanish	hot (to taste) = *picante* (the temperature term for 'hot' is *caliente*) *picante* = (a) hot, peppery, highly seasoned (b) *fig.* remark: sharp, stinging, cutting
French	hot (to taste) = *cuisant, piquant* (the temperature term for 'hot' is *chaud*) *cuisant* = hot (pepper); smarting, burning (pain) *piquant* = (a) prickly, biting, cutting; (b) hot, pungent
German	hot (to taste) = *scharf* (the temperature term for 'hot' is *heiß*) *scharf* = (a) sharp (biting, cutting) (b) hot, highly seasoned
Dutch	hot (hot spices) = *scherpe* (the temperature terms for 'hot are *heet, warm*) *scherpe* = sharp; hot (spices)
Russian	hot = *ostryj* (the temperature terms for 'hot' are *gorjačij, žarkij*) *ostryj* = sharp; (*ostryj sous* = piquant sauce)[6]

As we can see, there is no single pattern common to all these languages. Only Latin is similar to English in that it makes an association between hot taste sensations and hot temperatures. German, Dutch, Russian and Ancient Greek are very different from English, but similar between themselves because their words for 'spicy' also mean 'sharp'. French reserves its equivalent of 'hot' to describe hot peppers, but otherwise uses 'piquant', as do Spanish and Italian.

But does this mean that there is no pattern that they all follow? The languages in our sample can be divided into two big groups depending on the words they use to describe hot taste sensations: (1) spicy = hot (English, Latin; French uses the word for 'burning' which also applies to burning pain); (2) spicy = sharp (German, Dutch, Russian, Ancient Greek) or piquant (French, Spanish, Italian).

What is interesting about the second group is that all the words used for describing hot taste sensations are associated with words for painful sensations of mechanical origin which all have a short, sharp, and intense quality. In many languages, the equivalent of 'sharp' is the general term which subsumes all of the following ones: (a) 'biting' (German, French; *Middle English Dictionary* and OED give 'biting' as a synonym for 'hot'); (b) 'cutting' (German, French, Spanish); (c) 'prickly' (French); (d) 'piercing' (Ancient Greek); and (e) 'piquant' (French, Spanish, Italian; English and Russian also have this word).[7]

On the whole, despite the diversity we see, a pattern that is common to all these languages is easily detected. For in all of them, words for taste sensations caused by spicy foods are also words for sensations caused by either noxious thermal or mechanical stimuli. In the next section we shall see that this pattern is, quite likely, not arbitrary but also grounded in our physiology.

3.4 The pain pathway

We have seen that there are good physiological reasons for the association between hot thermal stimuli and spicy taste sensations. In this section we shall see that the association between spicy taste sensations and painful sensations caused by mechanical stimuli may also be grounded in certain physiological properties of the nociceptive pathway.

Nociceptors, which are primary afferent nerves with peripheral terminals, have two major functions: (1) transduction, or 'receptor activation', when one form of energy (chemical, mechanical, or thermal) is converted into the electrochemical nerve impulse; and (2) transmission, when the coded information is relayed to the CNS (Fields, 1987).[8]

There are three major groups of primary afferents distinguished by the presence or absence of a myelin sheath (a kind of insulation that makes impulses travel faster), the diameters and the conduction velocities of their constituent axons and, therefore, by their function. These three major groups are: (1) the large diameter Aα fibre myelinated primary afferents; (2) the smaller diameter Aδ fibre myelinated primary afferents; and (3) the small diameter C fibre unmyelinated primary afferents. Aα primary afferents are not differential and can be excited by mild mechanical stimuli. They do not increase their discharge when more intense stimuli are applied to them, hence, they cannot signal the application of noxious stimuli. Moreover, subjects' reports show that their activity does not produce pain. Thus, they do not play any significant role in nociception.

In contrast to them, most Aδ and C primary afferents are nociceptors because they are maximally responsive to noxious stimuli. Aδ nociceptors respond to noxious mechanical stimuli, particularly to stimulation with sharp-pointed instruments. Although some of them respond to innocuous mechanical stimuli as well, they are not as sensitive to them as Aα mechanoreceptors. About half of Aδ nociceptors also respond to noxious heat (type II Aδ nociceptors). Type II Aδ nociceptors readily respond to raised temperatures and are called 'mechanothermal nociceptors'. Other Aδ nociceptors are high-threshold mechanoreceptors which respond only to temperatures in the higher range (from $\approx$ 53 °C).

Finally, the third major class are C unmyelinated afferents which constitute the most common element of peripheral nerves and the majority of which are nociceptors. The main class of C fibre nociceptors are C-polymodal nociceptors (C-PMNs hereafter) which respond to all types of noxious stimuli: thermal, mechanical, and chemical, and which are sometimes called 'receptors for injury'.

The contribution of the three types of nociceptors (the Aδ mechanosensitive nociceptors, the Aδ mechanothermal nociceptors, and the C-PMNs) to pain sensation can be summarized as follows: (1) the activation of Aδ fibres leads to 'sharp, intense tingling' (Fields, 1987, p. 24), and repetitive application of noxious stimuli produces a 'rapid, acute, sharp pain' (Julius and Basbaum, 2001, p. 203); (2) the activation of C fibres leads to more intense and prolonged painful sensation. Interestingly, these patterns of Aδ and C fibres activation correspond to subjective reports of pain sensation, the phenomena of first and second pain (LaMotte and Campbell, 1978). First pain is an 'early sharp and relatively brief pricking sensation' which is elicited by activity in Aδ fibres. Second pain is a 'later dull, somewhat prolonged sensation' elicited by activity in C fibres (Fields, 1987, p. 25). It was shown (Torebjork and Hallin, 1973) that C fibre activity is particularly associated with prolonged burning sensation. Fields (1987) also remarks that when brief thermal stimuli are applied, the second pain sensation often has a burning quality.

You may have noticed that the sensations of first and second pain are described in exactly the same words that different languages use to describe the sensation caused by chilli peppers. Besides, these two sensations are the ones that we can detect in our phenomenal experience. When one bites a chilli pepper, the first sensation is that of an 'explosion' which is sharp, short, and intense; while the second sensation is that of a 'fire' which is prolonged and has a burning quality. In this connection, it is interesting to know that VR1, which is activated by heat and capsaicin, was discovered on both C and type II Aδ nociceptors (Julius and Basbaum, 2001; Ma, 2002). Thus, it appears that not only the spicy-hot, but also the spicy-sharp association is grounded in the molecular constitution of our pain detecting mechanisms.

Of course, the study of ion channels is relatively young and surrounded by its own problems and controversies. Let me mention some of them. One such problem is that different mechanisms may underlie the transduction of thermal and mechanical stimuli. Thus, Caterina *et al.* (2000) discovered that mice lacking VR1 exhibited normal responses to noxious mechanical stimuli, but not to painful heat or vanilloids. However, other researchers (Schumacher *et al.*, 2000) discovered a capsaicin-receptor subtype which has mechanosensitive properties and is responsive to high temperatures, thus suggesting that noxious mechanical stimuli may have similar molecular pathways. Another group of researchers (Ringkamp *et al.*, 2001) discovered the existence of heat-insensitive and capsaicin-sensitive A-fibre nociceptors. It seems that this problem may be related to different types of mechanically induced pain. Subjectively, pain resulting from the application of sharp instruments, pressure or pinching has different qualities, and it is possible that that the mechanisms of transduction differ slightly in all these cases.[9]

Another problem is that the exact role of VR1 in thermal nociception is far from being completely understood (McCleskey and Gold, 1999). Davis *et al.* (2000) disrupted the mouse VR1 gene, but unlike in Caterina *et al.*'s (2000) study, in their experiments mice showed normal responses to acute noxious thermal stimuli which made them conclude that other mechanisms may be sufficient for normal sensation of noxious heat. Nagy and Rang (1999) also concluded that different molecular mechanisms may underlie the membrane responses to heat and capsaicin. Finally, with the discovery of VR1 expression in many areas of the CNS, some researchers suggest that VR1 may be involved in more than pain perception, and play a role in the control of emotion, learning and satiety (Mezey *et al.*, 2000).

There is also a further question of how the CNS processes the information relayed to it by the primary afferents. Since nociceptors integrate exposure to different kinds of stimuli, nociceptive signals have to be decoded in the CNS to produce different perceptions (we can distinguish between thermal hotness and spiciness). Our experience of pain is not the same thing as the activity of nociceptors, and is compounded from multiple inputs, including input from non-nociceptive afferents, and further cognitive and emotional processing in the brain (Julius and Basbaum, 2001, p. 203). Nonetheless, the understanding of how pain-producing stimuli are detected by nociceptors sheds light on why and how we perceive stimuli from different modalities as similar and name them accordingly (why peppers can be 'hot' or 'sharp').[10]

3.5 The standard assumption and the 'hot' polysemy

According to the standard assumption, which says that only one meaning of a polyseme is its literal meaning, the literal meaning of 'hot' is 'of noticeably high temperature'. Since all other meanings of a polyseme are supposed to be metaphorically derived from its primary or literal meaning, 'hot' as 'spicy' can only be a metaphoric meaning of 'hot'. Thus, it should be understood through 'hot' as 'of noticeably high temperature'.

As we have seen, the standard assumption ultimately requires an explanation in terms of conceptual primacy. This requirement was taken to its extreme by some cognitive linguists who identify conceptual primacy with experiential primacy. Thus, as far as the standard assumption goes, we should suppose that the experience of hot taste sensations is secondary with respect to the experience of hot thermal sensations. However, it is not clear in what ways our experience of hotness in the domain of thermal sensation is more basic than our experience of hotness in the domain of taste sensation. The neurophysiological research discussed in this chapter explains why we perceive certain foods as hot, and shows that perception of thermal and gustatory hotness is mediated by the same mechanisms (up to a point). Thus, it seems that using the word 'hot' for spicy foods is not a metaphorical way of speaking,[11] but rather a natural consequence of our physiological organization.

At the linguistic level, 'hot' as 'spicy' may be a later acquisition than 'hot' as 'of noticeably high temperature'. Does this reflect a similar sequencing at the conceptual level? If it did, the mechanism of metaphorical projection could probably explain its emergence. However, this appears to be problematic. The mechanism of metaphorical projection (or the formation of primary metaphors) is supposed to begin operating in an individual's early experience. However, the 'spicy'–'hot' association is not an association between two domains of experience made on the basis of properties co-occurrence, but an association that arises from the similarity of sensations mediated by the same neural mechanisms. An explanation appealing to some kind of semantic mediation, as in many classical metaphor theories, is not satisfactory either. One can say that we call chilli peppers 'hot' because eating them makes us sweat, just as we can sweat in a hot room. And that 'hot' acquired its second meaning via the following semantic association route: hot things make you sweat, chilli peppers make you sweat, chilli peppers can be metaphorically called 'hot'. However, this explanation will not tell us why, for example, we do not call bicycles 'hot': riding a bicycle makes one sweat but, for all that, bicycles are not hot. (Besides, the two domains are not correlated in any other way: 'warm' does not mean 'somewhat spicy'.)

We have seen that many other languages are different from English and similar to it at the same time. Many languages do not have the 'hot'–'spicy' association. Nonetheless, they all follow the same pattern: to describe the sensation caused by spicy foods they use words for 'sharp' and 'pricking'. We have seen that the neural mechanisms presumably underlying the 'spicy'–'sharp' association are similar to those underlying the 'spicy'–'hot' association. Thus, describing spicy foods with words corresponding to the English 'sharp' is not a metaphorical way of speaking either, but rather a natural consequence of our physiological organization. Besides, the 'spicy'–'sharp' association is even more difficult for the standard assumption theorists to explain. Neither experiential correlation (you do not eat chilli peppers with sharp objects), no semantic mediation (eating chilli peppers does not make you feel sharp) seem to be plausible explanations. Apart from perceptual similarity there is nothing that makes chillies 'hot' or 'sharp'.

How does this neural evidence relate to the questions of polysemy? As I emphasized in Chapter 2, it is one of cognitive linguistics' major insights that our conceptual structure is grounded in our bodily (neural) organization, and that an explanation for polysemy has to be sought in the conceptual structure rather than words alone. We can provisionally think of concepts as mental entities designating certain parts of our experience and assume that linguistic organization reflects, although does not constrain, conceptual organization. (If you have words 'cat' and 'dog', you most likely have the corresponding concepts CAT and DOG. But if you have only the word for cats and not for dogs, this does not imply that you do not have the concept DOG, or that you cannot form a category of dogs as different from cats. It implies only that the language you speak does not express the concept DOG).

Thus, the explanation of the 'hot' polysemy that I propose is that HOT is not a metaphoric concept for the experience of spicy foods, but a literal concept spanning the experience of spicy foods *and* the experience of high temperatures. The same goes for the concept SHARP which spans the experience of sharp cutting objects and the experience of spicy foods. The sensation that spicy foods cause us, due to the underlying neural mechanisms, can be assimilated either under the concept HOT or the concept SHARP. On the basis of the evidence discussed in this chapter I would predict that if a language has a word for the spicy food sensation, and that word has another physical meaning, the language will express either the spicy–hot or the spicy–sharp association.[12]

In order to support the conceptual view of polysemy, it has to be shown that the 'spicy'–'hot' and 'spicy'–'sharp' associations are not merely a matter of linguistic convention. A way to do this is to show that the association that is not explicit in a language is nonetheless conceptually available to speakers of that language. For example, native English speakers should be able to understand the 'spicy'–'sharp' association, even though the language expresses the 'spicy'–'hot' association. Below I provide some indications for why this indeed may be the case.

First, let us see what the *Concise Oxford English Dictionary* (COED hereafter) says about the gustatory meaning of 'sharp'. It appears that 'sharp' is somewhat ambiguous in English. COED defines it as '(of food or its flavour) pungent, acid'. However, 'pungent' and 'acid' are not exactly synonymous (one would not say 'a pungent lemon'). The COED definition for 'pungent' is 'having a sharp or strong taste or smell, esp. so as to produce a pricking sensation'. And its definition for 'piquant' is 'agreeably pungent, sharp, or appetizing'. Finally, the COED also gives 'pungent' as a synonym of 'hot', along with 'acrid' and 'biting'. Pungency is also a characteristic property of hot peppers. Thus, Caterina *et al.* write 'capsaicin, the main *pungent* ingredient in 'hot' chilli peppers, elicits a sensation of burning pain . . . ' (1997, p. 816), and Liu *et al.* write 'capsaicin, the vanilloid responsible for the *pungent* taste of hot peppers, binds to receptors found primarily in polymodal nociceptors' (1998, p. 569, my italics in both cases). So it seems that the gustatory meaning of 'sharp' must have significant overlaps with the gustatory meaning of 'hot'.

However, native speakers' intuitions differ from dictionary evidence. Most native speakers of English understand 'sharp' as meaning 'bitter' or 'acidic', not 'hot' or 'spicy'. Still, informally asking native speakers of British and American English how they would understand the sentence 'This food (dish) is too sharp for me', I also received the replies that, although this is not something they would say, they would understand 'sharp' as meaning 'pungent', 'too hot' or 'too spicy' (especially if uttered in an appropriate context by a foreigner). One particularly striking intuitive definition of 'sharp' (to taste) was 'something that hits you, like a shock', – a definition that describes very well one's experience of biting a chilli pepper. A similar questioning of native Russian speakers, for whom the conventional association is between 'spicy' and 'sharp', produced similar results: unconventional, but understandable. Occasionally dropping 'Kakoj žarkij perets!' ('What a hot pepper!') instead of 'Kakoj ostryj perets!' ('What a sharp pepper!') I did much to amuse my listeners but caused them no comprehension difficulty. Thus, although a formal study is necessary to fully evaluate this claim, it appears that the 'spicy'–'hot' association is conceptually available to native Russian speakers, and the 'spicy'–'sharp' association is conceptually available to native English speakers. However, the strength of linguistic conventions cannot be ignored: although 'This food is too sharp for me' can be understood by native English speakers to mean 'This food is too hot for me', much resistance may be provoked by the sentence's apparent un-Englishness. A formal study may also show to what extent the overlap between the gustatory meanings of 'hot' and 'sharp' found in the COED is reflected in native speakers' use and understanding of the language.

It may be interesting to speculate why some languages express the 'spicy'–'hot' association, while other languages have the 'spicy'–'sharp' association. Perhaps at the time when spices became known in England, 'sharp' had a firmly entrenched gustatory meaning (think of apples growing in a cool climate with their characteristic sharp taste). The two gustatory sensations had to be linguistically distinguished, and the word 'hot' may have thus acquired the meaning 'spicy'. In Russian there are two words corresponding to the English 'sharp': 'ostryj' y 'rezkij', all of whose occurrences can be translated by the English 'sharp'. But they differ in their collocations. (Collocation is the company that a word keeps with other words: you can ask yourself why 'rancid' occurs with 'bacon' or 'butter' but not with 'milk', even though 'rancid' is 'gone bad', which can happen with milk as well as with butter.) Thus, although there exists a partial overlap between the uses of 'ostryj' and 'rezkij' ('sharp pain' can be translated as either 'ostraja bol' or 'rezkaja bol'), they are used in different company. The sharp taste of apples is 'rezkij', not 'ostryj', while peppers are 'ostrye', not 'rezkie'. But, to confuse a student of language further, sharp apples are added to dishes to make them taste a bit hotter ('dlja ostroty').[13]

To sum up. In this chapter we have seen that there are good 'embodied' reasons for describing spicy taste sensations with words corresponding either to the English 'hot' or 'sharp'. On the strength of linguistic conventionality the gustatory meanings of 'hot' and 'sharp' may appear metaphorical. However, neither metaphorical projection no semantic mediation seem to be good explanations of the pattern observed in different languages. Since the 'spicy'–'hot' and the 'spicy'–'sharp' associations are grounded in the way our sensorium works, I have suggested that the gustatory meanings of 'hot' and 'sharp' should not be considered metaphorical. In the next chapter I expand on this suggestion, introducing into the discussion another interesting type of physical–physical polysemy, the so-called synaesthetic metaphors.

4
Across Sensory Modalities

4.1 Bright sounds and loud lights[1]

In the last chapter we talked about the 'hot' polysemy. Another interesting example of physical-physical polysemy are so-called synaesthetic metaphors. 'Bright sounds' and 'loud colours', 'sharp tastes' and 'heavy smells' pervade our speech. Expressions such as these are called 'synaesthetic' because they make associations between different sensory modalities. Synaesthesia (from Greek *syn*, 'together' and *aisthesis*, 'perception') is a particular kind of perceptual experience in which the perception of a stimulus from one sensory modality is accompanied by perceptual experience from some other modality. Thus, in the most common case of synaesthetic experience – coloured hearing – sounds induce simultaneous perceptions of colour. As we shall see, the perceptual nature of synaesthesia has been firmly established by recent research. For a relatively small number of people, synaesthesiae are real, just as our ordinary perceptual experiences are real for us.

However, we are all capable of cross-modal associations that are in some respects similar to synaesthetic perception. 'Bright sounds' and 'loud colours' make perfect sense to us. Such expressions are usually considered metaphorical because properties denoted by the adjectives 'bright' and 'loud' are, apparently, properties of only one sensory modality, in this case vision and audition. As the reasoning commonly goes, we can predicate 'bright' of sounds because of some similarity relation between visual brightness and a certain effect that sounds have on us. But what is this similarity relation? Almost immediately one notices that 'bright sounds' or 'loud colours' express a different type of similarity than 'Juliet is the sun' or 'Billboards are warts on the landscape'. As Lawrence Marks and Marc Bornstein remark:

[a]bstract, conceptually based similarities are typically verbal, and often they are conveyed through metaphor. However, many simpler and equally important forms of similarity have roots closer to biological and sensory-perceptual function. Sensory similarities commonly rely on directly given perceptual equivalences rather than on conceptualized or constructed verbal analogies. (1987, pp. 49–50)

It is this last type of similarity, similarity due to perceptual equivalence, that has been extensively investigated by Marks and colleagues (Marks, 1974, 1975, 1978, 1982a, 1982b; Marks et al., 1987; Marks and Bornstein, 1987). One assumption underlying their research was that synaesthetic perception is comparable with cross-modal associations made by non-synaesthetes, and that synaesthesia is possibly is a very strong manifestation of some universal principles of perception. Another assumption was that the interpretation of synaesthetic expressions reflects perceptual similarities that we detect between different sensory modalities.

Marks' experiments with adults (1982a, 1982b) established that: (1) perceptual matches between auditory and visual stimuli are easily made and are the same for all people; (2) subjects' ratings of perceptual stimuli with respect to their intensity in terms of a different modality are strikingly uniform (for example, visual stimuli rated with respect to loudness, or auditory stimuli rated with respect to brightness); and (3) subjects' ratings of verbal expressions describing auditory and visual perceptions are also uniform for both literal and metaphoric meanings (for example, 'sunlight' is judged as both brighter and louder than 'moonlight'). Thus, the interpretation of synaesthetic expressions appeared to follow and depend on some universal patterns in the perception of cross-modal similarity. In order to further test this hypothesis Marks et al. (1987) conducted a series of experiments with children (aged from 3.5 to 13.5) designed after Marks' experiments with adults.

The first experiment compared pitch with brightness. Marks et al. (1987) found that from an early age children understand the perceptual equivalence between high-pitched and bright, and low-pitched and dim. The ratings of verbal stimuli on brightness and pitch scales showed that literal distinctions tend to be larger than metaphoric ones (the difference between 'sunlight' and 'moonlight' is larger with respect to brightness than pitch). Metaphoric interpretations generally followed literal interpretations so that bigger literal distinctions lead to bigger metaphoric distinctions. (For example, perceptual values of 'sunlight' and 'moonlight' are established earlier than those of 'cough' and 'sneeze', and children find it easier to rate the former two nouns in both literal and metaphoric settings.)

The experiment also confirmed the existence of a previously observed asymmetry between the visual and auditory modalities. Auditory expressions suggest visual parallels more easily than visual expressions suggest auditory parallels (for example, 'high-pitched sunlight' is easier to understand than 'bright sneeze'). Finally, the interpretation of compound expressions was dominated by adjectives. Adjectives were easier to translate across modalities than nouns: for example, 'high-pitched' and 'low-pitched' were more easily judged with respect to brightness than 'sunlight' and 'moonlight' with respect to pitch (pp. 27–8).

The second experiment compared loudness with brightness, and again it was clear that children of all ages have a good grasp of this perceptual similarity. Children's ability to understand metaphorical cross-modal comparisons was shown to depend on whether they could make adequate literal distinctions. And as in the previous case, Marks et al. noticed adjectival dominance in the interpretation of compound expressions: children's ratings of 'dim thunder' and 'bright whisper' tended to reflect the difference between the adjectives, not the nouns (p. 50).

Finally, the third experiment tested children's understanding of the similarity between pitch and size. It turned out that this cross-modal equivalence is not systematically understood by younger children, and becomes consistent only by the age of 13. As in the first experiment, there was a significant asymmetry between acoustical and size nouns because pitch differences were easier to translate into size differences than the other way round. Interestingly, although adjectival dominance was observed again, it covered literal but not metaphoric meanings (p. 66). The third experiment also had a second half whose goal was to find out whether the similarity between pitch and size is present in colour names. The assignment of pitch and brightness to colours was consistent among children (as among adults): 'yellow' was judged the highest in pitch and brightness, while 'blue' was associated with low-pitched and dim. Generally, the attribution of pitch to colours seemed to reflect differences in brightness, because the ordering of colours with respect to pitch followed their brightness ordering.

Overall, the results of the three experiments seemed to confirm Marks et al.'s expectation that the perception of cross-modal similarities is universal, systematic, and present in early childhood. The ability that children demonstrated in interpreting pitch–brightness and loudness–brightness cross-modal expressions pointed in the same direction.

4.2 Seeing sounds and tasting shapes

In the last section we saw that all people are capable of forming crossmodal associations between different modalities. For a long time it had been thought that synaesthetes are no different, that they are just fanciful people with artistic inclinations, whose reported experiences of hearing colours, seeing sounds or tasting shapes had to be taken as a metaphorical way of speaking. There had been a strong tendency to explain synaesthetic perception through some kind of semantic mediation. For instance, this idea is explicitly present in Osgood, Suci and Tannenbaum who say that synaesthetic imagery is intimately tied with metaphor and that both are semantic relations (1957, p. 23). The situation changed dramatically in the last 15 years or so when the attention of experimental researchers was drawn to this curious phenomenon, and a number of studies established its perceptual character.

Thus, Richard Cytowic (1989a, 1993) extensively argued against equating synaesthesia as a particular genetically mediated aspect of perception with cross-modal matches made by non-synaesthetes. Although synaesthetic percepts usually follow the patterns of cross-modal associations – louder sounds evoke brighter and larger photisms – there is an important difference between the two. According to Cytowic, synaesthetes experience shapes and colours when hearing sounds, while non-synaesthetes only think that loud sounds correspond to bright colours. Cytowic's work also showed that there are no obvious correspondences between different synaesthetes' responses to stimuli. For instance, coloured hearing does not follow the universal pattern of correspondences between pitch and colour suggested by Marks *et al.* (1987).[2] So, what sets synaesthesia apart from non-synaesthetic cross-modal associations?

Synaesthesia occurs relatively rarely in individuals (with estimates varying from one in 200 to one in 20 000 people; Ramachandran and Hubbard, 2001b, p. 6) and is found predominantly in women (with the ratios somewhere between three to one and eight to one; Baron-Cohen *et al.*, 1993; Cytowic, 1989b; Cytowic, 1995). It runs in families (Baron-Cohen *et al.*, 1996), and most likely has a genetic basis (Bailey and Johnson, 1997). In synaesthetic perception any combination of senses is possible, or even multiple combinations of senses as in the case of Luria's (1968) famous patient who responded to auditory stimuli with parallel visual, tactile and taste sensations. The most common and the most studied type of synaesthesia is chromatic–graphemic synaesthesia characterized by stable number-colour or letter-colour associations (Baron-Cohen *et al.*, 1993). Another common type is coloured hearing, or chromesthesia, in which spoken words or music induce a parallel sensation of colour. Colour is the most commonly induced synaesthetic percept and it can be evoked not only by auditory stimuli, but also by smells, tastes and touch sensations (Cytowic, 1989a, p. 26). Other synaesthesiae include musical taste and smell, visual smell, perceptions of shaped or auditory pain, and polymodal synaesthesiae.

The most striking features of synaesthesia are its involuntary[3] and automatic character, as well as the durability and consistency of synaesthetic percepts. These three features have served as the basis for establishing the 'reality' of synaesthetic perception experimentally (Baron-Cohen *et al.*, 1993; Mattingley *et al.*, 2001; Mills *et al.*, 1999; Odgaard *et al.*, 1999; Ramachandran and Hubbard, 2001a, b; Smilek and Dixon, 2002). Synaesthetes perceive the parallel sensation as a natural part of a stimulus, not as a distinct sensation (Cytowic, 1989a). The range of synaesthesiae is normally restricted and the induced percepts are unelaborated. Synaesthesia is usually unidirectional, such that auditory stimuli induce sensations of colour, but colours do not induce auditory synaesthesiae (Cytowic, 1995) For most synaesthetes, their synaesthetic perceptions are accompanied by strong emotional feelings, such that seeing a number printed in the wrong colour may cause them emotional distress (Cytowic, 1989a; Ramachandran and Hubbard, 2001b). Several authors also make a connection between synaesthesia and creativity, pointing out that many famous artists, poets and musicians were synaesthetes (Dailey *et al.*, 1997), while others doubt that synaesthesia enhances creativity (Dann, 1998).

Since the study of synaesthesia is very young, its neural basis remains unclear. Even the most studied case of chromatic–graphemic synaesthesia reveals the diversity of synaesthetic experience. Some synaesthetes experience parallel colour sensations when visually presented with number graphemes, in others parallel colour sensations can be caused by the concept of a number in the absence of a visually presented stimulus (Dixon *et al.*, 2000). These considerations and the lack of uniform data on brain activation during synaesthesiae have recently led researchers to the view that different patterns of brain activation are involved in different kinds of synaesthesia (for competing explanations see Grossenbacher and Lovelace, 2001; Ramachandran and Hubbard, 2001b; Smilek and Dixon, 2002).

There is one further issue in the discussion of synaesthesia that is worth mentioning. Baron-Cohen who views synaesthesia as a breakdown in modularity, a 'leakage' between sensory channels (Baron-Cohen *et al.*, 1993) remarks that the existence of clearly maladaptive cases of synaesthesia (informational overload) support to the evolutionary argument that natural selection would have favoured modular senses (Baron-Cohen, 1996; on the notion of modularity see Fodor, 1983). Nonetheless, he admits that most synaesthetes do not consider their synaesthesiae as a disadvantage. Similarly, Cytowic (1995) notes that he has not encountered a single case of synaesthesia that would be strongly disruptive to an individual's perceptual experience as in Luria's (1968) famous subject who had difficulty understanding the content of a speaker's speech because of the intensity of the induced colour sensations.[4] His work also showed that most synaesthetes would not want to lose their synaesthesia, and often use it as a mnemonic device. Not only are their synaesthetic associations characterized by high stability over time, their memories are superior, and they are capable of recalling in great detail conversations and prose passages (Cytowic, 1995). In this respect, one could wonder whether synaesthesia may after all be adaptive.

What I want to suggest here is that synaesthesia may be a mechanism of compensation for certain symbolization deficits. Grossenbacher and Lovelace remark on the curious fact that in most cases 'synaesthetic inducers are stimuli that were created to convey meaning' (2001, p. 37), that is, letters of the alphabet or numbers which bear an arbitrary relation to the concepts they express. And although Cytowic emphasizes that synaesthetes are 'normal in the conventional sense' and have an overall high intelligence, he also notes that a number of cognitive deficits seem to be concomitant with synaesthetic perception. In particular, they include mathematical deficiencies (lexical-to-digit transcoding), right-left confusion, and a poor sense of direction for vector maps (1995, section 2.9).

Similarly, Ramachandran and Hubbard (2001b, p. 15) mention Spalding and Zangwill's (1950) report of a subject who lost his synaesthesia after a gunshot wound. Some years after the injury he showed difficulty in tasks involving numbers, and complained of experiencing spatial problems. Interestingly, the phrasing of his complaint involved reference to his 'number plan' which disappeared after the injury. A synaesthete's description of his or her mnemonics for numbers reported by Cytowic also suggests that synaesthetic colour sensations may serve as an alternative to more abstract representation: 'I know it's 2 because it's white' (1995, section 2.8). It is thus possible that synaesthesia is more prominent in people who have difficulty associating arbitrary symbols with meanings, and is the nature's mechanism of compensation for symbolization deficits. So far synaesthesia researchers have not considered this possibility. However, if the connection between synaesthetic perception and symbolic abilities receives experimental confirmation, it may throw new light on the phenomenon of synaesthesia and its possible adaptive value.[5]

4.3 How different are synaesthetes and non-synaesthetes?

Cytowic (1989a, 1995) insists on a sharp distinction between synaesthetic perception and non-synaesthetic cross-modal associations. Marks (Martino and Marks, 2001) believes that there must be a common core to synaesthetic perception and the ability to form cross-modal associations. In this section we shall consider what this common core may be.

The involuntary and automatic character of synaesthetic associations, which are probably formed at early stages of perceptual processing, sets them apart from non-synaesthetic cross-modal associations, which occur after the processed stimuli have been made available to consciousness. Besides, Cytowic (1989a) notes that there are qualitative differences in the distribution of responses to a stimulus between synaesthetes and non-synaesthetes. He compared synaesthetes' and non-synaesthetes' choices of geometric shapes in response to tastes, and their coloured hearing in response to single piano notes. The results of the two matching tasks showed that synaesthetes choose only some restricted areas of the response domain, displaying an absolute mapping between modalities, while non-synaesthetes tend to include in their responses all available options (that is, their responses, although systematic, are context dependent; see Martino and Marks, 2001, p. 64).

However, there is one important point that Cytowic says nothing about: how do non-synaesthetes make systematic cross-modal matches? Cytowic claims that the non-synaesthetic controls in his experiments made associations between modalities consciously, whereas the synaesthetes' choices are made unconsciously. But, there is some unclearness as to what counts as a conscious decision in a stimulus matching task. As Cytowic notes, one of the control subjects initially selected for the experiment refused to participate in it on the grounds that there was no logical way for tastes and shapes to go together (1989a, p. 76) – this was evidently a conscious decision. But if most people associate sweet tastes with round shapes and sour tastes with conical shapes, and cannot give any clearly articulated reason for their choices, then there must be something more to cross-modal associations than a conscious decision. Perhaps, the similarity of choices made by non-synaesthetes has to do not with shared abstract meanings (what could those be, anyway?) but some common perceptual mechanisms. How could one otherwise explain non-synaesthetic subjects' consistent association of sweetness with roundness, or loudness with brightness? Thus, although there are good reasons to distinguish synaesthetic perception from non-synaesthetic cross-modal associations, the ability to form cross-modal matches also needs an explanation.

The work of Marks and colleagues showed that people have no difficulty correlating stimuli in visual and auditory modalities. Louder sounds and higher pitches correspond to brighter visual stimuli, and the same patterns of correlations exist for both synaesthetes and non-synaesthetes (Marks, 1978). Similarly, Hubbard (1996) showed the existence of uniform correlations between lightness and pitch, and lightness and melodic interval (lighter stimuli are associated with ascending melodic intervals, darker stimuli with descending melodic intervals). It is also possible that there are robust cross-modal correspondences between vision and olfaction, because Gilbert et al.'s (1996) subjects who were asked to describe odours by colour were consistent in their descriptions when retested two years later. Overall, as Stein and Meredith (1993) note, people can rank all kinds of stimuli on a continuous scale, and thus make judgements of equivalence across modalities (including judgements about pain, desire or expectations; 1993, p. 17).

There is also a large body of literature showing that in multisensory integration, stimuli from one modality can modulate the perception of stimuli from a different modality. Thus, auditory stimuli, which are processed faster than visual stimuli, can increase reaction speed to visual stimuli, if a visual stimulus precedes an auditory stimulus by the difference in processing time (Stein and Meredith, 1993). Auditory stimuli may also enhance early perceptual processing of spatially congruent visual stimuli (McDonald et al., 2000).[6] Interestingly, some data show that perceptual facilitation follows the pattern of cross-modal associations: high-pitched tones are classified faster when accompanied by white colours, and low-pitched tones when accompanied by black colours (Martino and Marks, 2001; for similar vision-touch interactions see Martino and Marks, 2000).

What makes cross-modal associations possible? Stein and Meredith (1993) say that there are three main explanations (primarily concerning the associations between vision and audition). The first explanation postulates the existence of a separate neural pool which has access to individual inputs from modalities held in modality-specific form. The second explanation is that all sensory information is redescribed in the format of vision. And the third explanation is that sensory information may be held in amodal form, such that stimuli from different modalities can be compared on the basis of their amodal physical characteristics such as intensity, size, number, spatial location and direction. However, as Stein and Meredith note, the data are not sufficient to choose among the three explanations, and it is possible that all of the three schemas coexist in different areas in the brain. Nonetheless, even at the level of single neurons (polysensory neurons) there is simultaneous coding of within- and across-modality information. Since intensity is represented in the nervous system by the frequency of action potentials, it is possible that the subjective perception of similarity across modalities may have as its neural basis 'similar levels of activity in common multisensory neuronal pools throughout the brain' (pp. 18–19; cf. Marks *et al.*, 1987, p. 73; Marks and Bornstein, 1987, p. 58).

Marks *et al.*'s (1987) experiments with children were intended to test the existence of a universal perceptual core of cross-modal similarities which presumably underlies the interpretation of synaesthetic metaphors. The results showed that even very young children were consistent in their judgements of similarity between visual and auditory stimuli. This suggested that the ability to perceive cross-modal equivalences is universal rather than idiosyncratic, and that it probably is an innate property of perception (Marks and Bornstein, 1987, p. 62). An alternative hypothesis would be that cross-modal similarities are derived from experience, by associating the observed regularities in everyday life. However, as Marks *et al.* noted, it seems very unlikely that co-occurrences of brightness and loudness, for instance, should produce a universally reliable connection. Besides,

> [e]ven if experience does teach us to associate loudness with brightness or pitch with size, it is much harder to specify a source for an "ecological" connection between pitch and brightness. The association between relatively high pitched sounds and bright lights or light colors seems not to have an obvious external source. But it surely has an early developmental origin. (1987, p. 72)

The question whether children and infants can perceive cross-modal similarities has long been debated by psychologists. According to the Piaget school (Piaget, 1952), sensory systems are different at birth, and experience has to contribute to the integration of stimuli from different modalities. According to the opposite view, sensory modalities are not completely differentiated in newborns and form some kind of a 'primitive unity' (Gibson, 1966; Bower, 1977; Turkewitz and Mellon, 1989; see also Stein and Meredith, 1993, p. 11). Today, most psychologists agree that the detection of cross-modal equivalences is present from birth and that experience contributes to differentiation rather than integration among modalities (Baron-Cohen, 1996). Infants' sensitivity to similarity between stimuli in visual and auditory, as well as visual and somatosensory, modalities seems to have been established beyond doubt (Lewkowicz and Turkewitz, 1980; Meltzoff and Borden, 1979; Rose et al., 1978; Wagner et al., 1981). Since the ability to detect cross-modal similarities was shown to be present in infants as young as one month old (Lewkowicz and Turkewitz, 1980), it seems justifiable to conclude that it is an innate ability rather than a capacity acquired from experience with objects.

It has to be remarked that an alternative non-Piagetian explanation of multisensory integration in infants has recently been proposed. According to the currently accepted view, infants are able to recognize objects in different modalities (for example, to visually recognize a pacifier they sucked on but did not see), because of their ability to make judgements of equivalence between modalities based on some abstract or amodal features of stimuli (Meltzoff and Borden, 1979; Rose, 1990; Spelke, 1987). According to the alternative view (Maurer, 1997), all infants are synaesthetes at least for the first months of life, such that stimuli from one modality trigger sensations in other modalities.

This view has some support in neuroanatomical studies, since in many newborns of non-human species (hamster, cat) there are neural connections between visual, auditory and somatosensory areas of the brain (Maurer, 1997). There are also studies showing that the brains of newborn animals appear to be more multisensory than adult brains of the same animals because they 'exhibit multisensory convergence in structures known to be unimodal at maturity' (Stein and Meredith, 1993, p. 14). This view is also consistent with an explanation of synaesthesia as defective pruning of connections between different brain areas (Ramachandran and Hubbard, 2001; see also Harrison and Baron-Cohen, 1996).[7] On the whole, although this is a challenging view for developmental psychologists, more evidence will be needed to support it. What may speak against it, however, is the highly idiosyncratic and restricted range of synaesthetic associations which are not characteristic of cross-modal associations exhibited by adults and young children.

To conclude the discussions of the last two sections, let me summarize the main points of interest that arose from our brief consideration of synaesthetic and non-synaesthetic cross-modal perception. Thus, it seems clear that we can take for granted the following three statements: (a) synaesthetic perception is qualitatively different from the ability to perceive cross-modal equivalences; (b) the ability to perceive cross-modal similarities[8] is universal and, most likely, innate; and (c) synaesthetic and non-synaesthetic cross-modal associations may have a common neural basis, although nothing definite can be said about this presently. With this in mind, we can now move on to the discussion of how and whether perceptual similarities are manifested in a systematic way in language.

4.4 Cross-modal associations and synaesthetic metaphors

We have seen that perceptual similarity between stimuli from different modalities, such as the similarity between loudness and brightness, may be a universal and innate property of perception. However, what is of major interest to us here are synaesthetic metaphors, such as 'bright music' or 'loud colours'. Marks and colleagues' experiments showed that synaesthetic metaphors are easily rated by both children and adults, and that their understanding is uniform across subjects. Thus, the question that has to be answered now concerns the mechanisms that underlie the interpretation of synaesthetic metaphors. Let us begin with Marks et al.'s (1987) views on the subject.

According to Marks et al., verbal processes gain access to perceptual knowledge, and thus 'verbal (semantic) knowledge taps perceptual knowledge' (1987, p. 77). Perceptual knowledge is understood as the structure of perceptual domains (organized in a continuum) available either consciously or unconsciously to the perceiving organism, whereas verbal knowledge is a conscious knowledge of the labels that properly designate different dimensions of perceptual experience. Verbal knowledge of cross-modal similarities is thus the knowledge of which labels can be substituted one for another in order to comply with the rules of cross-modal perception. As Marks et al. say:

> perception and conception of cross-modal similarity are closely connected. We view the resemblances . . . as quintessentially perceptual . . . and we believe that they in turn become available, perhaps automatically, to the more abstract system of knowledge embodied in language. One end result of the extension of perception to language is the capacity . . . to interpret cross-modal expressions in a systematic manner; but this capacity, even when based on innate cross-modal correspondences does not emerge as soon as children establish verbal labels for the pertinent aspects of perceptual experience . . . . (1987, p. 74)

According to the representational part of their story, the structure of perceptual dimensions is paralleled in the multidimensional conceptual space. This means that the establishment of perceptual cross-modal correspondences is accompanied by the establishment of corresponding gradations in sensory meanings. For example, if children judge 'bright sound' to be louder than 'dim sound', they must have already established verbal correlates of the perceptual equivalence between loudness and brightness. The multidimensionality of meaning implies that in the course of development representations of sensory meanings are organized into graded continua (p. 77).

Since brightness is not a perceptual attribute of sounds, 'bright' is not a proper linguistic label in describing auditory experience (Marks, 1982a, p. 177). However, since cross-modal perception is psychologically real and the understanding of synaesthetic expressions is uniform, Marks et al. concluded that synaesthetic metaphors reveal perceptual knowledge. Or in other words, that cross-modal similarities in language have the form of similes or metaphors (1987, p. 1). The developmental question raised by this is that, since cross-modal metaphors are expressions of intrinsic perceptual similarities, children's ability to understand them does not imply that they recognize them as metaphors. Marks et al. say that two answers are possible: (a) either children do not discriminate between perceptual categories the way adults do, and thus do not have criteria for metaphoricity; (b) or they know when they violate conceptual boundaries, and thus can distinguish metaphors from literal uses. Marks et al. choose an intermediate position saying that the expression of cross-modal similarities becomes metaphoric 'whenever the modalities become independent perceptual categories' (1987, p. 82).

On the whole, there is some plausibility to Marks et al.'s representational story, according to which there are parallel perceptual and conceptual spaces, such that the understanding of synaesthetic metaphors is achieved through the comparison of relative positions words occupy in the conceptual space. However, their story cannot be the right story, and we shall presently see why.

According to Marks et al., perceptual experiences and meanings are multidimensional, such that development involves 'both the creation of additional dimensions of meaning and the differentiation of holistic psychological entities into component domains' (1987, p. 75). And development is supposed to proceed the following way. First, labels for experiences in different modalities become established (for example, 'bright'). Then, with the organization of elements of perceptual dimensions by their order, gradation and polarity, the conceptual space becomes structured in a similar way. (For example, the ability to evaluate the loudness of auditory stimuli leads to the ability to judge the relative loudness of denotations of such words as 'squeak' and 'thunder'.) The capacity to understand cross-modal similarities depends on the establishment of a system of linguistic labels for each sensory modality, such that labels are transferred across modalities according to their position in the conceptual space. But the verbal knowledge of cross-modal equivalences itself is derived from implicit perceptual knowledge. Below I summarize what I find problematic in this account.

Sensory meanings are holistic: first of all, what I find problematic is that 'sensory meanings' are supposed to be points on a mental rating scale. While it is true that knowing what 'thunder' means probably involves knowing that thunder is loud, it does not have to involve knowing that thunder is louder than a squeak. On Marks *et al.*'s account, however, all sensory meanings from the same modality interdetermine each other, that is, the relative perceptual values of the denotations of 'thunder' and 'squeak' are part of the meaning of these words. And this implies a vicious regress: unless one knows the loudness values of all auditory nouns, one cannot know what any of them means. Surely, this is not the case. Similarly for modal adjectives. While it is true that knowing what 'loud' means probably involves knowing that some auditory stimuli are louder than others, it cannot be part of the meaning of 'loud' that drum notes are usually louder than piano notes, and so on.

Note that this is not trivial. Thus, to give another example, 'bright' contributes its meaning to the expressions 'bright sunlight' and 'bright moonlight' just as well as 'sunlight' and 'moonlight' do, but it is not part of the meaning of 'bright' that sunlight is usually brighter than moonlight. Speaking generally, conceiving of sensory meanings as multivalued or continuous poses an irresolvable problem of compositionality. Thus, according to Marks *et al.* what is needed for being able to perform rating tasks is the establishment of some prototypical sensory meanings corresponding to objects and properties, but prototypes do not compose (Fodor, 1998a). Consider also the example of 'sneeze'. Marks *et al.* say that at a certain stage in development children do not have a well-defined position for 'sneeze' in the 'conceptual auditory space' (p. 81), although they may know what it refers to. But does this show that they do not know the meaning of 'sneeze'? It is one thing to know what 'sneeze' means/refers to, but it is another thing to know that sneezes are normally high-pitched. So, it appears that it is not the meaning of 'sneeze' but rather the meaning of 'high-pitched' that was tested in the scale rating tasks.[9]

Perceptual properties are unambiguously mapped onto language: perhaps, the view of sensory meanings as having a scalar organization was partly inspired by the observation that visual adjectives are easily judged with respect to their loudness and pitch. And since both children and adults judge 'bright' as louder and higher in pitch than 'dim', Marks *et al.* concluded that BRIGHT, LOUD and HIGH-PITCHED stand in some unarbitrary relation to DIM, SOFT and LOW-PITCHED, which are representations in the conceptual space parallel to the perceptual space. This observation is indeed important. But consider the following example. If one has to judge 'bright music' on the scale 'loud–soft', it will be closer to the 'loud' end of the scale. However, 'bright music' does not mean 'loud music': we can very well describe music played softly as 'bright'.

Thus, if the dependence of language on perception was as clear-cut as Marks *et al.* want it to be, this would imply that 'loud' and 'bright' are synonymous, the only difference between them being that one is a literal and the other a metaphorical label for the same sense impression. However, changing the loudness of music does not thereby change its brightness. Similarly, Marks *et al.*'s account would imply that 'high-pitched colours' and 'loud colours' must be synonymous because, perceptually, brightness stands in the same relation to pitch as to loudness. But as neither is the case, then clearly there is something more intricate going on in here than mere verbal reflection of phenomenological similarity.

Final point: metaphors in perception: since concepts are implicitly identified with perceptual categories in Marks *et al.*'s account, their use of words is not always very exact. Marks (1982a) uses the expression 'synesthesia in language'. Marks *et al.* (1987) write that cross-modal similarities become metaphoric when the modalities become independent perceptual categories, and thus, that 'cross-modal similarities are not metaphoric to infants' (p. 83). Marks and Bornstein (1987) say that some synaesthetic metaphors are present in early childhood, whereas others emerge from experience (p. 55). One might get the impression that, contrary to what was said previously, metaphor is considered not as a way to express perceptual experience but as this experience itself, that is, that the perceptual similarity between loudness and brightness is itself metaphoric.

Such an interpretation can be found, for instance, in Haskell who says that Marks and Bornstein (1987) present 'a model for the origins of sensory metaphor' (1987, p. 3). It is also consonant with the views of some cognitive linguists. Thus, Sweetser mentions metaphorical structuring of 'our perceptions of the world' (Sweetser, 1990, p. 9). However, it is not consistent with Marks *et al.*'s views that metaphor is a matter of the application of verbal labels. And nowhere in their text do they suggest that perception itself may be metaphorical (what ecological value, anyway, could we ascribe to *perceiving* objects or events as if they were something else?). It is also evident that Marks and Bornstein (1987) themselves do not consider cross-modal perception as metaphorical. They clearly say that young children's implicit perceptual knowledge of cross-modal similarities parallels their implicit verbal knowledge of cross-modal similarities which 'adults use in comprehending certain important kinds of metaphors' (p. 53). Thus, one would not be justified in concluding that the perception of cross-modal similarities is an example of metaphorical perception; perceptual similarities and synaesthetic metaphors have to be distinguished.

What I shall argue now is that if language followed perceptual equivalences in a one-to-one manner (for example, if 'bright music' meant 'loud music'), the asymmetries observed in the experimental results would not have arisen.

Consider first the asymmetry between literal and metaphorical graphic representations of verbal stimuli. Marks *et al.* (1987) note that literal distinctions tend to be larger than metaphorical ones because the children judged the difference between 'moonlight' and 'sunlight' to be larger with respect to brightness than pitch. Similar results, showing that metaphorical effects are usually smaller than literal ones, were obtained by Marks in his experiments with adults:

> The conclusion from these data is that visual nouns do not simply impart intensity; they do not automatically imply loudness by means of their brightness.... Moreover, the modified words or phrases themselves did not, in any simple or systematic way, translate their loudness into brightness or their brightness into loudness. *Thunder*, though enormously louder than a *whisper*, was not at all brighter. (1982a, p. 184)

In 1982 Marks considered brightness as a psychophysical attribute of auditory experience, and explained the observed effect by saying that 'thunder' and 'whisper' differ in loudness more than in brightness because brightness is a composite of loudness and pitch. But in 1987 Marks *et al.* rejected this explanation. It follows that: (a) either brightness is some attribute of the auditory modality that has to be formulated more precisely; or (b) brightness is an attribute of the visual modality, and the transfer of the predicate 'bright' to auditory words and experiences is accomplished at the semantic level. However, this second explanation fails to tell us why there are stable perceptual correlations between brightness and loudness.

Another asymmetry noticed by Marks *et al.* (1987) is that acoustic verbal stimuli are easier to judge with respect to their brightness than visual verbal stimuli with respect to their loudness and pitch (for example, 'sneeze' is easier to judge with respect to brightness than 'sunlight' with respect to pitch). As they note, this asymmetry has some similarity with synaesthetic perception where auditory stimuli invoke photisms more often than visual stimuli invoke sound impressions. They conclude that the source of the asymmetry may be in perception rather than cognition:

> The direction of asymmetry in synesthesia parallels that in verbal metaphor. If synesthesia is perceptual in origin and nature, as we suspect, then asymmetry in synesthesia would suggest . . . that asymmetry in metaphor too may reside in some as-yet-undetermined, presumably neurophysiological, characteristic of perceptual processing. (p. 81)[10]

Consider now some examples of the visual-auditory asymmetry. 'Soft sunlight' appears less metaphorical than 'loud sunlight', which in turn is less metaphorical than 'high-pitched sunlight'. And, as Marks *et al.* would probably put it, all three are visual properties described in auditory terms. However, it is not clear that 'soft' is primarily an auditory term (one could have used instead 'quiet sunlight'). Similarly for visual-auditory transfers: 'large thunder' vs. 'small thunder' are obviously more informative expressions than 'bright sneeze' vs. 'dark cough', although if we consider synaesthetic expressions as mere reflections of perceptual correspondences they should be judged as equally acceptable. Thus, as we have already seen, the rating experiments may give us an insight into the conceptualization of perceptual correlations, but they cannot be give us the meanings of the expressions in question.[11]

Finally, I would like to comment briefly on the use of verbal stimuli in Marks *et al.*'s experiments. Marks *et al.* observed an asymmetry between the visual and auditory modalities because auditory expressions suggested better parallels for visual expressions than the other way round. The examples that produced the asymmetry were 'high-pitched sunlight' and 'bright sneeze', where 'high-pitched sunlight' was easier to interpret. It would be interesting to see whether using 'bright voice' instead of 'bright sneeze' would have produced a different result, especially as 'sneeze' is not ordinarily a subject of any specific descriptions compared with 'voice'.[12] I suspect that changing the stimuli in this and other cases would have eliminated certain asymmetries and unexpected results. Overall, the considerations I presented in this section show that the question about the meaning of synaesthetic adjectives such as 'bright' and the question about conceptual structure supporting their interpretation have to be distinguished from the question about cross-modal perceptual equivalences which may have as their basis comparable intensity of stimuli.

4.5 Synaesthetic adjectives and the standard assumption

In a later work, Melara and Marks (1990) suggested that the source of cross-modal equivalences is in semantically based interactions (that is, the way our language influences how we perceive correspondences between modalities). This view is also found in recent work by Martino and Marks (2001) who prefer not to draw a strict distinction between synaesthetic perception and the ability to form cross-modal matches which they call 'weak synaesthesia'. According to them, 'strong synaesthesia' occurs at a low-level sensory locus, and 'weak synaesthesia' is mediated by a high-level semantic locus.

I have already mentioned that Martino and Marks (1999) obtained experimental results showing that the interaction between sensory modalities follows the pattern of cross-modal associations. Thus, in selective attention tasks subjects classify high-pitched tones faster when those are accompanied by 'unattended' white colours, and low-pitched tones are identified faster in the presence of dark colours. One possible explanation for these 'congruence effects' is that cross-modal similarities are mediated by some commonality in neural coding. Martino and Marks propose an alternative explanation, called the semantic-coding hypothesis, according to which congruence effects 'involve high-level mechanisms, which develop over childhood from experience with percepts and language'. The semantic-coding hypothesis includes the following claims:

> First, although cross-modal correspondence may arise from sensory mechanisms in infants, these correspondences reflect postsensory (meaning-based) mechanisms in adults. Second, experience with percepts from various modalities and the language a person uses to describe these percepts produces an abstract semantic network that captures synesthetic correspondence. Third, when synesthetically corresponding stimuli are perceived, they are recorded from sensory

representations into abstract ones based on this semantic network. Fourth, the coding of stimuli from different modalities as matching or mismatching depends on the context within which the stimuli are presented. (2001, pp. 64–5)

However, the four claims of the semantic-coding hypothesis present a number of problems. The most obvious one is that semantically based interactions cannot be present in early infancy. But if the ability to detect cross-modal similarities in infancy and early childhood is mediated by sensory mechanisms, it is not clear why this sensory mediation should disappear at the age when, as Martino and Marks suggest, a person acquires the knowledge of the 'secondary' meanings of synaesthetic adjectives. Moreover, earlier work by Marks (see section 4.1) showed that both children and adults can match perceptual stimuli by their intensity in the absence of verbal stimuli. Besides, subjects can make judgements of similarity between a large number of stimulus domains, establishing perceptual equivalence, for instance, between brightness and the amount of pain (cf. Stein and Meredith, 1993: 17). It is thus not clear that ranking the amount of pain on a brightness scale involves semantic mediation through the 'bright'–'dim' network (for 'bright' and 'dim' are not the predicates that normally occur in descriptions of pain sensations).

Martino and Marks say that perceptual cross-modal correspondences are mediated by higher-level mechanisms, and provide two arguments in favour of the semantic-coding hypothesis: contextual dependence of congruence effects and the appearance of congruence effects in response to verbal stimuli. Unlike true synaesthetes, non-synaesthetes are sensitive to the contextual presentation of stimuli, and match all available stimuli from two domains compared. Besides, in selective attention tasks involving categorization of tones or colours, congruence effects are observed when both tones and colours vary, but not when either of the stimuli remain constant (Martino and Marks, 2001, p. 65; Melara, 1989).

Martino and Marks interpret this data in favour of the semantic-coding hypothesis, saying that the sensory account of cross-modal correspondences would predict higher processing speed for congruent matches in both conditions. However, they do not consider the possibility that stimuli not attended consciously by a subject may nonetheless enter into the processes of multisensory integration, and that the constancy of a stimulus across trials would lead to habituation effects thus reducing its influence on the processing of the attended stimulus.

Martino and Marks' own explanation according to which variation in stimuli creates a context for their evaluation and 'highlights' a synaesthetic association does not by itself support the view that perceptual cross-modal correspondences are semantically mediated.

As a further support for the semantic-coding hypothesis, which says that both sensory and linguistic stimuli are recorded into an abstract representation which serves as a basis for cross-modal associations, Martino and Marks provide the fact that congruence effects can be elicited by linguistic stimuli. Thus, the classification of high- and low-pitched tones is facilitated not only by the presentation of white and black colours correspondingly, but also by the words 'white' and 'black'. These data indeed provide stronger support to the semantic-coding hypothesis. However it does not eliminate the existence of perceptually mediated cross-modal associations. It is perfectly possible that both perceptually and semantically mediated cross-modal associations coexist.[13]

In this respect, one may wonder why Martino and Marks want to deny the existence of perceptually mediated cross-modal associations in adults. The most plausible explanation is that they need to account for synaesthetic expressions which are the most obvious realization of 'weak synaesthesia' (2001, p. 65). From this perspective, Martino and Marks's approach is a clear manifestation of the standard assumption, according to which only one meaning of a polysemous adjective can be its literal meaning. Thus, in the summary of features characteristic of 'strong' and 'weak' synaesthesia (2001, p. 63), they include literal semantic associations for strong synaesthetes and metaphorical semantic associations for weak synaesthetes (or non-synaesthetes). In the light of our discussion in section 4.2 and Martino and Marks' own characterization of synaesthetic processing as occurring at a low-level sensory locus, the statement that associations formed by synaesthetes are literal semantic associations appears to be contradictory. Synaesthetic associations are not semantically mediated, and synaesthetes do not exhibit any disturbances of perceptual or semantic knowledge (for example, they are normally aware that synaesthetic percepts are not identical with their veridical perceptual experience).

But what about the statement that associations formed by non-synaesthetes are metaphorical semantic associations? Martino and Marks do not show that cross-modal associations have no underlying perceptual basis; the only thing they show is that linguistic stimuli can contribute to perceptual facilitation in selective attention tasks. Thus, there is no reason to consider perceptual cross-modal associations as metaphorical. The notion of metaphoricity can only appear in the discussion of synaesthetic expressions such as 'bright music' or 'sweet smell'. And the reason that the notion of metaphoricity appears in that discussion is that synaesthetic adjectives are supposed to literally denote a property in only one sensory modality. (Recall that according to Marks *et al.* (1987), children begin to understand synaesthetic expressions once 'the proper labels' are established.) However, we are never told why this should be so. The standard assumption has never been anything more than an assumption.[14]

4.6 The no-polysemy view of conceptual structure

In the last chapter – *The 'hot' polysemy* – we talked about expressions that seem to be metaphorical, but most probably are not. In my view, synaesthetic adjectives form another group of such expressions. On the standard criteria of metaphoricity, 'bright music' and 'loud colours' are metaphorical expressions because they violate 'conceptual boundaries'. And they are said to violate conceptual boundaries because 'brightness' is a proper term in the domain of vision, whereas 'loudness' is a proper term in the domain of audition (cf. Marks *et al.*, 1987, p. 83). However, there is something peculiar about 'bright music' and 'loud colours' because there is no explicitly specifiable similarity relation which would justify the metaphorical transfer, if this is what underlies the production and understanding of such expressions. (As I show in the preceding sections, the best available explanation which postulates the existence of parallel perceptual and conceptual spaces leads to unacceptable meaning holism and predicts false synonymy between adjectives denoting synaesthetically equivalent perceptual properties.)

In Chapters 1 and 2 I showed that metaphor researchers who accept the standard assumption are led to endorse (either implicitly or explicitly) the view that literalness has to do with some kind of conceptual primacy. However, both children and adults can easily judge visual and auditory stimuli with respect to their brightness or loudness. As Marks *et al.* (1987) had to conclude, the understanding that 'bright' applies to sounds metaphorically appears only when children have learned that 'bright' applies literally only to visual stimuli. Up to that point, the auditory 'bright' is not appreciated as metaphorical, even though children can evaluate auditory stimuli with respect to their brightness. In the light of this consideration and the failure of the parallel perceptual-conceptual spaces hypothesis, it is not clear what could warrant the conclusion that 'bright' derives its literal meaning from the fact that brightness is primarily a property in the visual modality. Thus, when we consider synaesthetic expressions, the question of whether a label applies literally or metaphorically becomes first of all the question of linguistic convention; but conventions do not set up conceptual priorities.[15]

Thus, I would like to propose here a new account of physical-physical polysemy which I call the no-polysemy view of conceptual structure (for the moment I will provide only a broad outline, and discuss it in more detail in Chapter 10). I suggest that there is nothing to prevent one from thinking that 'bright' does not *properly* describe stimuli only in the visual modality, but also stimuli in other modalities, even though the physical properties depicted by 'bright' in 'bright light' and 'bright music' are not the same. A better way to phrase this is to say that the concept BRIGHT (cf. Martino and Marks' 'abstract representation') that one entertains in connection with bright music or bright lights is one and the same psychologically primitive concept. That is, in understanding 'bright music' or 'bright light' the adjective 'bright' maps onto the psychologically primitive concept BRIGHT. This, however, will not make 'bright' in 'bright light' and 'bright music' have the same meaning because in one case 'bright' is predicated of light and in the other case 'bright' is predicated of music. But music and light are not the same (and compounds need not mean the same either; as I argue later the level of concepts and the level of meaning have to be kept separate).

Now, if we consider the notion of reference in the loose sense of what speakers of a language refer to (tend to refer to) when they utter ' . . . ', we can see that there is nothing to prevent us from determining the reference of the auditory 'bright' (given, of course, that we can establish when someone is using the expression erroneously). If the overwhelming majority of speakers reliably and consistently applied 'bright music' to some kinds of music and not others, this would show that 'bright music' has a more or less precise extension, and is not a matter of 'anything goes'. (And as we have seen from the discussion of Marks *et al.*'s experiments, synaesthetic expressions reliably evoke the same responses from all subjects.) Thus, there are good reasons to expect subjects to show far greater consistency in their responses to 'bright music' than, for instance, 'pink music', and this suggests that the two expressions cannot be treated in the same way.

It is a common practice among many researchers (philosophers in particular) to appeal to dictionaries when deciding what counts as a literal or metaphoric meaning of an expression. And it is a difficult task for lexicographers to decide whether an entry has to be marked *figurative* or not. Consider the following extract from the OED entry on 'bright':

bright
1. Shining; emitting, reflecting, or pervaded by much light
   a. said of luminaries (1000)
   b. of polished metals, precious stones, and other objects whose surfaces reflect light (1000)
   c. of illuminated surfaces, of the day in sunshine, etc. (1000)
   d. of transparent substances: clear, translucent (1709)
2. Clear or luminous to the mental perception (1000) ...
4.a. Of vivid or brilliant colour ... (1375) ...
5. Of sounds: a. Clear, shrill, ringing. b. Said of the mental effect of a note (1000).

In the absence of the standard assumption what is to tell us which of these entries contains the primary or literal meaning of 'bright'?[16]

The no-polysemy view of conceptual structure says that dictionaries (or lexicographers) are pretty good at capturing our intuitions: there is a single psychologically primitive concept BRIGHT onto which all instances of 'bright' map in the process of language understanding. Still, what meaning each and every instance of 'bright' has depends on its particular domain of application. Thus, the no-polysemy view denies that the one and only literal meaning of 'bright' is its visual meaning (which of them, anyway, is the best candidate?). At this point I close the discussion of the no-polysemy view in this section. Since it is bound to provoke much resistance, before we can take it on again a number of issues have to be considered in the following chapters – issues that, hopefully, will help us to take that resistance down.

4.7 How could have psychologically primitive concepts come about?

In recent years, the evolutionary stance has taken a strong hold over psychological research. Many people believe today that only in 'the light of evolution' can we ever hope to completely understand our own cognitive abilities (cf. Plotkin, 1997; see also Barkow *et al.*, 1992; Pinker, 1994, 1997). In this section I present a rough sketch of the possible evolutionary origin of psychologically primitive concepts.

First, let us return to the views of Richard Cytowic, who insists on a strict distinction between synaesthetic perception and non-synaesthetic cross-modal associations. In his critique of older approaches to synaesthesia, Cytowic (1989a) emphasizes that the nature of language and cross-modal associations with respect to synaesthesia have been misunderstood because both synaesthesia and cross-modal associations were considered as derivative aspects of language. Following Norman Geschwind he suggests that, on the contrary, cross-modal associations are requisite for language:

> The ability to acquire speech has as a prerequisite the ability to form cross-modal associations. In sub-human forms, the only readily established sensory-sensory associations are those between a non-limbic (i.e. visual, tactile or auditory) stimulus and a limbic stimulus. It is only in man that associations between two nonlimbic stimuli are readily formed and it is this ability which underlies the learning of names of objects. (Geschwind, 1964, p. 155, quoted in Cytowic, 1989a, p. 72; see also Cytowic, 1993, p. 122)[17]

This suggestion is intimately connected with Cytowic's hypothesis about the neural basis of synaesthesia as a disconnection of the phylogenetically older limbic areas from the newer cortical areas, and his view of the limbic system as a 'seat' of synaesthesia. An even more intriguing suggestion is that synaesthesia is a fundamental quality of sensation, which became less and less significant with the evolution of the mammalian cortex and the separation of associative areas from receptive areas. It is in this sense that Cytowic considers synaesthetic perception as a result of a common mammalian fusion of senses which may still exist, but does not arise to consciousness.

These views of Cytowic have not received a widespread acceptance. His neurophysiological explanation of synaesthesia has not so far received confirmation (Frith and Paulesu, 1997; Humphreys, 1990; Ramachandran and Hubbard, 2001b). His view of synaesthesia as 'a remnant of how early mammals perceived the world' (1989a, p. 176) were said to 'strain the reader's credulity' (Stein and Meredith, 1993, p. 9). The ability to form cross-modal associations involving two non-limbic stimuli (for example, vision and audition) is clearly present in a large number of other species (Korb, 1995). True, cross-modal associations between non-limbic stimuli are normally made by animals only in connection with the limbic influence (for example, to receive a reward or avoid being hurt), but that does not mean that they cannot integrate auditory and visual information (see Fuster *et al.*, 2000). But even if synaesthetic perception is not at the beginning of language origins, does this mean that Geschwind's suggestion has no interesting consequences for a theory of the evolution of human cognitive capacities?

In his 1965 article, Geschwind suggested that human ability to develop speech arose from the ability to form non-limbic cross-modal associations, which he connected with the emergence of the angular gyrus region and the parietal association area (p. 274) absent in non-human primates. Recenly, Wendy Wilkins and Jennie Wakefield (1995) have taken up and modified Geschwind's suggestion. They proposed that the development of the parieto-occipito-temporal junction[18] (which is absent in the pongid brain) lead to the appearance of a neuroanatomical substrate for the ability to form modality-neutral representations, which, combined with the structure-imposing contribution of the Broca's area, resulted in the emergence of conceptual structure which could support language.

We have seen that humans have no difficulty detecting similarity between stimuli from different modalities. Wilkins and Wakefield provide further evidence which shows that humans, including infants, can form amodal representations of such properties as ascendency/descendency, continuity/discontinuity and hardness, even though stimuli may come from clearly separated modalities, as vision and audition, or vision and the tactile modality (1995, p. 169). Unlike humans, nonhuman primates, although capable of cross-modal integration, cannot form amodal representations of properties:

> in the chimpanzee, physical identity seems to serve as a bridge between vision and touch whereas attributed common properties (e.g. 'strength of stimulus', 'local continuity/discontinuity') do not. (Ettlinger, 1981, p. 585; quoted in Wilkins and Wakefield, 1995, p. 169)[19]

On the basis of these data Wilkins and Wakefield suggested that one of the distinctive features of human cognitive capacity is the ability to abstract properties that can be generalized across situations. In their view, this ability may have served as the basis for linguistic lexicalization.

There is some inconclusiveness concerning the role that Wilkins and Wakefield ascribe to the interaction of the parieto-occipito-temporal junction and Broca's area as the neuroanatomical structure which 'produces' the conceptual structure (p. 175). A number of researchers commenting on Wilkins and Wakefield's article presented evidence for the existence of these neuroanatomical structures and the same polymodal connectivity in nonhuman primates, as well as doubted the role of these structures in the cognitive tasks that Wilkins and Wakefield assigned to them (see Dingwall, 1995; Jacobs and Horner, 1995; Maryanski, 1995; Mitchell and Miles, 1995).

Still, there are a number of important insights in Wilkins and Wakefield's account. Unlike many researchers in cognitive sciences who concentrate primarily on the role of vision or spatial orientation in concept formation, Wilkins and Wakefield emphasize that there must be a connection between, say, the concept of an object and representations of that object received from different sensory modalities: conceptual structure cannot be confined to representations from only one sense modality (1995, p. 175). Another important contribution of their article is that human language is believed to have arisen from changes in representational and conceptualizing capacity rather than from increased communication needs (see commentaries by Hurford and Kirby, 1995; Newmeyer, 1995). Or, in the words of Derek Bickerton, language is 'a more sophisticated way of representing (that is, knowing) a world external to the creature' (1990, p. 102).

In the last section I suggested that synaesthetic adjectives map onto corresponding psychologically primitive concepts. As we have seen, the understanding of synaesthetic adjectives presents no difficulty even to young children, and their interpretations are uniform across subjects.[20] The question now is: how can we make sense of synaesthetic polysemy from this representational point of view?

Let us begin with considering the types of cross-modal transfers of which we are capable. First, there is the ability to recognize an object presented in one sensory modality after it had been presented in a different sense modality. Nonhuman primates are capable of performing such tasks (Ettlinger and Wilson, 1990). Second, there is 'transmodal perception' (Costall *et al.*, 2001): if an object appears soft to the eye, there is a good chance that it will be soft to the touch; if something smells sweet, there is a good chance that it will taste sweet (do you know of a single kid who has not tested whether a sweet-smelling shampoo would also taste sweet?). Nonhuman animals are also capable of this kind of perception. Finally, there is the ability to perceive stimuli in different sensory modalities as exhibiting properties normally associated with one modality, for example, to perceive tactile stimuli, colours or sounds as soft. And this presumably is the uniquely human ability. However, note that whereas the first two abilities do not require that one possess concepts (such as SOFT), the third ability clearly does. (For example, it involves being able to attend to a particular property of the input from a sensory modality without associating it with such limbic reinforcers as pleasantness or unpleasantness.)

There is another curious fact to consider. Whereas humans are capable of drawing an almost infinite number of distinctions among objects, chimpanzees are not able to progress beyond two category classifications (Langer, 2000). Our ability to draw more and more specific distinctions is reflected in the large number of nouns human languages have (for example, taxonomies). Compared with nouns, adjectives form only a small fraction of lexical items (Dixon, 1982). Besides, most adjectives can be used to describe properties from practically all sensory modalities. Given the discriminative capacity manifested in categorization abilities with respect to objects, it is curious that it is not reflected in the categorization of properties.

It is in this connection that I find Wilkins and Wakefield's account particularly striking. It is possible that the emergence of human conceptual structure coincided with the reorganization in the processing of perceptual information. And this could have resulted in the ability to abstract and represent particular properties of the sensory input. If things were indeed this way, one natural consequence of this would be the emergence of concepts for properties which are not tied to a single sensory modality. Synaesthetic adjectives may well reflect this particular feature of our conceptual organization: properties that appear to be more salient in one sensory modality than others can nonetheless be detected in these other modalities.[21]

5
Double-Function Terms

5.1 A puzzle

In the previous chapter I suggested that so-called synaesthetic metaphors may not be metaphors after all. In this and the next chapters I address the issue of physical–psychological adjectival polysemy (for example, 'sharp' in 'sharp knife' and 'sharp person') in order to suggest how the no-polysemy view of conceptual structure can handle this group of expressions.

Physical–psychological adjectives are also known as double-function adjectives or double-function terms. This is how they were labelled by Solomon Asch who initiated the whole inquiry back in the 1950s and said that:

> There seems to be an outstanding fittingness in speaking of 'bitter truth' or 'dark purpose'. So much is this the case that these models of expression have for us every mark of being literal. (1955, p. 30)

The same intuition that there is something undeniably 'fitting' in the use of physical adjectives to talk about psychological properties is found in John Searle who believes that double-function adjectives express some simple facts about our sensibility:

> Temperature metaphors for emotional and personal traits are in fact quite common and they are not derived from any literal underlying similarities... Similarly, taste metaphors for personal traits are not based on properties in common. We speak of a 'sweet disposition' or a 'bitter person', without implying that the sweet disposition and the bitter person have literal traits in common with sweet and bitter

tastes which exhaust the utterance meaning of the metaphorical utterance. Of course, sweet dispositions and sweet things are both pleasant, but much more is conveyed by the metaphor than mere pleasantness. (1993, pp. 98–9)

In this chapter I describe the results and conclusions of Solomon Asch' work and attempt to show the significance of his considerations. But before we begin, I would like to introduce an *a priori* constraint on accounts of physical–physical and physical–psychological polysemy. This constraint is due to Li (1997) who remarked that if we recognize that language is a biological system, then we had better avoid redundant explanations in favour of subsuming different phenomena under more general principles. That is, because language as we study it is a 'black box', it may be useful to recognize 'a general function F of a system in the face of F's different manifestations' (p. 176).[1] The 'black box' we are going to deal with here is the following: as input we have information from sensory modalities plus some innate constraints on knowledge and perception, as output we have what appears to be a metaphorical way of speaking about psychological properties. The question is: what should be going on in individual speakers' minds so that they find it natural to use the same predicates for different physical and for psychological properties? The black box constraint requires that physical–physical and physical–psychological polysemy be explained by the same principle.

5.2 Asch on double-function adjectives

Asch's inquiry into double-function adjectives was provoked by his research into the formation of impressions of other people via linguistic descriptions, which revealed that the same terms are overwhelmingly used to refer to both physical and psychological properties. Thus, in his 1955 study he compared a number of double-function adjectives across historically and geographically unrelated languages. They included 'warm', 'cold', 'hot'; 'dull', 'bright', 'pale', 'shining'; 'straight', 'twisted', 'crooked'; 'sweet', 'bitter'; 'colourful', 'colourless'; 'rough', 'smooth', 'slippery'; 'dry', 'wet'; 'clear', 'cloudy'; 'deep', 'shallow'; 'high', 'low'; 'broad', 'narrow'; 'rounded', 'sharp'; 'hard' and 'soft' (1955, p. 31). The languages compared to English were Old Testament Hebrew, Homeric Greek, Chinese, Thai, Malayalam and Hausa. The objective of the study was to find out whether these languages employ the same adjectives[2] for describing physical and psychological properties, and whether psychological meanings of double-function adjectives are uniform across languages.

Asch found that all these languages have adjectives with both physical and psychological meanings. Besides, some physical–psychological pairs are identical to the English ones (for example, 'straight'–'crooked'). The situation with other adjectives is a bit more complicated because their psychological meanings are not identical across languages (for example, 'hot'–'cold'). However, as Asch remarks, there is some indisputable similarity between the psychological meanings of these adjectives in different languages:

> For example, the morpheme for 'hot' ... stands for rage or wrath (Hebrew), enthusiasm (Chinese, Malayalam), sexual arousal (Thai), energy (Hausa), or nervousness (in Shilha, a Berber language, the phrase 'his head is hot' = he is nervous). Similarly, the morpheme for 'cold' ... stands for self-possession (Hebrew), indifference or hostility (Chinese), loneliness (Thai), laziness or apathy (Hausa). (1955, p. 33)

In 1955, Asch was not prepared to provide a theoretical explanation for the fact that a large number of adjectives fulfil a dual referential function, noting only that most subjects themselves preferred the intrinsic rather than the associative explanation. That is, they thought that, in some respects, we experience other people as we experience physical objects rather than thinking that such uses are conventional and results of historical accidents (or transfers of meaning). However, he did not accept these explanations on the grounds that such introspective evidence is itself in need of explanation. Further work had to be done.

The results of this work were published in 1958 (with the addition of Burmese to the cross-linguistic data). Asch remarks again on the particular appropriateness of physical terms in descriptions of psychological properties. He also observes in passing that there are hardly any exclusively psychological adjectives, and that psychological meanings of dual predicates in context are apparently independent for language speakers of their meaning in other contexts. Considering cross-linguistic data on the morphemes for 'sweet', 'bitter' and 'sour', Asch stresses the 'impressive agreement' among them which cannot be merely a matter of positive or negative evaluation. The psychological meanings of these taste terms are clearly differentiated: 'sweet' never stands for courage or honesty, while 'bitter' and 'sour' do not designate aggressive attitudes. That is, the psychological meanings of dual-function adjectives express more than some ethical judgement.[3]

In his 1958 article Asch also has a classified list of cross-linguistic divergences. They include: (a) cases of meaning restriction when an adjective denotes only a physical property; (b) different ranges of psychological meanings for an adjective; and (c) cases where it was difficult to establish an adjective's psychological meaning. I discuss these findings in the next section. Presently, it will suffice to say that no contradictory instances were found (such that an adjective corresponding to 'straight' in its physical meaning would correspond to 'crooked' in its psychological meaning), and that differing meanings of an adjective never turned out to be heterogeneous, but rather were 'specializations of a more general property in which they all share' (1958, p. 90). The following conclusion begged for acceptance: there is no one-to-one agreement between languages, but the agreement there is seems to be law-governed and substantial.

Asch noticed that in using such double-function adjectives as 'hard' one refers to one's phenomenal experience and describes the mode of interaction with the object in question (hardness is resistance to change). When applied to descriptions of people, double-function adjectives also denote a mode of interaction. Despite the differences in content and complexity, the schemas of interaction, according to Asch, are experienced as 'dynamically similar'.

> The conclusion we draw, and one we consider essential to a solution of the present problem, is that the terms under discussion refer not alone to unique sensory qualities, but to functional properties or modes of interaction. They do not denote exclusively the 'raw materials' of experience; they are also the names of *concepts*. (1958, p. 93)

Finally, Asch's last inquiry into double-function adjectives (Asch and Nerlove, 1960) concerned their understanding by children of different age groups. One of its objectives was to find out whether children were aware of the double use and understood the connections between the two meanings. Their understanding of the physical meanings of 'sweet', 'hard', 'cold', 'soft', 'bright', 'deep', 'warm' and 'crooked' was tested on a number of objects, after which each child was asked whether these adjectives could describe persons. In the first group (aged from three years and one month to four years and eleven months), 'sweet' was the only adjective understood by the majority of children in its psychological meaning. When asked about the psychological meanings of other adjectives, the children normally exhibited an indignant reaction, and in a few cases when they agreed that these adjectives could describe people, they took them to refer to people's physical properties.

In the second group (aged from five years and ten months to six years and one month), the physical meanings were still dominant, although in a number of cases some of these adjectives were already used by the children to describe psychological properties ('sweet', 'soft', 'hard', 'bright'), and explanations for them were mostly given in affective terms (likeable – dislikeable). In the third group (aged from seven years and six months to eight years), there was a significant increase both in the use and understanding of these adjectives' psychological meanings, although the children had difficulty formulating the relation between the two meanings and insisted that there was no similarity between them ('They are two different kinds of *deep*'; 1960, p. 53). The children in the fourth group (aged from nine years and three months to ten years) showed further increase both in the understanding of psychological meanings and in their ability to find grounds for similarity. Finally, in the fifth group (aged from ten years and eleven months to twelve years and one month) there was a significant advance in comprehension and in the general adequacy of explanations given by the children.

These results were not expected by Asch and Nerlove, as it turned out that psychological meanings of double-function adjectives are acquired as *independent* meanings, without any contact with their physical meanings. It was totally unexpected that similarity plays such a small role in the process of acquisition. Nonetheless, Asch and Nerlove thought that

> [t]he failure to use or understand a term is not evidence of failure to have the corresponding experience. It would indeed be strange to hold that children are insensitive to a person's properties such as *warm* or *cold* on the ground that they have not included them in their speech. (1960, p. 56)

No simple conclusions were drawn from these experiments. However, they suggested that individual language development does not have to follow historical language development. A possible objection to this, according to which children are aware of the relation of meaning similarity but are unable to express it, was rejected by Asch and Nerlove for the lack of evidence. Asch and Nerlove's own explanation of their data included the existence of a 'bridging procedure' which connects two stages of comprehension: from physical–emotional to distinctly psychological uses (from '*warm* people make you feel warm' to '*warm* people are kind'). Overall, Asch and Nerlove's data showed a clear tendency in the development of the understanding of double-function adjectives, but they did not give a clear indication of psychological conditions responsible for these changes, nor did they fully clarify the relationship between physical and psychological meanings of double-function adjectives.

5.3 Discussing Asch's research: cross-linguistic study

When I first came across Asch's work I was amazed by how contemporary it sounds. Particularly in the context of cognitive semantics research on metaphor which largely endorses the associationist explanation, according to which double-function adjectives are the result of stable associations between physical and psychological stimulation. The associationist explanation was explicitly rejected by Asch (1958) who doubted that the association of a psychological event with a component of the corresponding physical event works for most double-function adjectives.

The no-polysemy view of conceptual structure which I introduced in the previous chapter says that there is less metaphoricity in language than is usually supposed. According to the no-polysemy view, polysemous adjectives of the synaesthetic and double-function types (the black box constraint) map onto the corresponding psychologically primitive concepts, which themselves are not polysemous (for example, 'deep' in 'deep water' and 'deep grief' map onto the psychologically primitive concept DEEP). For the moment, you can think of psychologically primitive concepts as some innate patterns of organizing information about properties of experiences. The question we need to answer now is whether the existence of such psychologically primitive concepts is compatible with the divergences in the data on psychological meanings of double-function adjectives collected by Asch.

First, recall that no contradictory instances were found across historically and geographically unrelated languages and, as Asch noted, the differing instances seem to be 'specializations of a more general property in which they all share' (1958, p. 90). Consider some of them (from Asch, 1955):

Cold: self-possession (Hebrew)　　Hot: rage/wrath (Hebrew)
　　　indifference (Chinese)　　　　　　enthusiasm (Chinese, Malayalam)
　　　hostility (Chinese)　　　　　　　　sexual arousal (Thai)
　　　loneliness (Thai)　　　　　　　　　worry (Thai)
　　　laziness/apathy (Hausa)　　　　　energy (Hausa)

Now consider the range of psychological meanings for the corresponding English adjectives (from the *Oxford English Dictionary*)[4]:

Cold: lack of ardour
       lack of warmth
       no intensity of feeling
       lack of enthusiasm
       lack of heartiness
       lack of zeal
       indifference
       apathy
       unexcitability
       unimpassioness
       not flurried
       not hasty
       deliberateness
       lack of sexual passion
       lack of feelings
       cold-bloodedness
       lack of emotions

Hot: excitability
       intensity of feeling
       anger
       sexual desire
       feverishness
       violent exertion
       suffering
       intensity
       violence
       rage

As one can see, the range of psychological meanings that English has for 'cold' and 'hot' includes the psychological meanings of corresponding adjectives in the languages studied by Asch. 'Cold' in English does not just mean 'unemotional' or 'apathetic' but has a whole range of related meanings. Similarly, Russian adjectives for 'cold' and 'hot' convey the same range of meanings without being restricted to any one of them. This suggests that other languages may also express the full range of psychological meanings of 'cold' and 'hot' instead of being associated with only one of them. Some of Asch's examples show that this indeed may be the case. 'Cold' in Chinese means both 'hostile' and 'indifferent'; 'hot' in Thai means both 'worried' and 'sexually aroused'. Thus, the psychological meanings of 'cold' and 'hot' cannot be uniquely given by listing their synonyms or near-synonyms.

Similarly, if we consider more carefully such adjectives as 'sweet', whose psychological meaning may differ across languages, we shall discover that unification is possible. Below is the list for the psychological meaning of 'sweet' in different languages (from Asch, 1958, p. 89):

Hebrew   sweet to the soul (said of pleasant words) (Prov. 16: 24)
Greek   sweet laughter, voice (etymologically linked with the verb 'please')
Chinese   a sweet smile (colloquial); sweet, honeyed words = specious words

Thai   to be sweet is to faint; to be bitter is medicine = beware of people with whom you have relations
Hausa   I don't feel sweetness = I don't feel well
Burmese   face sweet = pleasant-faced; voice sweet = pleasant voice; speech sweet = pleasant speech

At first sight, these instances may appear to be incompatible. However, as Asch himself remarks, the evidence for this statement was limited. By analogy to the previous examples, I believe that the incompatibility would disappear if more evidence were available from the languages in question. Consider one such example. Russian has an adjective for 'sweet' which can be used to describe some psychological property. As it happens, both 'sweet' as 'pleasant' and 'sweet' as 'specious' are available depending on context. When we talk about the physical meaning of 'sweet' ('not salt, sour or bitter', 'having the pleasant taste characteristic of sugar'), we may devise testing procedures for finding out whether something is sweet or not. Nevertheless, this is a different matter from whether a speaker judges something as 'sweet-and-pleasant-to-the-taste' or as 'sweet-but-a-bit-too-much' (that is, the physical meaning of 'sweet' does not incorporate evaluative judgements). Similarly, there are no reasons to think that the psychological meaning of 'sweet' cannot be given independently of evaluative judgements (it is possible to call someone 'sweet' regardless of whether you think that being a sweet person is a good or a bad thing).

Discussing the divergences in the data, Asch remarks that it is better to compare languages as systems rather than individual units of these languages. Thus, when an adjective denotes only a physical property, it may be the case that another word has already met the need of expressing some aspect of the psychological reality. For this reason the adjective in question may not be imbued with a psychological meaning. Similarly, when it is difficult to establish the precise psychological meaning of an adjective, it may be the case that a fuller understanding of the syntactic properties of a language in relation to its semantics would clarify how one or the other meaning is chosen by hearers. For example, in Thai 'spoiled heart' means 'to be sad', whereas 'heart spoiled' means 'to be discouraged' (Asch, 1958, p. 90; note, however, that even in this example there is some general property shared by both instances of 'spoiled').

Overall, a more careful look at the data shows that there are fewer divergences than may seem at first. Besides, the psychological meaning of a double-function adjective cannot be identified with a single synonymous expression as should be expected if its psychological meaning were derived metaphorically. Unlike the standard view, the no-polysemy view treats psychological meanings of polysemous adjectives as their literal meanings, and is thus perfectly compatible with the cross-linguistic data.

5.4 Conceptual atomism

As we have seen in Chapters 1 and 2, most metaphor researchers subscribe to the standard assumption according to which only one meaning of a polysemous adjective can be its literal meaning. One specific contention that makes part of the standard assumption (and also lends some support to it) is the view that the literal–metaphorical distinction follows from transfers of predicates across domains of experience or semantic fields. In this section I argue that the semantic fields explanation does not work for synaesthetic and double-function adjectives.

The notions of 'meaning atomism' and 'meaning holism' are central to many discussions in the philosophy of language. Roughly, the issue under discussion is whether the meaning of a word is only its denotation (meaning atomism), or whether sense relations are meaning constitutive (meaning holism). According to meaning atomism, to know what 'cat' means you only need to know what kind of things are in the extension of 'cat'. According to meaning holism, to know what 'cat' means you also need to know in what relation it stands to other words in its semantic field, that is, the field of animate beings. The whole issue is very complicated, but for our purposes here this simple definition will be sufficient (for a substantial critique of meaning holism see Fodor and Lepore, 1992; for the problems that meaning holism causes in connection with the questions of learning see Dummett, 1973, pp. 599–600).

The idea that the meaning of a word is given by its relation to other words in a language is especially prominent in semantic fields theory (Kittay, 1987; Lehrer, 1974; Lehrer and Kittay, 1992), one particular version of meaning holism. According to semantic fields theory, words belong to semantic fields, and metaphorical interpretation involves mapping the relations from one field onto another. Thus, for example, 'Juliet is the sun' is interpreted by mapping the field of celestial bodies (or is it the field of light- and heat-emitting objects?) onto the field of humans. The interpretation of psychological meanings of double-function adjectives is supposed to proceed the same way. Thus, in the interpretation of the psychological meaning of 'warm' the field of temperature sensations is mapped onto the field of humans. However, there are some problems with semantic fields theory. The most important objection to it is that the dependency of the meaning of a word on the meanings of other words in the same field cannot preserve referential relations, because changing the meaning of one word in a field would imply changing the meanings of all words in that field (Hintikka and Sandu, 1994).[5] Besides, there is an irresolvable problem of semantic fields individuation for a vast majority of words (Ludlow, 1991).

I mention semantic fields theory specifically because one may object to the no-polysemy view by saying that the meaning of a word is determined by its relations to other words within a language, and that these relations differ across languages. Thus, Morgan writes:

> I checked for figurative use of 'blue', 'yellow', 'green', 'cold', 'warm', 'square', 'bad news', 'sunset', 'dawn', 'moon', 'sun', 'wolf', 'pig', 'fox' and 'dirt'. I found as many differences as similarities. None accepted 'warm' as a figurative counterpart of 'cold'. I was told that in Arabic, there are two words for 'cold', only one of which has Searle's figurative use. One could conclude from this that one has to *learn* that 'warm' is used figuratively to mean friendly, responsive, and so on. (1993, p. 131)

However strange it may sound, Morgan's examples are in fact more compatible with meaning atomism than holism. Here is why. One may assume that the meaning of 'cold' is intrinsically related to the meanings of 'warm', 'hot', 'cool' and any other words that one happens to consider as relevant to the domain of thermal sensation ('scorching', 'freezing', and so on). But in this case one will be lead to conclude that the absence of such other words in the vocabulary of some language would make it impossible for us to find out what an expression of this language means. (For example, whether a word should be translated into English as 'hot' or 'cold' or with the help of some other word.) One solution to this kind of the radical interpretation problem may be to limit the domain of thermal sensations to four basic terms – 'warm', 'cold', 'hot' and 'cool'. But this is not an acceptable option for a holist, since it presupposes the existence of some independent grounds for establishing the number of basic terms in a semantic field (independent from the pattern of sense relations in a language).

In contrast to such views, I believe that there are more similarities than differences between people of different languages and cultures, and that this is so because we are members of the same species. Thus, we can take just one step further and say that conceptual similarity is to be expected: that 'hot' and 'cold' mean precisely HOT and COLD across languages. In this respect, there is no need for them to be conceptually related. One need not know or remember anything about cold things in order to be able to react in an adequate way to hot things. And if one is a sophisticated enough creature (a human being?), one may have the concept HOT but not the concept COLD. Still, there could be three objections to the atomistic view. The first one is that the words 'hot', 'cold', 'cool' and 'warm' are definitely related. The second one is that there are unlikely to be languages that have a word for 'hot' but lack a word for 'cold'. And the third one is that people use the conceptual relation between 'hot' and 'cold' in their reasoning.

These objections seem to express the naive view that since hotness and coldness are both normally present in our experience, the corresponding concepts must be necessarily present and related in one's conceptual system.[6] Imagine a hypothetical parasite (migrated here from Dretske, 1995, p. 82) that attaches to its host only when the latter has a body temperature of +18 °C. That is, the temperature is registered to be +18 °C by its temperature-detecting mechanisms (and we can establish this by outside observation). Imagine also that we endow our parasite with a minimal representational capacity and a minimal conceptual system and assume that it is such that it is able to form part of a larger human conceptual system if extended. Imagine finally that the only temperature-related concept the parasite has is WARM, which is about the temperature at which it attaches to its host. This way the parasite may represent the temperature of +18 °C either as the temperature of +18 °C or as WARM (but since it is responsive only to the temperature of +18 °C, WARM for it is exactly the temperature of +18 °C). The temperature of the parasite's host may drop to −18 °C (due to refrigeration) or raise to +58 °C reflecting changes in the external world, but this would not affect the parasite's representational capacities. It would still have the concept WARM but not COLD or HOT (although it may have the concept OTHER-THAN-WARM). Thus, WARM, HOT and COLD do not necessarily have to be conceptually related.

Humans are a bit more complicated than hypothetical parasites. They have all these concepts, and no language is known that has a word for 'hot' but lacks a word for 'cold'. Whether one takes hotness and coldness to be properties of things or subjective qualities, it is obvious that humans' survival is affected by both poles of the continuum. Thus, there is nothing surprising in the fact that human languages express both concepts. On the contrary, inhabitants of the planet K40 have a conceptual system just like ours, but differ from us in some respects. They cannot sense 30 °C (only 31 °C) differences in temperature; the average temperature on their planet is +550 °C and never falls below +530 °C; and the only danger that comes to them from the environment are severe increases in temperature from 100 °C. In this connection, they are most likely to have in their language a word for 'hot' but not for 'cold' (using instead a word for 'okay').

But, you may say, humans are not K40ans and seem to rely on the conceptual relation between HOT and COLD in their reasoning. I do not deny that. However, the fact that they do and the question of conceptual atomism are different issues. Things in the external world may possess any temperature in the continuum from absolute zero to $+\infty$ °C, but it is the sensitivity of perceiving and representing systems that determines how parts of the continuum are conceptualized. The fact that HOT and COLD are connected in human reasoning reflects the fact that humans are influenced by that difference in their activities. K40ans, for example, are more interested in the relation between hotness and okayness.

Psychological meanings of double-function adjectives exhibit even less necessary conceptual relatedness. Even though in the vast majority of languages both 'hot' and 'cold' have psychological meanings, it does not follow that an individual has to know the psychological meaning of one in order to know the psychological meaning of the other. To show this one can simply extend the argument about their physical meanings. Thus, when one knows what 'a cold person' means, one knows what behaviour this kind of person is likely to exhibit in various situations. This is sufficient for understanding 'He's a cold person' and for inferring that he might have reacted in such and such way in a situation. But in order to understand 'a cold person' one does not need to know how a warm person or a hot-tempered person would have behaved in the same situation.

In short, as I hope to have shown in this section, arguments from meaning holism fail to give substance to the idea that the content of concepts expressed in a language is relative to the number of words that this language has in some or other semantic field. For this reason, linguistic variability does not undermine the no-polysemy view of conceptual structure.

5.5 Discussing Asch's research: language acquisition study

As we have seen in section 5.2, Asch and Nerlove's (1960) research on children's understanding of double-function adjectives provided some evidence on the developmental timetables in the acquisition of their psychological meanings. However, there was no evidence that the acquisition of psychological meanings of double-function adjectives is affected by the knowledge of their physical meanings. From this Asch and Nerlove concluded that the inability to describe the similarity between features of experiences does not entail the lack of such experiences and suggested that a bridging procedure was operating between physical–emotional and psychological meanings.

From the no-polysemy view of conceptual structure, a different interpretation of the results can be proposed. If the research did not show that the acquisition of psychological meanings made any contact with the physical meanings, why seek a connection when there is none? As a third-age-grouper in Asch and Nerlove's experiments remarked in response to the question about the psychological meaning of 'deep': 'They are two different kinds of *deep*' (1960, p. 53).[7] As a psychologically primitive concept, DEEP depicts those aspects of reality that exhibit the property of being deep, but in order to know the meaning of 'deep' in different contexts one needs to have knowledge of those objects that 'deep' is predicated of. The fact that younger children reacted indignantly to the suggestion that physical adjectives they knew may have psychological meanings does not by itself show that psychological meanings depend on physical meanings. As we shall see below, there are certain constraints that may explain the later acquisition of psychological meanings.

However, before we consider them, it has to be remarked that there is still little agreement between researchers on children's understanding of alternative word meanings. This disagreement is especially striking when children's spontaneous speech is compared with their performance in experimental settings (Winner and Gardner, 1993, p. 431). And even experimental research often produces different results. Thus, Gardner (1974) showed that the application of descriptive terms across unusual domains does not present a serious difficulty for children. (The verbal stimuli in his experiments included 'cold'/'warm', 'hard'/'soft', 'happy'/'sad', 'loud'/'quiet' and 'light'/'dark' in application to visual-colour, visual-physiognomic, visual-abstract, auditory, tactile and verbal-kinaesthetic modalities.) Interestingly, on the task that required applying verbal stimuli to faces pre-schoolers made 67 per cent correct matches. This can be taken as evidence to the effect that even very young children are capable of associating personalities (through facial expressions) with physical adjectives. In contrast with Asch and Nerlove's (1960) results, the application of adjectives 'hard' and 'soft' across domains was easy even for the youngest subjects (aged three years and five months; Gardner, 1974, p. 88).

Given that there are age-related differences in children's understanding of double-function adjectives, how can one explain them? Winner and Gardner (1993) consider one possible explanation, according to which children's difficulty with the psychological meanings of double-function adjectives is due to the difference in their ability to understand perceptual and non-perceptual metaphors. On this account, what develops is the ability to appreciate relational or structural similarity. However, a number of studies indicate that even very young children can understand non-perceptual similarity, and that by the age of three or four children already rely on structural similarity in drawing analogies (Winner and Gardner, 1993, p. 433–5; Brown, 1989; Goswami, 1992). Thus, Winner and Gardner (1993) conclude that a more plausible explanation is that children's ability to perceive similarity between domains is present from the very beginning but is constrained by their knowledge of domains compared (cf. Gibbs, 1994, Chapter 9). On the one hand, Winner and Gardner consider the psychological meanings of double-function adjectives as their metaphoric meanings: 'we attribute to mental states and personality traits properties literally true only of physical objects'. But on the other hand, they seem to reject the interpretation according to which children are unable to perceive the similarity between 'physical hardness and lack of emotional warmth' (1993, p. 433).[8]

According to the no-polysemy view of conceptual structure, the psychological meanings of double-function adjectives are not their metaphoric meanings. How, then, can we account for the age-related differences in children's understanding of them? I suggest that these developmental differences are due to some general constraints operating in vocabulary acquisition and selective attention to stimuli.

A question that had long puzzled developmental psychologists is how children know what objects a word refers to (for example, how do they know that 'chair' refers to chairs rather than seats of chairs, and so on)? Today many psychologists agree that there are certain constraints on children's acquisition of vocabulary. One such constraint is children's tendency to avoid synonymy. That is, when they hear a new word in the context of a familiar object, they start looking for a new object or a new property to which this word could apply (Markman, 1989). We can call this 'one word–one meaning' constraint operating in development. And although it is clearly beneficial in early lexical acquisition, it imposes a restriction on the acquisition of alternative word meanings.

Thus, besides having difficulty with the psychological meanings of double-function adjectives, three and even five years old children have difficulty with other types of polysemy, regarding 'neck of a bottle' or 'arm of a chair' as nonsense (Curtis, 1985). Similar problems accompany first-graders processing of homonymy, as they have difficulty switching from one meaning of a homonym to another (Cramer, 1983). Children of older age groups (nine-year-olds) experience difficulty with ignoring content when asked to make judgements about syntactic form (for example, 'The cats are barking so loudly'; Bialystok, 1993).

Morton and Trehub (2001) interpret these results as due to attentional constraints operating in children's understanding of language. They further provide their own data showing that these constraints operate within a broader range. Thus, in interpreting utterances with conflicting content and paralinguistic cues (a situation with positive emotional implications such as 'My mommy gave me a treat' described in a sad voice), children and adults attach different significance to content and paralinguistic features. Although young children and even infants are sensitive to vocal cues to emotion and respond to them in appropriate ways, four- and five-year-olds in Morton and Trehub's experiments failed to perceive the conflict between propositional content and paralinguistic features of utterances, making their judgements on the basis of content only. Even seven- and eight-year-olds, while noticing that the utterances contained conflicting emotional features, 'still maintained that the speaker had expressed her feelings well' (2001, p. 838). The situation changes by the age of nine or ten when children start to rely more on paralinguistic cues than content, which is how adults perform on this task.

Taking these data into account, I believe that it is possible that children's difficulty with the psychological meanings of double-function adjectives has to do with some general attentional constraints operating in development.[9] The age-related pattern of changes in children's reliance on content or paralinguistic cues in Morton and Trehub's experiments parallels the pattern of changes in children's understanding of psychological meanings of double-function adjectives in Asch and Nerlove's (1960) experiments. The existence of attentional constraints may also help in explaining the conflicting results obtained by Asch and Nerlove (1960) and Gardner (1974).

As mentioned earlier, three years and five months old children in Gardner's experiments successfully mapped such adjectives as 'hard' and 'soft' onto faces, which is in contradiction with Asch and Nerlove's results. It is possible that the discrepancy in the results may be explained if we consider the attentional efforts required by the experimental tasks. Thus, in Gardner's study children had to decide which word better described a face, and their performance suggests that they understood what it is for a facial expression to be 'hard' or 'soft'. In Asch and Nerlove's study, children were required to give verbal interpretations of the psychological meanings of double-function adjectives after their attention had been drawn to their physical meanings. This may have imposed an excessive demand on their language processing abilities.

Overall, currently available data on children's understanding of language does not contradict the no-polysemy view of conceptual structure. On the contrary, the no-polysemy view can make sense of Asch and Nerlove's observation that the acquisition of psychological meanings is independent of their physical meanings. (That is, psychological meanings are not acquired by extending physical meanings with the help of analogy or metaphor.) Age-related differences in children's understanding of psychological meanings can be explained if one takes into account the existence of certain general constraints that operate in development. However, currently available data are also insufficient to arrive at a single conclusion about children's understanding of the psychological meanings of double-function adjectives. More detailed studies, taking into account the difference in children's abilities to correctly understand words and give reasons for why a word was understood in a particular way (cf. Vosniadou *et al.*, 1984), as well as differences in experimental settings will be necessary.

6
Double-Function Terms Again

6.1 Adjectival polysemy in psycholinguistic research

In the previous chapter we saw that the no-polysemy view of conceptual structure can be extended to account for physical–psychological adjectival polysemy. Unlike the standard assumption theories, the no-polysemy view denies that psychological meanings of double-function adjectives are their metaphoric or secondary meanings. A standard assumption theorist may object to this by invoking evidence from psycholinguistic studies in normal and brain-damaged subjects. The purpose if this chapter is therefore to show that some assumptions people have as far as the literal-metaphorical distinction is concerned are not so well grounded as they may appear.

Thus, to show that the standard view is advantageous over the no-polysemy view one may use evidence from semantic priming experiments. In semantic priming experiments, one word is spoken or flashed on a computer screen (the prime), and then, after different time delays (SOA – stimulus-onset-asynchronies), a string of letters appears on the screen (the target). Subjects have to decide as quickly as possible whether this string of letters is a word or not. Generally, if the second word (the target) is related to the first word (the prime), subjects take less time to make their decision, and the second word is said to be 'primed for' by the first word. Different priming patterns are obtained for ambiguous words (words with more than one meaning) presented in isolation and in context, as well as at different delays. These differences in priming can be generalized and used to make hypotheses about the mental lexicon, that is, about how different meanings of words are represented in people's heads. If the data shows that different priming effects are obtained for the two meanings of a polyseme, this can be interpreted as showing that one of its meanings is its literal (or dominant) and the other is its metaphoric (or subordinate) meaning. This way the literal–metaphorical distinction may appear to be a natural fact about the organization of the mental lexicon.

Below I analyse the viabilty of this view, first discussing Williams' (1992) experiments on physical–psychological adjectival polysemy, and then offering some more general considerations that, in my view, lend support to the no-polysemy hypothesis.

Prior to Williams' (1992) experiments it had been established that meanings of homonyms ('bank' as a financial institution and riverside) are represented independently of each other in the mental lexicon (Tabossi *et al.*, 1987). That is, in priming experiments all meanings of a homonym become initially activated independently of context, but context almost immediately favours the selection of the appropriate meaning. The purpose of Williams' experiments was to establish whether the meanings of polysemes are also independently represented in the mental lexicon or whether they are interrelated and exhibit some kind of hierarchical structuring. It was supposed that if polysemes are mentally represented in the same way as homonyms, all their meanings should also be initially activated in semantic priming tasks.

The experimental materials included polysemous adjectives that have both physical and psychological meanings: 'awkward' ('clumsy' vs. 'embarrassing'), 'tight' ('taut' vs. 'compact'), 'dull' ('dreary' vs. 'stupid'), 'firm' ('solid' vs. 'strict'), 'smooth' ('even' vs. 'slick'), 'deep' ('low' vs. 'profound'), 'dirty' ('soiled' vs. 'obscene'), and 'strong' ('mighty' vs. 'intense'). The results of the single word priming task were compared with priming effects in sentence contexts at delays of 250, 500 and 850 msec. The experiment showed that in isolation the two meanings of a polysemous adjective ('strict' vs. 'solid') are equally primed for by that adjective ('firm'). However, in sentence context, the results were asymmetrical between central ('solid') and non-central meanings ('strict'). In those cases when the context suggested the central meaning, the non-central targets were not primed for. By contrast, when the context suggested the non-central meaning, the central targets were primed for (even at delays of 850 msec after offset). Although there was also some degree of priming in the non-central condition, it was unstable over items and subjects (Williams, 1992, p. 201).

Thus, the results of this experiment showed that the irrelevant meanings of polysemous adjectives do not become suppressed as the irrelevant meanings of homonyms do. This suggested to Williams that the meanings of a polyseme are neither independent in language comprehension nor equal in their representation in the mental lexicon, but are interrelated in an important way such that some of them persist even in irrelevant contexts.

In order to establish more clearly the difference between central and non-central meanings, the second experiment was conducted. It employed a direct relatedness judgement task, where subjects were asked to judge the relatedness of target words to sentences (tested against related and unrelated pairs of central and non-central targets). After seeing a sentence on a screen and acknowledging that they understood it, the subjects were required to press either *yes* or *no* button in response to a target depending on whether they judged it to be related 'in a general way' to the overall meaning of the sentence. Sets of testing materials consisted of four sentences with the following order of conditions – central related, central unrelated, non-central related, non-central unrelated – as in the following example (from Williams, 1992, p. 216):

Firm
The headmaster decided that the boy would do better with a firm teacher. SOLID
The headmaster decided that the boy would do better with a young teacher. SOLID
The woman did not like her hotel room because it had a firm bed. STRICT
The woman did not like her hotel room because it had an unmade bed. STRICT

The second experiment showed that at long delays non-central meanings stopped interfering with the subjects' responses, and target interference with the sentences' overall meanings was confined to those cases where a central target followed a non-central use of an adjective. Thus, 'solid' was more likely to interfere with the overall meaning of the first sentence in the example cited, rather than 'strict' with the overall meaning of the third sentence. However, the second experiment also showed a high degree of item and subject variability, with a significant interaction between centrality and relatedness for the subjects but not for the items.[1]

Overall, Williams' (1992) study, in which some contextually irrelevant meanings of polysemous adjectives persisted even at sufficiently long delays, shows that unlike the meanings of homonyms, the meanings of polysemes are interrelated. This is exactly how the difference between homonymy and polysemy is usually defined, but what is the nature of this interrelatedness?

As Williams says, in order to account for meaning interrelatedness in polysemy and asymmetric experimental results, two facts need an explanation: (a) the presence of asymmetry in the activation of central and non-central meanings of a term; and (b) the absence of perfect asymmetry in the priming of central and non-central targets (the effect of non-central targets is noticeable at short but not at long delays). And although Williams admits that the results of his experiments do not uniquely favour either the 'ecological' (centrality determined in terms of meaning frequency) or the 'intellectual' (centrality determined in terms of the structural aspects of conceptual organization) approach to the question of meaning interrelatedness in polysemy, he appears to be more sympathetic to the view that meaning representations are hierarchically structured.

How does one account for the asymmetric results from the point of view of meanings hierarchies? According to Williams, although the single word priming task revealed no difference in computing the prime-target relations for central and non-central targets, the target itself might license 'the extension of the prime's meaning where necessary' (1992, p. 210). Further, as the experimental results showed, computing the relation between a central target and the context favouring a non-central reading does not become more complicated and the target is primed for. Williams' explanation for this is that, for central targets, the extension of the prime's meaning is compatible with the context because the extended meaning may be already implicit within the context and, because of the hierarchical concept structure, explored during the activation process. Unlike central targets, non-central targets are computed only in felicitous contexts; in non-felicitous contexts extensions of a prime are blocked by the context. Finally, although on certain trials the relation between a prime and a non-central target was successfully computed, this fact is considered insignificant by Williams on the grounds that subjects have a tendency to overinterpretation.

Thus, the results of Williams' experiments strongly suggest that meanings of polysemous adjectives are interrelated and interdependent. Some meanings (central meanings) are privileged, and this may be due to their position in the hierarchical meaning structure. As it happens, central meanings in Williams' experiments are also physical meanings of the adjectives included in the study. Thus, the conclusion that non-central meanings are metaphorically extended psychological meanings seems inevitable, but is it?

6.2 Discussing Williams' results

As we have seen, Williams himself is more favourably inclined towards explaining asymmetric priming effects as due to the hierarchical meaning structure rather than meaning frequency. In the hierarchical meaning structure the central (physical) meaning of a polysemous adjective dominates its non-central (psychological) meaning. One way to understand this is that psychological meanings of polysemous adjectives are secondary and derived from their primary physical meanings. This understanding would be consistent with Williams' observation that central meanings were implicit in contexts biased towards non-central meanings, and with the choice of experimental materials, where the centrality of meanings was established with reference to their concreteness and frequency. Etymologically, all but two adjectives ('dull' and 'tight') had earlier physical meanings.

Thus, according to Williams, the meanings of polysemous adjectives are organized in the mental lexicon in such a way that physical meanings are central in the hierarchy and extendible to psychological meanings, which are their derivatives. Such organization should explain the differences in priming effects. However, the two experiments did not show the existence of such organization. In some cases, owing to subject and item variability, priming effects from non-central targets were equally significant. This is noted by Kilgariff who doubts that the experimental paradigm of semantic priming is practical

> for determining the numbers of senses for a substantial number of words. The results of the experiments are just not sufficiently stable: as Williams says, the priming task 'suffers from a large degree of item and subject variability'. (1997, p. 99)

What I intend to show in this section is that the no-polysemy view, according to which psychological meanings of polysemous adjectives are not their metaphoric meanings, is compatible with the results of Williams' study, and may even be a better explanation of the observed asymmetries. And first of all, let us have a closer look at the experimental materials. Consider the following two sentences:

> Everyone thought that he should become a salesman because he was so smooth. EVEN
> The builder worked hard until the wall was quite smooth. SLICK[2]

According to Williams, in the first sentence the context biases the non-central meaning towards the central target. 'Even', which is the central meaning of 'smooth', is implicitly active within the representation of 'smooth'. In the second sentence, the computation of the relation between the prime and the target is blocked by the context.

However, if we consider the range of meanings of the two targets themselves, we shall see that 'even', apart from its physical meanings, also has a psychological meaning close to that of 'smooth'. And 'slick' has a physical meaning compatible with the interpretation of 'smooth' in the context of 'smooth wall'.[3] 'Even' can mean 'equable' or 'calm' (of a person's temper), and this interpretation does not conflict with the 'salesman' context, even if the sentence meaning changes slightly. Similarly, 'slick' can be rendered as 'sleek, smooth' or 'slippery', which are also quite felicitous in the 'wall' context. Thus, it is no accident that the second sentence which contains a non-central target word evoked a large number of *yes* responses (59 per cent).

But what about other sets of sentences where non-central targets did not evoke many positive responses? Consider the following two sentences:

The first hour of the party was rather awkward. CLUMSY
The gymnast's movements were judged as rather too awkward. EMBARRASSING

On the one hand, 'clumsy' means 'awkward in movement or shape, ungainly', and if we substitute 'ungainly' for 'awkward' in the first sentence, the overall meaning of the sentence will not change much. On the other hand, 'embarrassing' means 'causing (a person) to feel awkward or self-conscious or ashamed', and this meaning is overruled by the overall meaning of the second sentence (someone else judged the gymnast's movements as awkward). Here is another example:

The school teacher was criticised for not being firm. SOLID
The couple wanted a bed that was firm. STRICT

On the one hand, 'solid' can mean 'staunch and dependable', which is quite felicitous in the 'teacher' context. On the other hand, 'strict' means 'precisely limited or defined; without exception or deviation' or 'requiring complete compliance or exact, reinforced rigidity', neither of which is felicitous in the 'bed' context. And the last example:

She was difficult to get along with because her moods were so strong.
MIGHTY
He always helped his friends move house because he was so strong.
INTENSE

Here, on the one hand, 'mighty' means 'powerful or strong, in body, mind, or influence' or 'great, considerable' (colloquial), and these meanings are felicitous in the context of moods.[4] On the other hand, the range of meanings for 'intense' includes: (1) '(of a quality, feeling, etc.) existing in a high degree, extreme, forceful'; (2a) '(of a person) feeling, or apt to feel, strong emotion'; (2b) 'expressing strong emotion'; (3) '(of a colour) very strong or deep'; (4) '(of an action, etc.) highly concentrated'. None of them expresses the physical ability necessary for moving house, and thus the search for a possible relation is banned by the context.

According to Williams, mental representations of polysemous adjectives are structured hierarchically in such a way that, for example, physical strength forms the central node of STRONG, and an additional, though related, node corresponds to those instances of 'strong' where the physical interpretation would be undesirable. This second node, presumably, appeared as a result of a metaphorical (historical) extension of meaning. In the processing of polysemous adjectives, the central node is accessed first and persists, even if the context requires moving to the additional node. Thus, the difference in priming effects would follow directly from the structure of conceptual organization. However, it is important to keep in mind that Williams' proposal for the organization of the mental lexicon is an idealized version of 'what would have been there' barred instability of priming effects, high degree of subject and item variability and the tendency to overinterpretation among subjects.

According to the no-polysemy view, 'strong' does not have 'physically strong' as its only literal meaning or, in terms of conceptual organization, as the central *node* which is accessed first in the process of language understanding. Rather, 'strong' maps onto the psychologically primitive concept STRONG which spans both physical and psychological manifestations of that property (how different meanings of 'strong' and other polysemous adjectives are computed in context is discussed in Chapter 10). As we have seen above, the asymmetries in priming effects observed in Williams' experiments may not have resulted from different conceptual representations corresponding to central and non-central meanings. A more careful look at the experimental materials shows a larger number of meaning overlaps between the primes and central targets than between the primes and non-central targets. Besides, when there were meaning overlaps between the primes and non-central targets, the non-central targets were judged as related to a sentence' overall meaning. In this sense, the no-polysemy view may be more consistent with Williams' data. Furthermore, the no-polysemy view is also consistent with the results of the single word priming experiments, which did not produce differing priming effects for central and non-central targets. The no-polysemy view can also accommodate high item variability and subjects' tendency to overinterpretation.[5]

There is also one more general problem arsing in connection with the study of meaning in the semantic priming paradigm: the problem of meaning individuation (cf. Kilgariff, 1997). For example, Williams' study restricted the range of meanings of 'strong' to one physical ('strong for the purpose of moving house') and one psychological meaning ('strong moods'). However, if the full range of meanings is taken into account, it might be more difficult to decide which of them should be forming the central node in the conceptual structure. 'Strong material' and 'strong hands' both seem straightforwardly literal. But clearly, 'strong hands' are not strong because they are made of strong materials, and 'strong materials' are not strong because they are good for lifting things (although they may be good for us to use them in devices for lifting things). However, even on Williams' account, they are both literally strong. Does it have to follow that one of them rather than the other forms the central node in the conceptual structure? And how would one account for synaesthetic uses of 'strong', as in 'strong light' or 'strong smell'? Are they accessed before the psychological meanings of 'strong'?

Unfortunately, I know of no studies that bear on that issue directly. However, several researchers have challenged the ordered-access model showing that all meanings of an ambiguous word are initially activated regardless of context, even though the degree of activation may be sensitive to relative meaning frequency and contextual influences (Lucas, 1999; Seidenberg *et al.*, 1982; Simpson, 1994; Simpson and Burgess, 1985; Simpson and Kang, 1994; Tabossi and Zardon, 1993). Thus, if one wants to avoid circularity, one cannot base the account of literal meaning on the primacy of access (cf. Giora, 1997, 1998, 1999, 2002; see also Gibbs, 1994, 2002).[6] Whether an account of literal meaning can be based on data from differential semantic processing in cerebral hemispheres is discussed in the remainder of this chapter.

6.3 The processing of alternative meanings by cerebral hemispheres: the beginnings

Today it is an accepted fact among neuropsychologists that most cognitive tasks require the participation of the two cerebral hemispheres. A number of language-related tasks are dependent on the proper functioning not only of the left but also the right hemisphere. Several studies have shown that damage to the right hemisphere can lead to the destruction of a number of cognitive abilities which constitute an important part of our linguistic communication. They include the comprehension and production of humour, affect, nonliteral utterances and indirect speech acts, as well as the more general ability to organize incoming linguistic information into a coherent discourse (for detailed lists of references see Burgess and Chiarello, 1996; Paradis, 1998). However, here we shall be concerned with only one aspect of the research into the division of linguistic labour between the two hemispheres – the processing of metaphors and polysemes.

Even those who are not very familiar with this area of research have most probably heard of a number of findings which suggest that whereas the left hemisphere stores literal meanings of words, the intact right hemisphere is necessary for the processing of metaphoric language. Thus, clinical studies indicate that people with damage to the right hemisphere have difficulty understanding metaphors. These findings may be used by a supporter of the standard assumption to argue that a look at the hemispheric differences in language processing may tell us the difference between the literal and the metaphorical; that differential processing of the various meanings of polysemous adjectives may be interpreted as showing that they have only one literal meaning, and that their other meanings are not independent, but derived from their literal meaning. In this respect, the purpose of the remaining sections of this chapter is to show that currently available data on the distribution of meaning processing between the two hemispheres do not lend support to the standard assumption, and that the no-polysemy view is consistent with empirical evidence.

Let us begin with the classical study of alternative meaning processing by brain-damaged subjects that was conducted by Winner and Gardner (1977). Inspired by the work of Asch on double-function adjectives, Winner and Gardner sought to establish how the division of linguistic labour between the two hemispheres relates to the understanding of 'connotative' aspects of language. In their experiments subjects were asked to match 18 phrases (9 double-function of the type 'heavy heart' and 9 synaesthetic of the type 'colourful music') with sets of 4 coloured pictures (representing the appropriate metaphoric meaning of a phrase, its literal interpretation, a salient property denoted by the adjective, and a salient object denoted by the noun), and then give verbal explications of the phrases. The comparison was made between normal subjects and three groups of brain-damaged patients (damage to the left hemisphere, to the right hemisphere, and patients with dementia).

The results of the experiment showed that: (a) normal adults chose more metaphoric pictures than any other group; (b) patients with left hemisphere damage (LHD hereafter) chose slightly fewer metaphoric pictures; (c) patients with right hemisphere damage (RHD hereafter) and dementia chose significantly fewer metaphoric pictures than normal adults. From the point of view of their characteristic reactions (1977, p. 723), (a) RHD patients chose as many literal as metaphoric pictures and, unlike other groups, did not find the literal pictures strange or absurd; (b) patients with left anterior lesions chose a significant number of metaphoric pictures (67 per cent); (c) patients with left posterior lesions chose 46 per cent of metaphoric and 24 per cent of literal pictures (the remainder were only-noun and only-adjective interpretations); (d) patients with dementia made an equal number of metaphoric and literal choices; and finally (e) normal controls chose metaphoric pictures 73 per cent of the time and were ready to correct their choices when asked to do so.

In the second part of the experiment, when subjects were asked to give verbal explications of their choices, an interesting pattern of responses was discovered. Patients with LHD performed poorly on the task, repeating words in the sentences, while patients with RHD were able to offer paraphrases. Thus, there was some interesting dissociation between the pictorial choices made by RHD individuals and their verbal explications, which, however, did not disturb the patients themselves. Below is an illustration of this from Winner and Gardner:

> Four of these patients, however, initially resisted the sentences as meaningless and then proceeded to interpret them appropriately. Thus, upon hearing a sentence containing the expression 'bright smell', one patient said: 'The word bright is in the wrong place. I wouldn't say bright smell, though it could be a *nice* smell.' Another, when asked to paraphrase a sentence containing the clause 'a dark song', said adamantly that he had never heard of describing a song as 'dark'; but he then readily paraphrased it as

meaning 'slow and dreary'. . . . Thus, although metaphoric expressions *sounded* wrong to these subjects, their linguistic comprehension remained relatively unimpaired. A dissociation seemed to exist, in brief, between what they *thought* they knew, and what *in fact* was known. (1977, p. 724)

From the results of their study Winner and Gardner concluded to the dominance of the left hemisphere for the denotative aspects of language, and the right hemisphere for the connotative aspects of language. Still, it has to be remarked that they doubted that there is a strict distinction between functions of the two hemispheres with respect to figurative language processing. The performances of anterior aphasics, posterior aphasics (showing the poorer overall performance), and patients with dementia were as had been expected. The unexpected finding was the dissociation between adequate verbal explications and literal picture selection in RHD patients. In the absence of other evidence (visuo-spatial deficits) and taking into account the general inappropriateness of responses and emotional reactions of RHD patients, Winner and Gardner suggested that their performances might be considered as a 'qualitatively different mode of metaphor appreciation', rather than a total lack of the ability to understand alternative meanings. Another interesting observation from the present perspective is that no group of patients showed any difference in the processing of synaesthetic and double-function, which agrees with the black box *a priori* requirement on the processing of various meanings of polysemous adjectives.

6.4 The processing of alternative meanings by cerebral hemispheres: later studies

Winner and Gardner's (1977) study is sometimes cited as having shown that while the left hemisphere (LH thereafter) is responsible for literal language processing, the right hemisphere (RH thereafter) is responsible for the processing of figurative language (Paradis, 1998; but see Anaki *et al.*, 1998). However, it did not show that RHD patients are completely incapable of appreciating alternative meanings of words. Rather it showed that they are prone to attend to only one meaning of an ambiguous word. In this section, we shall see that later studies did not fully clarify the issue, and that the study of how brain damage affects language processing does not support the literal-metaphorical distinction with respect to polysemous adjectives.

The two later studies often cited as having established the role of the RH as metaphor processor were conducted by Brownell and his colleagues (1984, 1990). Brownell et al.'s (1984) study addressed the sensitivity of LHD and RHD patients to the alternative meanings of double-function adjectives. The subjects in their study were asked to pair an adjective with another adjective which they judged to 'go together' with the first adjective (for example, 'wise'–'foolish' or 'wise'–'deep'). Their study showed that: (a) RHD patients avoided pairing adjectives with their metaphoric synonyms; (b) aphasic patients, on the contrary, based their judgements on metaphor and polarity, and ignored denotative aspects (antonymy); (c) normal controls were more flexible in their choices, making use of both denotation and connotation. From this the researchers concluded that 'the right hemisphere has as its particular province sensitivity to connotative aspects of meaning' (1984, p. 256). They also suggested that their study reflects the organization of a normal individual's knowledge of word meaning, which consists of separable lexical stores contained in different parts of the brain (p. 263).

Brownell et al. (1990) addressed the same question by asking their subjects to chose two words most similar in meaning from a group of words containing a target, a synonym, and a foil. Target words were either adjectives with alternative metaphoric meanings or nouns with alternative non-metaphoric meanings (for example, 'deep'–'wise'–'lake'). The purpose of the study was to find out whether the metaphor deficit in RHD subjects is restricted to metaphoric processing or whether it reflects the general inability to access alternative word meanings. The study showed that RHD subjects performed worse than LHD subjects on both conditions. However, a comparison of correct responses for groups of subjects indicated that there was a difference in the RHD subjects' appreciation of metaphoric and non-metaphoric alternative meanings, which was not the case with the LHD subjects. These results were interpreted by Brownell et al. (1990) as showing that RHD subjects cannot appreciate metaphoric meanings even at the single word level.[7]

Nonetheless, Brownell et al.'s (1984, 1990) results did not receive confirmation in other studies. Tompkins' (1990) subjects received an auditory lexical decision task, in which the targets were double-function adjectives and the primes were either their physical or psychological meanings (for example, 'dull'–'sharp' or 'smart'–'sharp'). The RHD subjects were not significantly different in their reaction times, and their lexical decisions were facilitated by both literal and metaphoric primes.

These results show that automatic processing of alternative meanings is preserved in RHD subjects and is comparable to that of normal subjects by all parameters, except for absolute speed.

Similarly, experiments conducted by Giora and colleagues (Giora et al., 1997; reported in Giora, 1999), in which the subjects were asked to give verbal explications of such expressions as 'a hard man', did not show any metaphoric deficit associated with RH damage. On the contrary, normal and RHD subjects performed well on the task, whereas LHD subjects had difficulty comprehending these expressions. Regarding these findings, Giora remarks on the inconsistency of their results with those obtained by Brownell et al. (1984), and emphasizes that their study both included a larger sample of subjects and stricter criteria of patient selection (Giora, 1999, p. 926).

Recently, Zaidel et al. (2002) have administered the Right Hemisphere Communication Battery (RHCB; Gardner and Brownell, 1986) to groups of RHD and LHD subjects. The RHCB includes, among others, pictorial and verbal metaphor subtest (as used by Winner and Gardner, 1977), and alternative word meanings subtest (as used by Brownell et al., 1990). Their study showed that both groups of patients performed worse than normal controls but that there were no differences between patient groups. Besides, the scores of LHD patients were lower than those of RHD patients on the three tasks that are of interest to us here (see Zaidel et al., 2002, p. 519). On the alternative word meanings subtest both groups of patients chose more synonyms than alternative meanings, and thus a selective RH deficit in choosing alternative/metaphoric word meanings was not supported.

Analysing the divergences in the studies of alternative meaning processing by RHD subjects and conducting their own study, Chobor and Schweiger (1998) came to a completely different conclusion on the issue. They doubted the clear-cut interpretations by Brownell et al. (1984, 1990) and questioned the localization of lexical ambiguity resolution in the right hemisphere. The puzzle of Winner and Gardner's (1977) study, in which RHD subjects were able to provide paraphrases of metaphoric expressions, was not solved by Brownell's et al. (In fact, Brownell et al.'s study did not show that RHD patients had difficulty *understanding* alternative psychological meanings of polysemous adjectives.)

Instead, Chobor and Schweiger suggested that cognitive processes required for the understanding of ambiguous words may be localized to the frontal lobes, and that the anterior/posterior dichotomy rather than left/right hemispheric asymmetry may be more important in the investigation of lexical ambiguity (1998, p. 121). Damage to the frontal lobes had long been known to impair abstract thought (Goldstein, 1948) and, in particular, the proper functioning of the frontal lobes had been shown (Luria, 1966) to underlie the ability 'to simultaneously hold more than one category (or concept) in one's mind' and to shift between categories (Chobor and Schweiger, 1998, p. 121; see also note 21 to Chapter 4). Evidently, performing a mental shift between categories is precisely the kind of cognitive operation that is necessary for the understanding of lexical ambiguity. Thus, the objective of Chobor and Schweiger's (1998) study was to establish whether there is a relation between the comprehension of lexical ambiguity and the ability to shift between categories.

Chobor and Schweiger tested normal and traumatically brain-damaged subjects on three types of ambiguity (homonymy, polysemy and metaphor)[8] using lexical decision (reaction time) and matching tasks. The tasks were combined in order to allow for a comparison between automatic and conscious processing. The study showed that on automatic retrieval (lexical decision task) subjects with traumatic brain injury took longer to respond to all types of ambiguity, and were particularly show in their responses to metaphor. However, the results of the matching task did not show any main effect for the two groups of subjects, and the differences between categories of words were relatively small. The same patients were also administered tests of abstraction, and their performance on the reaction time task showed a much greater degree of correlation with abstraction tests than tests of the right hemisphere function (patients who got low scores on abstraction tests reliably performed worse on the lexical decision task). This correlation also predicted that patients' responses would be slower to words related to the target in meaning than to words unrelated to the target in meaning.

Chober and Schweiger (1998) interpret these results as showing the relative intactness of semantic interpretations in traumatically brain-damaged patients, which is nonetheless accompanied by a retrieval deficit. These results confirmed their initial suggestion that subjects having problems with abstraction should show reduced sensitivity to alternative meanings of words, particularly to related rather than unrelated meanings. The presence of a significant correlation between abstraction deficits and difficulty with related alternative word meanings suggests that the involvement of the frontal lobes in lexical disambiguation tasks may be of greater importance than that of the right hemisphere.[9] Finally, as one can see from the overview of the studies above, it would be preposterous to conclude that related alternative meanings of words are selectively represented by the right hemisphere (and thus destroyed after right hemisphere damage). Since the main premise of the argument from differential semantic representation in cerebral hemispheres to the literal–metaphorical distinction is not supported, one cannot conclude that polysemous adjectives have only one literal meaning, and that their other meanings are metaphorically derivational.[10]

7
Words and Concepts

> The notion of a concept, like the related notion of meaning, lies at the heart of some of the most difficult and unresolved issues in philosophy and psychology. The word 'concept' itself is applied to a bewildering assortment of phenomena commonly thought to be constituents of thought.
>
> (Georges Rey, 1994, p. 185)

Up to now I have been using the word 'concept' either provisionally defining it or relying on the reader's intuitive grasp of it. Now it is time to get more precise on the issue.

I am taking here a mentalistic stand towards concepts, according to which concepts are mental entities that become activated when one encounters strings of letters or sounds which constitute meaningful units in one's language; that become activated when one wishes to produce such strings of sounds and letters; and that are active in all kinds of thought processes involving such units. Proceeding in the wake of informational semantics, we can say that concepts are mental entities through which we are connected to the external world, such that the referents of our concepts in the world cause us to have them. Following Fodor (1998a), we can also say that words are names for concepts, and that concepts are mental particulars forming parts of mental representations. Finally, for the moment, we can also take it for granted that concepts are constitutive of word meanings, and return to this question later.[1]

One may doubt the existence or usefulness of the theoretical level of concepts, but clinical research into the linguistic functioning of the brain suggests that concepts are 'real' entities that and essential for one's semantic competence. Hardly anyone would disagree that 'linguistic' brain disturbances which affect the ability to retrieve correct words are qualitatively different from 'conceptual' brain disturbances which lead to a significant loss of the ability to comprehend words and sentences. (An example of the former is anomia; a particularly striking example of such disturbance was reported by Baynes and Iven, 1991, see Pinker, 1994, pp. 311–12, or Gazzaniga *et al.*, 1998, p. 309; an example of the latter would be echolalia; for the need to distinguish between the two types of disturbances see Tranel and Damasio, 1999.)[2]

On the basis of an extensive study of naturally occurring speech errors, Garrett (1975, 1976, 1984) suggested a model of the sentence production process which includes a 'message level':

> This is not a linguistic level, strictly speaking, but rather consists of the elaboration of the basic concepts which a speaker wishes to talk about. The first truly linguistic level is the 'functional level'. At the functional level, lexical items are found for concepts. (from Caplan, 1987, p. 274; see also Garrett (1982) for the notions of pre-linguistic (in message production) and post-linguistic (in message comprehension) levels of knowledge)

Thus, some recurrent speech errors should be classified as errors of the 'functional' rather than the 'message' level. Such are, for instance, the errors made by agrammatic patients who have a tendency to use nominalizations instead of verbs, as in (1) 'The girl is flower the woman' (describing the picture of a girl presenting flowers to a teacher); and (2) 'The man kodaks . . . and the girl . . . kodaks the girl' (describing the picture of a man taking a photograph of a girl; Badecker and Caramazza, 1985; quoted in Caplan, 1987, p. 279). It appears that in these patients there are no impairments at the message level: the nominalizations used are semantically related to the verbs one would have used to describe the pictures, and an average listener can understand the intended meanings of the final outputs. On the other hand, impairments at the 'functional level' are evident: 'to flower' and 'to kodak' are not words of the standard English vocabulary. Given that an average listener will not have difficulty understanding the intended meanings, how does he/she understand these garbled sentences? Or in other words, what concepts are 'flower' and 'kodak' mapped onto?

Philosophers do not normally consider the phenomena described above as central to the issue of concepts. They tend to think of concepts as something like discriminatory capacities or modes of presentation of objects, properties and relations. Those presumably have realization in the brain, but this is not what makes them concepts. I agree that functional explanations are indispensable, and that to know where in the brain we may one day locate the concept LOVE will not be sufficient to know what makes it to be what it is. The reason I mentioned above some examples from clinical studies is to show that there is a good case for inquiring into concepts, whatever they prove to be in the end.

I mostly restrict my inquiry here to those concepts that correspond to (are activated by, are evoked by, and so on) polysemous adjectives of the synaesthetic and double-function types.[3] Here is how the story goes: presumably, there is a concept SHARP[4] that is activated when either sharp stimuli or 'sharp' (the written or the spoken form of the word) are attended by us (and we are in full possession of necessary discriminatory capacities). However, the number of dictionary definitions for the word 'sharp' is enormous (the OED has 13 entries and even more sub-entries). 'Sharp' can be used across a huge number of domains in connection with practically everything, including physical properties of objects known to us by different kinds of sensory stimulation, interpersonal relations and more abstract entities: knives may be sharp, sounds may be sharp,[5] tastes may be sharp, brains may be sharp, replies may be sharp, look-outs may be sharp, attention may be sharp ('I paid him sharp attention'), and so on.

And here is what a theory of concepts has to clarify: do all the various meanings of 'sharp' map onto the same concept SHARP? Or do they map onto separate indexed concepts $SHARP_1$, $SHARP_2$, and so on? Or does only one of them (the primary 'sharp') map directly onto the concept SHARP? And what about its other meanings which presumably are its metaphorical derivations? Do they map indirectly onto the concept SHARP? Or do they map indirectly onto some other concept following the procedure of metaphorical transformation? And if so, how can we find out which concepts they map onto?

In Chapters 8 and 9 I recount some stories about concepts to see if they satisfy the *a priori* requirement I introduced in Chapter 5 as the black box analogy: namely, that in studying language one must try to avoid redundant explanations in favour of subsuming different phenomena under more general principles. Since language is a 'black box', it may be useful to recognize 'a general function F of a system in the face of F's different manifestations' (Li, 1997, p. 176). On the basis of this consideration, I suggest that the employment of the same words across multiple domains of experience has to be explained in the most possible economical way. Thus, in the following two chapters I argue that so far a satisfactory theory of concepts corresponding to polysemous adjectives has not been found. After that, in Chapter 10 I spell out in detail the no-polysemy view of conceptual structure, according to which all occurrences of polysemous adjectives such as 'sharp', 'soft' and 'bright' map directly onto the corresponding supramodal concepts SHARP, SOFT and BRIGHT. All the difficult questions and objections provoked by the no-polysemy view are addressed after the discussion of current alternatives.

8
Back to Cognitive Semantics

8.1 Sweetser's mind-as-body metaphor

Eve Sweetser characterizes linguistic categorization as depending not only on our referential capacities but also, and most importantly, 'on our metaphorical and metonymic structuring of our perceptions of the world' (1990, p. 9). In Chapter 2, discussing Lakoff and Johnson's work, I formulated a number of objections to the general validity of experientialist proposals. In this chapter I consider a particular set of *quasi* metaphors (synaesthetic and double-function adjectives) for which cognitive semantics cannot provide a sufficiently simple and uniform explanation.

According to Sweetser (1990), Lakoff and Johnson did not notice that individual conceptual metaphors form part of a larger system which is the pervasive understanding of the internal self through the bodily external self. She thus proposed the existence of a more global the mind-as-body conceptual metaphor which connects the analogous areas of internal and external sensation via metaphorical mapping. And although her work is more known for the study of Indo-European perception verbs with dual referential function, it also contains some passages dealing with synaesthetic and double-function adjectives.

Sweetser holds that semantic change always proceeds in the same way, and that only cognitive semantics can explain this fact. This explanation comes from postulating historically parallel 'metaphorically structured, non-objective connections between senses' (1990, p. 27) which have as their source humans' understanding of their experience of the world. Semantic change always proceeds from concrete (physical and social) to abstract (emotional and mental) meanings. And the question that cognitive semantics has to answer is how and why the vocabulary of physical perception is linked in all languages to the vocabulary of 'intellect and knowledge'. Considering double-function adjectives, Sweetser objects to a direct associative explanation and says that:

> uses such as *bitter* anger and *sweet* personality seem relatively distinct from any direct physical taste-response of sweetness or bitterness. I would regard such uses of *bitter* and *sweet* as metaphorical: the anger is unpleasant to our emotions in a way analogous to that in which a bitter taste displeases our tastebuds. (1990, p. 29)

Sweetser's main reasons for proposing a metaphorical explanation are the unidirectionality of semantic change and the existence of a large range of mappings between the domains of external and internal self. Her argument was mostly directed against semantic features analysis, which she contrasts with the metaphorical system of interconnections, or highly motivated links between 'parallel or *analogous* areas of physical and internal sensation' (1990, p. 45). These areas include logical necessity as the mental analogue of sociophysical force ('a strong argument'); intellection as the analogue of vision ('a clear presentation'), and so on. In the next section I argue that Sweetser's theory cannot account for conceptual representations of synaesthetic and double-function adjectives.

8.2 Enter criticisms

Semantic change and the validity of etymological explanations

First of all, my doubts about the mind-as-body metaphor theory concern the validity of etymological explanations for synchronic semantics. Discussing older approaches to semantic change, Sweetser writes:

> If we took these feature-based semantic etymologies in general at their face value, the resulting Proto-Indo-European vocabulary as a whole would be an improbably abstract one. (1990, p. 24)

However, the same kind of objection applies to Sweetser's own approach, which assumes that semantic change always proceeds from the physical and concrete to the psychological and abstract. According to feature-based etymologies, the proto-people had an improbably abstract vocabulary. However according to Sweetser, the proto-people must have talked extensively about all sorts of complicated physical and social states, but started talking about psychological states after some evolutionary change. This seems to be highly unlikely.[1]

That is, I find it problematic to believe that the physical and social worlds are more accessible to one's direct understanding than the worlds of emotion and reasoning (Sweetser, 1990, p. 31), or that introspection and interpersonal relations become subject of thought and conversation relatively late after the first appearance of the protolanguage. Cognitive semantics holds that the 'conceptual system emerges from everyday experience' (Sweetser, 1990, p. 1), but it is not clear what makes or lets cognitive semanticists decide that an individual's internal world and his or her interpersonal and social relations are not part of his/her everyday experience. For it is most likely that one's everyday experience includes emotions (cf. Damasio, 1999) and introspection, which might well be a direct source of concepts for internal states (cf. Barsalou, 1999). Besides, if one thinks of folk theories, it is evident that there are at least as many folk theories explaining people's character, behaviour and reasoning as those explaining the physical structure of the world (thus, physical explanations of ancient myths are often based on psychological explanations).[2]

Roger Lass (1997) made a case against unidirectionality with respect to grammaticalization studies.[3] I believe that a similar case can be made against the idea of unidirectionality with respect to semantic change. Sweetser (1990) argues that mappings from the physical to the psychological or mental (sometimes contrasted as concrete and abstract) are unidirectional. However, she herself gives examples to the contrary: 'words meaning mental attention or understanding can come to mean physical hearing', 'Gk *katalambano*: "seize" (used metaphorically also to mean "understand") became Mod.Gk *katalambaino* "understand"' (1990, pp. 35, 28).[4]

Similarly, Williams notes that English words 'dull', 'mild', 'soft', 'empty' and 'keen' were derived from non-sensory fields, and thus provides evidence that 'touch and dimension, areas of relatively concrete reference, draw on words representing more abstract meanings' (1976, p. 469). It may be argued that abstract source words are themselves later derivatives of concrete words, but it is not clear what the value of this assumption would be, since it is unlikely that the 'initial' vocabulary contained words only for physical entities and events.[5] Furthermore, the OED entries for various meanings of polysemous adjectives are not conclusive as to their primary and derived meanings. (Besides, there is a question of whether insignificant time differences in the appearance of documented distinct meanings reflect the amount of time required for these meanings to have been conventionalized or whether they are mere historical accidents.) Thus,

> The first entry for 'sharp' as 'having a keen cutting edge' dates from 825
>
> The first entry for 'sharp' as 'acute or penetrating in intellect or perception' dates from 888
>
> The first entries for 'bright' as 'shining, emitting, reflecting, or pervaded by much light' said of luminaries or polished metals, precious stones, and other objects whose surfaces reflect light date from 1000
>
> The first entry for 'bright' as 'clear or luminous to the mental perception' dates from 1000
>
> The first entry for 'bright' as [of sounds] 'clear, shrill, ringing' dates from 1000
>
> The first entry for 'hot' as 'adjective expressing a well-known quality or condition of material bodies, due to a high degree of molecular energy; producing one of the primary sensations' dates from 1000
>
> The first entry for 'hot' as 'excited; showing intensity of feeling' dates from 971

It is curious to note that in some cases entries for what seem to be more prototypical meanings in fact date later than entries for meanings that seem to be metaphorically derived. Thus, the first entry for 'cold' as '(of soil) slow to absorb heat' dates from 1398, while 'cold' as 'void of ardour, warmth or intensity of feeling' dates from 1175.

Finally, a more general case against the validity of etymological considerations for synchronic semantics can be made from John Lyons' description of the two ways by which lexical items change their meaning:

> the generalization of the Latin 'panarium' ('bread basket') to the French 'panier' ('basket') with the specialization of the old English 'mete' ('food') to the Modern English 'meat'. (1968, p. 266)

The point is that at any past time, the difference between the concepts MEAT and FOOD must have been available to speakers of English (whether or not at that time they referred to food as 'mete'). One question arises inevitably: how far in history should we look (cf. Lyons, 1977) to find some primitive language which would have only a few expressions for the primitive people's thought, such that the primary meanings of these expressions were later extended to include all expressions that are part of the Indo-European languages in their present form? The thing is that etymological studies cannot provide any compelling evidence about concepts.

Synaesthetic expressions and direct perceptual explanations

Even if we assume for the moment that Sweetser's explanation of double-function adjectives is correct, there will remain the question of how to derive meanings of synaesthetic expressions and amodal adjectives. Sweetser considers 'clear' as a term proper to the visual modality that becomes a term in the domain of intellection because of the parallels between vision and knowledge. However, 'clear' applies across the whole range of sensory modalities (for example, 'clear sound' or 'clear taste'; moreover, 'to hear clearly' seems to be as literal as 'to see clearly'). Does this mean that our understanding of, say, audition is based on our understanding of vision?

One explanation of 'synaesthesia in language' from the point of view of cognitive semantics can be found in Shen (1997). However, the only explanation he offers is that mappings from more 'accessible' concepts onto 'less accessible' ones seem more 'natural' than the other way round. Conceptual accessibility is determined for Shen by two factors: the directness of contact between the perceiving sense and the perceived entity (for example, touch and taste are more easily mapped onto sound and sight than the other way round), and the existence or lack of a special perceiving organ for a modality (for example, touch does not have a special organ and thus is the easiest for mapping).

However, this explanation is not entirely plausible: touch is not an undifferentiated modality but comprises thermal sensitivity, pain detection, pressure detection, and so on (Kuraev *et al.*, 2000, p. 181). The fact that the sense of touch is realized by cutaneous receptors which cover the entire body surface does not entail that there is no special organ for touch (or a separate sensory modality). Besides, Shen's explanation does not provide an answer to the question why some auditory terms are more easily mapped onto visual stimuli than other auditory terms and why some visual terms are more easily mapped onto auditory stimuli than other visual terms (Marks *et al.*, 1987; see also Chapter 4). The very notion of 'accessibility' is suspect: how is vision more accessible than audition? accessible to what? (see Chapter 4 on multisensory integration). Generally, Shen's account is an attempt to give a statistical rather than a conceptual analysis: it says that some modalities are semantic sources for other modalities, but does not say how the transfer of terms across modalities is made possible. In particular, it does not say why there are feasible transfers from the so-called higher modalities to lower modalities (for example, 'loud taste'). The very claim that some sensory modalities are understood on the model of other sensory modalities is empty in the absence of any account of how the sensory modalities are understood on their own.

And although there are indeed correspondences between sensory modalities in terms of stimuli intensity, a direct perceptual explanation does not work as an account of how synaesthetic adjectives acquire their meaning (see Chapter 4). Thus, the denotations of 'bright' and 'loud' are comparable in terms of stimulus intensity, but 'bright music' does not mean 'loud music'. Besides, there is something about 'bright music' (unlike 'pink music', for example) that may allow one to establish its denotation with a relatively high degree of precision (see Chapter 10). Thus, if one tries to give an explanation of synaesthetic expressions in terms of direct experiential correspondences, one inevitably arrives at a point where such correspondences are not sufficient to explain the correspondences in conceptual organization. And clearly, this is not a satisfactory account of synaesthetic polysemy.[6]

Dual explanations for conceptual structure

Now, let us return to the mind-as-body metaphor theory in connection with double-function adjectives.[7] One of its instances is the use of taste predicates in descriptions of persons. However, when Sweetser says that the use of taste predicates in talking about persons operates in the metaphorical/analogical mode, she ignores the fact noticed several years ago by Asch that 'sweetness' and 'bitterness' of personalities do not simply convey a positive or negative evaluation, but have a rather precise range of meanings across languages: 'sweet' never means 'courageous', and 'bitter' never means 'overtly aggressive'. Similarly with temperature metaphors: the application of 'cold' and 'hot' to personalities cannot be explained simply by saying that cold things are unpleasant (ice-cream?! beer?!) while warm things are pleasant. And as we have seen in Chapter 5, despite the variation in the range of meanings expressed by the morphemes corresponding to the English 'cold' in different languages, all of these meanings are intelligible to speakers of other languages, and their range is not arbitrary but obeys some generally valid principles.

According to Sweetser (and other cognitive semanticists), people tend to understand one thing as another while not considering them objectively the same. When the rhetoric is taken out of this claim, it is hard to see how it can be cashed in terms of conceptual representation (Murphy, 1996). One simple way to account for conceptual representations corresponding to the various meanings of polysemous adjectives is to assume that there are separate concepts corresponding to each of their meanings (since, after all, most of them are dead metaphors). However, inherent in the notion of conceptual metaphor (including the mind-as-body metaphor) is the assumption that the metaphoric structuring of concepts operates in on-line linguistic processing. Thus, when you touch a surface, and the thought 'It is cold' or 'It's a cold surface' occurs to you, the concept COLD is activated. However, when you talk to someone, and the thought 'He is cold' or 'He's a cold person' occurs to you, we should expect the activation of the same concept COLD together with a simultaneous or consequent activation of some other concept X that would be activated on its own were not the expression 'a cold person' a metaphorical one.

But what is that other concept? It cannot be UNEMOTIONAL (or any other near-synonym that appears to be the most appropriate in the context of thought), since the range of psychological meanings for 'cold' is much broader than that, and it is not clear that the context selects only one acceptable paraphrase of 'cold'. Besides, the concept COLD is activated anyway, and unless one assumes *a priori* that the valid activation of the concept COLD can occur only in contexts compatible with the interpretation 'having cold temperature', it is not clear why the process of interpretation should be relayed to the concept UNEMOTIONAL (and the like).

One may respond to this by saying that the reason why 'cold' has a metaphorical application to descriptions of people is precisely because the concept X is not UNEMOTIONAL or anything of the kind, but because it is an unexpressible concept. However, this would be a very mysterious position to take. First, because the range of the psychological meanings of 'cold' can be expressed using other words. Second, as has been noted by many critics of cognitive semantics (see Chapter 2), because in order for a word from one domain to metaphorically apply to some other domain, one must already have concepts for that other domain.

Finally, Sweetser's approach presupposes that the understanding of psychological meanings of double-function adjectives either has to proceed through two stages of concept activation or involve the simultaneous activation of two different concepts (competing for processing resources). But this would lead to a significantly greater complexity in the processing of psychological meanings of double-function adjectives than is suggested by the current data (see Williams, 1992 and the discussion in Chapter 6; see also Gibbs, 1994).

An even more serious problem for the mind-as-body metaphor theory is that it has to introduce two different types of conceptual representations corresponding to synaesthetic and psychological meanings of polysemous adjectives. According to cognitive semanticists, the reason for metaphoric restructuring of conceptual domains is the existence of different levels of understanding: the direct understanding of bodily based experience, and the indirect, metaphorical, understanding of all other types of experience. Thus, psychological meanings of polysemous adjectives have to be understood through their physical meanings because the understanding of the mental is structured by the understanding of the physical.

However, since all meanings of synaesthetic adjectives concern aspects of embodied experience, one cannot apply to them the same reasoning strategy. This implies that psychological and synaesthetic meanings of polysemous adjectives should be processed differently, which, however, does not happen (cf. Winner and Gardner, 1977). The point is that if one's explanation for the derived meaning of 'cold' in 'cold person' cannot be applied without significant modification to the derived meaning of 'cold' in such expressions as 'cold light', then this explanation is not satisfactory from the point of view of both cognitive economy and the requirement for simplicity that any scientific explanation can be expected to comply with.

Speaking more generally, if one wishes to avoid circularity, one cannot appeal to the mind-as-body metaphor to argue that some meanings of polysemous adjectives are primary or basic, because the mind-as-body metaphor theory depends on that very assumption. Thus, Sweetser (1990, p. 30) says that the existence of such expressions as 'a strong argument' is due to the epistemic domain being structured analogously with the sociophysical domain. However, in our understanding of the sociophysical domain we employ a set of concepts (STRONG, WEAK, and so on) that we already should possess before we can understand that domain.

Thus, Sweetser has no independent argument for the sociophysical domain having some kind of conceptual primacy. And it may well be that in thinking about the epistemic domain we employ the same concepts as in thinking about the sociophysical domain, such that our understanding of the epistemic domain is not mediated by our understanding of the sociophysical domain.[8] The response to which cognitive semanticists normally revert when confronted with this standard critical consideration is to claim that people understand one kind of things in terms of another. However, this claim is invalidated if one considers that even in the course of everyday reasoning (deciding whether a nail is strong vs. deciding whether an argument is strong) the applicability of the same term in two different domains is tested by different procedures (Blackburn, 1984).[9]

Overall, cognitive semanticists of the Lakoff–Johnson–Sweetser trend still have not presented a theory of conceptual representation[10] which could be evaluated independently of the claim about the metaphorical structuring of concepts. Synaesthetic and double-function adjectives present a special problem for cognitive semantics since it fails to provide a uniform explanation of these two types of adjectival polysemy, thus violating the black box requirement. Besides, the mind-as-body metaphor theory predicts higher processing demands for the understanding of alternative meanings of synaesthetic and double-function adjectives, but this prediction is not supported by currently available psycholinguistic evidence.

9
Polysemy in Lexical Semantics

9.1 Semantics and conceptual structure: the beginnings

A good while before cognitive linguistics became popular, lexical semanticists (at least some of them) began to develop an interest in concepts and conceptual structure. In a book called *Language and Perception* (1976), George Miller and Philip Johnson-Laird proposed to give a psychological theory of semantics, in which the relationship between perceptual and lexical structures is mediated by the conceptual structure. Conceptual thought is that which relates perception and language: '[p]ercepts and words are merely avenues into and out of this conceptual structure' (p. vii).

The reason that Miller and Johnson-Laird directed their attention to concepts is precisely the one that we find today in many research programs: if words such as 'red', 'loud', 'sour', and so on are found across languages, and since perception and cognition cannot be separated, then there must be some real physiological and psychological processes correlated with their use. Although not all theorists regard such entities as truly perceptual, one can still take them to be 'the basic atoms of the mind'. The conceptual structure is grounded in perception: perceptual properties and relations are conceptually represented in the form of predicates.

The widespread phenomenon of polysemy is a puzzle for any theorist who attempts to offer generalizations concerning the use of a polysemous word. What drives a polysemy theorist is the belief that different uses of a polyseme have to be related in some unarbitrary way. Introducing the notion of conceptual structure/mental representation into semantics gives one the tools to offer such generalizations. Miller and Johnson-Laird were primarily concerned with verbal polysemy (for example, the polysemy of the verb 'move'), attempting to provide a single formal schema that underlies different uses of a polyseme, and that can be modulated by context in each specific case. However, it is interesting to note that they have also posed the question that lead me to develop the no-polysemy view. In a passing remark they wondered:

> Perhaps it is a mistake to think that the concept expressed by a word like 'sharp', which can describe touch, taste, sound, intelligence, terrain, strictness, eagerness and objects, is legitimately applicable to touch and must be generalized for other applications; SHARP may be a concept of more than just a sensory quality... A sharp mind may be as good an instance of SHARP as a sharp pain; a warm person may be as good an instance of WARM as a warm tactual sensation. (1976, p. 360)

Unfortunately, they have not wondered enough to pursue this question any further. It is therefore the objective of this chapter to see whether an answer can be found in later work on lexical semantics.

9.2 Polysemy and conceptual structure

In this section we shall discuss Ray Jackendoff's (1983, 1992) semantic primitives approach to lexical polysemy, and Jerry Fodor's (1998a) distrust of the notion of polysemy itself. In his influential book *Semantics and Cognition* Jackendoff clearly articulated the position that semantic theory has to be 'responsible to the facts of grammar and cognitive psychology' (1983, p. 18). Grammatical theories alone cannot account for the sense-relatedness found in polysemy. The generalizations have to be made at the level of conceptual structure, a single level of mental representation onto which the information from peripheral systems (sensory modalities) and language is mapped and where it is made compatible.

According to Jackendoff, the elements of the conceptual structure are semantically primitive representations which span all conceptual fields and whose combination produces complex representations corresponding to different uses of a polyseme in context. This means that some lexical concepts do not have atomic representations corresponding to them but can be decomposed into more primitive elements. One of the most famous examples of such decomposition is the decomposition of 'kill' into CAUSE TO DIE or CAUSE TO BECOME NOT ALIVE. CAUSE is a primitive which can be combined with other primitives to produce the mental representation corresponding to 'kill'. The problems connected with this particular example are no less well-known. As Fodor (1970) noted, 'kill' cannot mean CAUSE TO DIE/CAUSE TO BECOME NOT ALIVE because, say, you may cause someone to die on Tuesday if you shoot him or her on Monday, but you cannot kill someone on Tuesday if you shoot him or her on Monday. This shows that 'kill' and 'cause to die' are not semantically equivalent.[1] Moreover, Fodor *et al.* (1975) provided experimental evidence that processing times do not differ for those words that were supposed to have complex semantic structure and those that were not (for example, 'kill'–'die'; see Jackendoff, 1983, pp. 125–7 for a critical evaluation of these results).

Nonetheless, Jackendoff believes that a decompositional approach to word meaning (mental representation) is necessary in order to account, among other things, for the syntax-semantics correspondence and the preservation of concept identity of polysemes across semantic fields.[2] A couple of examples can show the need to introduce structured concepts. Thus, as Jackendoff (1983) observes, if one assumes that 'see' has a unified meaning (or means exactly the same in all contexts), one cannot explain the difference in its meaning in the following two sentences: 'I must have looked at that a dozen times, but I never saw it' and 'I must have seen that a dozen times, but I never noticed it'. In the first sentence, 'see' means that something comes to the subject's visual awareness, whereas the second sentence denies that sense of 'see', where it means that the subject's gaze goes towards something. One way to deal with that difficulty is to assume that there are two distinct but homophonous verbs 'see$_1$' and 'see$_2$'. However, as Jackendoff writes, this is not a particularly good solution because very simple sentences such as 'I saw Bill' present an even bigger difficulty for such analyses: which of the two distinct senses of 'see' is intended in this sentence? is the sentence truly ambiguous? (1983, p. 151). It seems obvious that the sentence intends both senses, and that there is something wrong with treating 'see$_1$' and 'see$_2$' as distinct lexical items. A better way to account for the difficulty is to think of 'see' as unambiguous, with the two senses included in its representation such that both senses enter the interpretation by default, unless one or the other of them is cancelled by the context.

Another example, with which we shall be dealing in the rest of this section, is the verb 'keep'. At the very beginning of his 1983 book Jackendoff illustrates the need to account for semantic generalizations in terms of conceptual structure on the example of 'keep'. 'Keep' is used widely to express maintenance across semantic fields ('keep the book on the shelf', 'keep the book', 'keep someone angry'), and there is no grammatical explanation that would allow one to generalize over its uses. Jackendoff's generalization in terms of conceptual structure is known as the Thematic Relations Hypotheses (adopted and modified after Gruber, 1965) which pursues the goal of decomposing word meanings into primitive conceptual features. The primitives come from the spatial semantic field[3] and include the ontological categories [THING], [EVENT], [STATE], [PLACE], [PATH], [PROPERTY] and the functions [BE], [GO], [ORIENT], [STAY], [CAUSE], [LET]. Syntactic structures of sentences are translated into conceptual representations organized around ontological categories, and lexical items (verbs, in particular) are decomposed into functional relations. Thus, the sentence 'The book is on the shelf', which expresses a state, receives the representation: [State BE ([Thing BOOK], [Place ON SHELF])]. The sentence 'Suzanne kept the books on the shelf', which expresses an event and has an agent, is represented with the help of the binary function CAUSE and is rendered as:

[Event CAUSE ([Thing SUZANNE],
    [Event STAY ([Thing BOOKS], [Place ON SHELF])])]
(1983, p. 175)[4]

The advantage of the Thematic Relations Hypothesis is that it allows for generalizations across semantic fields via the univocal categories and functions borrowed from the semantic field of motion and location. 'Keep' occurs in a large number of semantic fields, but the unification is made possible with the preservation of spatial primitives and the introduction of semantic field features into the corresponding representations. Below are some examples of how the Thematic Relations Hypothesis allows for sense distinctions within different uses of 'keep' (after Jackendoff, 1983, 1992).

    Field: Temporal/Scheduling of activities
    (semantic field feature subscript: Temp)
    Example: Despite the weather, we kept the meeting at 6.00.
    Representation: [Event CAUSE ([Thing WE],
        [Event STAY$_{Temp}$ ([Event MEETING],
        [Place AT$_{Temp}$ ([Time 6:00])])])]

    Field: Possession (semantic field feature subscript: Poss)
    Example 1: Amy kept the doll.
    Example 2: Susan kept the money.
    Representation 1: [Event CAUSE ([Thing AMY],
        [Event STAY$_{Poss}$ ([Thing DOLL],
        [Place AT$_{Poss}$ ([Thing AMY])])])]

Field: Identificational/Ascription of properties
(semantic field feature subscript: Ident)
Example 1: Sol kept Gary a celebrity
(alternatively: Sol kept Gary famous).
Example 2: Sam kept the crowd happy.
Representation 1: [Event CAUSE ([Thing SOL],
 [Event STAY$_{Ident}$ ([Thing GARY],
 [Place AT$_{Ident}$ ([Type CELEBRITY])])])]
 alternatively: [Place AT$_{Ident}$ ([Property FAMOUS])])])]

Field: Circumstantial/non-causative
(semantic field feature subscript: Circ).
Example: Fred kept composing quarters.
Representation: [Event STAY$_{Circ}$ ([Thing FRED]i,
 [Place AT$_{Circ}$ ([Event i COMPOSE QUARTERS])])]

Field: Circumstantial/causative (semantic field feature subscript: Circ)
Example: Louise kept Fred composing quarters.
Representation: [Event CAUSE ([Thing LOUISE],
 [Event STAY$_{Circ}$ ([Thing FRED]i,
 [Place AT$_{Circ}$ ([Event i COMPOSE QUARTERS])])])]

This generalization allows one to capture the unchangeable part of the meaning of 'keep' across semantic fields. All sentences containing 'keep' have [STAY] or its causative as part of their conceptual representation. What changes from sentence to sentence is the semantic field feature which tells us whether the sentence is about positions in the physical space (the spatial 'keep') or roles in events or situations (the circumstantial 'keep'), and so on. Thus, this analysis allows one to subsume different uses of a verb ('keep' in our example) under a single semantic analysis, showing how all its uses are formally and unarbitrarily related in the conceptual structure.

In his 1992 book, *Languages of the Mind*, Ray Jackendoff reproduces this analysis in a more compact form, and it is this analysis that came under the attack of Jerry Fodor (1998a, pp. 49–56), who does not believe in structured concepts. Fodor's argument for his theory of atomic concepts includes, among other considerations, a critical analysis of Jackendoff' proposal, and with this we shall now deal.[5] As we have just seen, according to Jackendoff, 'keep' always has the same unchangeable meaning 'cause a state that endures over time'.[6] To put it in slightly different terms, 'keep' maps onto CAUSE TO STAY, and the meaning of 'keep' in context is derived from this concept plus a semantic field feature. However, as Fodor rightly notes, the only way to make Jackendoff's proposal work is to assume that CAUSE in univocal across semantic fields. That is, one has to assume that in 'Susan kept the money' and 'Sam kept the crowd happy', the relation of causation that obtains between Susan and the money and the relation of causation that obtains between Sam and the crowd are instances of the same relation. But if one grants that CAUSE can be univocal across semantic fields, why cannot one grant the same about KEEP?

The question whether CAUSE is univocal can be answered either in the positive or in the negative. If one replies in the negative, one loses the argument for 'keep' being polysemous (that is, one cannot support the intuition that all meanings of 'keep' are related). If one replies in the positive, one may still have a case, but one has to say what makes CAUSE univocal. To get the point of Fodor's argument, it has to be kept in mind that Fodor discusses Jackendoff's proposal in a chapter against definitions. Thus, lexical semanticists, in trying to solve the problem of polysemy in particular, postulate a level of conceptual representation at which lexical items are decomposed into some more primitive representational items. However, this amounts to saying that lexical items are definable, or that their meanings can be given with the help of definitions. The way that Fodor reads Jackendoff is that 'keep' means (expresses the concept) CAUSE A STATE THAT ENDURES OVER TIME or CAUSE TO STAY. Given that, and given that the univocality of 'keep' across semantic fields depends on the univocality of CAUSE across semantic fields, one may try to further decompose CAUSE into an even more primitive representational item X which would explain the univocality of CAUSE. But this option would clearly involve an infinite regress, and would not explain why CAUSE can be a primitive but KEEP cannot.

From here, according to Fodor, the only option that remains open to Jackendoff is to assume that in order to be univocal across semantic fields, a word need not receive a structured conceptual representation: 'keep' is represented as CAUSE TO STAY but 'cause' is represented as CAUSE. However, once one admits such a possibility, one can no longer argue from the intuition about univocality to structured concepts. There is simply no reason to prefer the explanation according to which 'keep' is univocal because its decomposition is univocal to the explanation which says that 'keep' is univocal because KEEP is univocal.[7]

Expanding and modifying Fodor's objections to Jackendoff's analysis (to make them more compatible with the formalisms reproduced above), I would suggest that the main problem for Jackendoff's version of decomposition arises from not postulating enough representational levels. The formalisms for encoding 'keep' are supposed to be conceptual representations onto which sentences containing 'keep' are mapped. However, whereas [CAUSE] is univocal across fields, [STAY] always comes with a semantic field subscript. In order to support the intuition that 'keep' is univocal across semantic fields, the concepts into which it is decomposed have to be univocal themselves. But this is not so: CAUSE is univocal across semantic fields, but STAY is not. In fact, what we find in Jackendoff's formalisms are five different concepts STAY which are distinguished by semantic field: $STAY_{(spatial)}$, $STAY_{poss}$, and so on. Thus, sentences containing 'keep' map onto conceptual representations which involve subscribed concepts, that is, the concept STAY is itself ambiguous. However, from the univocality of CAUSE and ambiguity of STAY one cannot conclude to the univocality of 'keep'. And this way, instead of having shown that all meanings of 'keep' are related at a deeper level of conceptual representation, Jackendoff will be forced to conclude that 'keep' is merely homonymous (that there is spatial 'keep', possessional 'keep', and so on).

We have just seen how the decompositional approach to polysemy developed by Jackendoff turns out to lead to an unexpected result: instead of supporting our intuitions about polysemy, it lends support to the view that the relatedness of meanings across semantic fields is an illusion. However, the intuition that all uses of 'keep' have something in common is pretty strong. And perhaps the best way to account for this intuition is to accept Fodor's ingeniously simple solution: we feel that all uses of 'keep' are related because they really are. In all its instances, 'keep' always expresses the same relation, the relation of *keeping* (1998a, p. 55). Lexical semanticists may find this idea implausible[8] but, as I argue in Chapter 10, the difficulty one may have accepting it is due to the fact that not enough discriminations have been made between representational levels. The point is that thought is not ambiguous, that there is no polysemy at the conceptual level. And since the decompositional approach discussed in this section fails to capture our intuitions, we shall have to find a different way to make sense of the two convictions that many people share: that different meanings of a polyseme are *related*, but that they are, at the same time, *different* meanings. However before we do that, we shall first discuss in the next section a more recent proposal for relating meanings of polysemes – the generative lexicon theory.

9.3 The generative lexicon

The expression 'to avoid the unnecessary proliferation of meanings', which has now become almost a slogan, was largely inspired by James

Pustejovsky's book *The Generative Lexicon* (1995). What primarily interests us here is Pustejovsky's treatment of adjectival polysemy, where the interpretation of an adjective depends on the qualia structure of the noun with which it combines in context. But first of all, let us begin with a brief exposition of the generative lexicon theory.

In the preceding chapters I have already mentioned several times the difference between two types of lexical ambiguity: homonymy and polysemy. What distinguishes them is the idea of meaning relatedness, and as such they should be represented differently. However, traditionally, homonymy and polysemy had been treated the same way, on the model of homonymy. All senses of a word, however related they may be, received separate representations in the lexicon. Thus, we would have not only BANK$_1$ (financial institution) and BANK$_2$ (riverside), but also, say, CHICKEN$_1$ (bird) and CHICKEN$_2$ (meat). Even intuitively one can feel that something is wrong with such lexicons: banks as financial institutions are not necessarily found on river banks, whereas there seems to be a necessary connection between chicken and its meat. Pustejovsky's generative lexicon is a theory that tries to capture this intuition. But besides the intuitive feeling of something having gone wrong, there are other limitations to what Pustejovsky calls 'sense enumeration lexicons'.

One such limitation is the inability to account for creative use of words in novel contexts. For example, adjectives such as 'good' can occur with an incredibly large number of nouns: 'a good umbrella', 'a good meal', 'a good teacher', and so on (Pustejovsky, 1995, p. 43). Sense enumeration lexicons account for the differences in the meaning of 'good' in these expressions by listing the corresponding senses of 'good': 'good$_1$' = functioning well, 'good$_2$' = tasty, 'good$_3$' = performing some act well, and so on. However, when a new 'good'-expression is encountered, for which there is no fixed sense stored in the lexicon, a new sense has to be added. The whole process is apparently limitless, and the intuition that new uses of 'good' are related to the other uses of 'good' is lost.

Pustejovsky's conviction is that the interpretation of words such as 'good' in novel contexts does not depend only on background world knowledge, but is constrained by lexical knowledge, by meanings of words (1995, pp. 55–7). Thus, in order to constrain the interpretation of words in context lexically, a greater internal structure has to be introduced into lexical representations. Take a polysemous noun such as 'book' which can refer to a physical object or book content (an example of logical polysemy in accepted terminology). Sense enumeration lexicons list the two senses and include into the representation of each sense two bits information: lexical category that it belongs to (for example, count noun) and a specification of the genus term (for example, printed material). By contrast, the richer semantic representation for lexical items proposed by Pustejovsky allows one to conflate different word senses into a single meta-entry or lexical-conceptual paradigm. This richer representation for lexical items has four levels: argument structure, event structure, qualia structure and lexical inheritance structure (1995, p. 61). We can use the same example BOOK[9] to see what these levels are.

Thus, the argument structure specifies the number and type of logical arguments and their syntactic realization. The argument structure for BOOK (recall that 'book' is a polysemous noun) specifies that it can denote a physical object or information (represented formally as: ARG1 = x:information, ARG2 = y:phys_obj).[10]

Event structure defines the event type of a lexical item, that is, whether it is a state or a process. Since 'book', unlike 'lunch' or 'examination', cannot denote a process, this structure is absent from its representation.

Qualia structure, essential for Pustejovsky's theory, specifies a lexical item's qualia roles, which include its formal, constitutive, telic, and agentive roles. The formal role for BOOK specifies that books qua physical objects hold books qua information (FORMAL = hold (y,x)). The constitutive role, which specifies the relation between an object and its constituent parts, is absent from the qualia structure of BOOK. The telic role of BOOK specifies its function, the purpose of its existence, which is to be read (TELIC = read (e,w,x.y)). Finally, the agentive role specifies how something 'comes into being', which is for BOOK to be written by somebody (AGENT = write (e',v,x.y)).

The reason for introducing qualia structures into representations of nouns is an attempt to explain the phenomenon of 'senses in context', to solve the problem of productive adjectival and verbal polysemy without multiplying the number of lexical entries beyond necessity. What qualia structures do is 'suggest' interpretations of words in context (Pustejovsky, 1995, p. 87). Thus, 'enjoy NP' can have an infinite number of senses in context. But introducing a separate entry for 'enjoy' in the lexicon for every possible combination would hardly be productive. The introduction of qualia structures into representations of nouns allows one to produce a reading for 'enjoy NP' which, moreover, is consistent with the verb's full range of complementation. Thus, we can have 'enjoy reading a book' and 'enjoy a book'. When we want to know what 'enjoy' means in the second sentence, we can check up the telic role for BOOK to produce the default interpretation of 'enjoy a book' as 'enjoy reading a book'. Now let us consider the generative lexicon's solution to some instances of adjectival polysemy, and we shall address other questions arising in connection with the generative lexicon theory in the next section when discussing Fodor and Lepore's (1998) critique of Pustejovsky's proposals.

It had been noticed a good while ago that (some) adjective-noun constructions resist the standard compositional model-theoretic treatment. Thus, whereas 'a red pen' can be understood as denoting something that is red and is a pen, 'a good pen' is not something that is good (a good thing) and is a pen (Jackendoff, 1983, p. 71). The meaning of such adjectives as 'good' depends on the nouns (the heads) they modify.[11] Besides, adjectival modification is inherently productive: 'good' and 'fast' can modify almost an infinite number of nouns. But, as Pustejovsky has argued, sense-enumeration lexicons do not do justice to the productivity of adjective-noun constructions. The introduction of qualia structures into representations of nouns helps one retain the intuition that all meanings of a polysemous adjective are related, and, at the same time, explain how these adjectives can acquire new senses in context. The generative device which produces the interpretation of a polysemous adjective in context is called 'selective binding'. Below we shall see how it is supposed to work.

Consider the expression 'a fast typist'. When we understand this expression we do not assume that it is about someone who is a typist and who is fast. The way we understand 'a fast typist' is that it is about a person who types fast. In the generative lexicon theory, the qualia structure for TYPIST (the telic role) specifies the most prominent activity of typists, which is typing. The adjective 'fast', which pertains to rates of processes, selects for the telic role in the qualia structure of TYPIST. Thus we arrive at the interpretation of 'a fast typist' as 'someone who types fast' (after Jackendoff, 1998a, pp. 62–3). This way we only need one entry for 'fast' because the creative use of the adjective 'fast' can be captured through richer lexical representations for nouns with which it combines. As Pustejovsky puts it: 'the same expression can serve countless purposes *because* the semantic features (meanings) change in context' (1998, p. 291).

However, even though Pustejovsky has reconsidered the framework of lexical semantics by introducing generative devices instead of conceptual primitives (1995, p. 293), it seems that there was no real change. Concepts remain complex, and meanings of words definitional. The attempt to explain adjectival polysemy by providing richer semantic representations for nouns and single 'unificationary' meta-entries for adjectives does not work because meanings (senses) of adjectives are still divided into basic and derived (1995, p. 304). This is particularly clear from Jackendoff's (1998a) discussion of polysemous adjectives from the position of the generative lexicon theory.

Both Pustejovky and Jackendoff believe that one cannot apply the formal semantic approach to the analysis of polysemous adjectives such as 'fast'. However it seems that the true reason for requiring a new analysis is not that if you look for an overlap between all fast things and all things that are typists you will not arrive at the meaning of 'a fast typist', but rather that 'fast' has a basic (or primary) meaning which pertains to rates of processes (as in 'fast waltz'). Therefore, you cannot simply apply 'fast' in its primary meaning to typists or roads ('a fast road') since neither are processes. The qualia structures are needed to tell one what processes are associated with these lexical items: typists by default type (thus, 'a fast typist' is someone who types fast); roads are objects over which one travels (thus, 'a fast road' is a road over which one travels fast).

But whereas one can agree that 'fast' is about processes, it is more difficult to agree that the process that 'fast' picks out in a context is the one that is specified in a noun's qualia structure. The standard objection to the 'fast typist' example shows that the interpretation suggested by the qualia structure can be overridden by an interpretation that does not follow from any of the roles within the qualia structure. Thus, in the sentence 'A fast typist won the race', the interpretation of 'a fast typist' is not 'someone who types fast' but rather 'someone who runs fast'. However, one cannot expect the qualia structure of TYPIST to specify all those things that typists may happen to be doing when they are not typing.

Other counterexamples can be found. Consider 'a fast game' which means that 'the motions involved in the game are rapid and swift' (Pustejovsky, 1995, p. 44). But the generative lexicon does not produce this interpretation. And here is why. 'A fast book' is 'one that can be read in a short time' (1995, p. 44). We arrive at this interpretation on the basis of information in the qualia structure for BOOK. The telic role for BOOK is to be read; thus, 'a fast book' is a book that can be fast-read, read in a short amount of time. The telic role for GAME is presumably to be played (that is what games are for). Following the generative procedure we should receive that 'a fast game' is a game that can be fast-played, played in a short amount of time (as in 'fast chess'; cf. 'fast lunch' or 'fast exam' which can also denote events). However, this is not the default interpretation of 'fast game'; and its default interpretation does not follow from the qualia structure.[12]

Consider now another polysemous adjective, 'sad'. According to Jackendoff:

> *sad* pertains to a person's emotional experience. It therefore can modify *woman* by simple composition, but not *event* or *movie*. Rather it must pertain to the emotional experience of characters found in the qualia structure of *event* and *movie*. . . . (1998a, p. 63)

Thus, the qualia structure of EVENT should specify that events have participants, and the qualia structure of MOVIE that movies are viewed by people. However, this will not completely resolve the ambiguity: if 'a sad movie' is to be understood as a movie that makes one experience sadness, we may still have to say whether it makes one experience sadness as one's personal experience or whether it makes one experience sadness on someone else's behalf. (After watching a war documentary one may perfectly well utter a detached 'It's a sad world', but not experience sadness at heart; feeling sad for other people is different from feeling sad for personal reasons). The need for refinements may go *ad infinitum*, but it is not clear how much of them the lexicon is required to capture and under what criteria.

Moreover, if we consider Pustejovsky's lexicon not as an abstract semantic theory, but as a psychological hypothesis concerning the conceptual structure, where qualia structures are parts of conceptual representations, a number of questions arise. If the interpretation of 'a sad event' or 'a sad movie' were indeed more psychologically complex than the interpretation of 'a sad woman' (as entailed by Jackendoff's analysis), then it should take longer to process the former two expressions than the latter one, and this should be reflected in psycholinguistic experiments. (However, even metaphor processing may not be more time-consuming than the processing of literal or primary meanings; see Blasko and Connine, 1993; Gibbs, 1994; Glucksberg, 2001.)

Thus, Pustejovsky–Jackendoff's analysis of polysemous adjectives does not take us much further than the starting point: if 'sad' is as immediately interpretable in 'a sad movie' as it is in 'a sad woman', and if in some cases it means 'to experience sadness' and in others 'to cause sadness', then the introduction of qualia structures still does not resolve its polysemy into a single entry. 'Sad' remains ambiguous much as it is in the enumerational lexicon: it means 'to experience sadness' in some contexts and 'to cause sadness' in other contexts. If one wanted to show that 'sad' is not polysemous, one would have to stipulate that the meaning of 'sad' is the same in 'a sad woman' and 'a sad movie'. That is, that 'sad' has only one meaning (a single entry in the mental lexicon) which it contributes to the interpretation of all 'sad'-expressions. To speak of basic and derived meanings pushes ambiguity further in instead of eliminating it.

One can probably already see why lexical semanticists working in the generative lexicon framework avoid the question of 'metaphorically polysemous' adjectives (such as 'bright' or 'sharp') and only deal with 'literally polysemous' adjectives (such as 'good' or 'fast'). Pustejovsky is quite explicit about the need to distinguish between logical polysemy, which can be generated within the lexicon, and 'more general operations of sense transfer such as metaphor, etc., which generative lexicon theory claims are extralinguistic transfer phenomena' (Pustejovsky and Boguraev, 1996, p. 9). This distrust of metaphor stems from the consideration that it does not exhibit the same patterns of regularity and systematicity across languages as the non-metaphorical creative polysemy (Pustejovsky, 1995, p. 4).[13] However, we have seen in the previous chapters that metaphorically polysemous adjectives of the synaesthetic and double-function types are found across historically and geographically unrelated languages and follow some regular and systematic patterns of meaning generation.

Perhaps there is a different reason for ignoring metaphorically polysemous adjectives than the lack of systematicity: the generative lexicon theory has no tools for dealing with them. Consider the two polysemes that we have been discussing all along: 'sharp' and 'bright'. Unlike 'fast' and 'sad' whose use across semantic fields or sensory domains is perhaps never metaphorical ('sad light' is 'light that makes one experience sadness', 'a sad remark' is 'a remark which expresses sadness'), 'sharp' and 'bright' behave differently. One cannot apply to them the generative lexicon analysis because in the generative lexicon theory adjectival polysemy is supposed to be resolvable not within adjectives themselves, as it were, but through the qualia structures of those nouns with which they compose.

It is clear that one cannot expect the interpretation of 'bright music' or 'sharp taste' to be generated by Pustejovsky's lexicon because the interpretation of these adjectives should be constrained by the qualia structures of the nouns 'music' and 'taste', the adjectives themselves being univocal. But we have seen above that the supposed univocality is only superficial: according to Pustejovsky and Jackendoff, there are after all primary meanings. So, the primary meaning of 'bright' pertains to visual stimuli and the primary meaning of 'sharp' pertains to cutting objects. Music is not a visual stimulus, taste is not a cutting object. But, if in the case of 'a fast typist' and 'a sad movie' we can find a compositional rule for generating non-primary meanings via the qualia structures of nouns (the function of typists is to type; the function of movies is to have an effect on their viewers), there is none that would similarly generate the interpretations of 'bright music' and 'sharp taste' (although, as with 'movie', one could say that the function of music is to have an effect on its listeners). Thus, the literal-metaphorical distinction is retained in its full force in Pustejovsky's semantics.

However, synaesthetic and double-function adjectives are interesting not only semantically (their various meanings are presumably contained in the lexicon, and their dictionary entries are often not even marked 'figurative'), but also psychologically (their various meanings seem to be interrelated rather than stored independently as separate entries). Pustejovsky's apparatus provides no tools to deal with them, and besides suffers from some internal inconsistencies of its own (psychological unsoundness, and the lack of meaning/concept univocality which the generative lexicon theory aimed to arrive at). Thus, we can take it that the generative lexicon theory cannot be the theory of concepts corresponding to metaphorically polysemous adjectives.

9.4 The disquotational lexicon and the problem of polysemy

In this section I discuss Fodor and Lepore's (1998) critique of Pustejovky's generative lexicon theory. This discussion serves two purposes: it throws further doubt on the generative lexicon theory as the right theory of conceptual representation, and at the same time claims that the disquotational lexicon offered by Fodor and Lepore as an alternative to the generative lexicon does not solve the problem of polysemy. The essence of Fodor and Lepore's critique is that lexical meaning is atomic and should be identified with denotation, whereas Pustejovsky's lexicon contains complex lexical entries which are intended to specify the inferences one is justified in making. According to Fodor and Lepore, this is never going to work,[14] and we can see how they develop their argument using some particular examples of verbal and adjectival polysemy.[15]

Take the verb 'bake'. According to Pustejovsky, it is polysemous between two readings: a creative activity as in 'bake a cake' and change-of-state as in 'bake a potato' (1995, p. 122). In order to avoid multiplying the meanings of 'bake' without necessity, Pustejovsky introduces the generative device called 'co-composition'. In the generative lexicon there is only one entry for BAKE whose qualia structure specifies that it is a change-of-state predicate, and whose agentive role is the activity of baking (AGENTIVE = bake_act). When 'bake' has 'potato' as its complement, the change-of-state reading follows directly from the qualia structure of BAKE ('potato' denotes a natural kind and potatoes cannot be produced by baking). However, when 'bake' has 'cake' as its complement, the story is different because the agentive role in the qualia structure of CAKE, which denotes an artefact, specifies that cakes are made by baking (AGENTIVE = bake_act(e1,w,y)). The creative activity reading in 'bake a cake' is generated via the composition of the qualia structures for BAKE and CAKE (their agentive roles match). Thus, we can say that the primary meaning of 'bake' is the change-of-state meaning, and that the creative activity meaning is generated from it in context.

This account of the 'bake' polysemy seems pretty straightforward. Nonetheless, Fodor and Lepore disagree that the story about the polysemy of 'bake' is that simple. According to Pustejovsky, if the complement of 'bake' is a natural kind, 'bake' receives the change-of-state reading, and if the complement of 'bake' is an artefact, 'bake' receives the creative activity reading. But as Fodor and Lepore note, this treatment of the 'bake' polysemy does not produce the correct interpretations of 'bake'-expressions in context. On the one hand, 'bake a cake' is itself ambiguous between a creative activity and heating up (frozen foods cakes). On the other hand, being an artefact does not by itself justify the creative activity reading: 'to bake a knife' and 'to bake a trolley car' resist it. From this Fodor and Lepore conclude that 'bake' is indeed lexically ambiguous, and its meanings cannot be reduced to one primary meaning.

Now consider the polysemous adjective 'good'. We have seen in the previous section how its precise interpretation depends on the noun it modifies/is predicated of. According to Pustejovsky, 'good' receives its interpretation from the qualia structure of the noun with which it combines. Most often it is the telic role: thus, if it is 'a good knife', then 'good' should be interpreted as 'good for cutting' because the telic role of KNIFE specifies that its function is cutting. But this interpretation may be overridden, as in the sentence 'That's a good knife, but it doesn't cut very well' where the adjective 'good' selects for the agentive role in the qualia structure of KNIFE and where it receives the interpretation 'a well-made knife' (Pustejovsky, 1995, p. 254, f. 19).

However, there are some problems with interpretations of 'good' following from the telic roles of nouns. This approach presupposes that all objects and entities referred to by nouns have functions. But, as Pustejovsky himself notes (1995, p. 45), whereas 'good weather' and 'good children' are both semantically well-formed literal expressions, neither weather nor children have clearly delineated functions (or any functions at all) that could be specified in the qualia structures of these concepts. According to Fodor and Lepore, it is possible that 'good' introduces a quantifier into the interpretation of 'good'-expressions. This way we can treat 'good' as context insensitive such that 'a good NP' always means 'one that is good for *whatever it is* that NPs are supposed to be good for' (1998, p. 286).[16] Returning now to Pustejovsky's treatment of the 'good' polysemy, it is doubtful whether any of the other three roles – formal, constitutive or agentive – in the qualia structures of WEATHER and CHILDREN can generate the interpretation of 'good weather' and 'good children': constitutive and agentive roles clearly do not ('good children' are not 'well-made children'). It is similarly unclear whether the formal roles of WEATHER and CHILDREN specify anything that can enter the interpretation of 'good weather' and 'good children' (for example, the knowledge that children are humans, or even young humans, is not very helpful for producing the interpretation of the expression 'good children').[17]

Thus far we have considered two examples from the generative lexicon theory that provoked Fodor and Lepore's critique with the following conclusions: either the ambiguity is not resolved ('bake'), or words treated as polysemous and thus context-sensitive are not such ('good'). According to Fodor and Lepore, there are cases of real polysemy as exhibited by such lexical items as 'bake' which is ambiguous between two meanings. The two meanings of 'bake' denote different processes, such that in order to understand which process is referred to 'bake'-sentences have to be disambiguated.[18] But there are also lexical items whose meaning does not change across contexts. One of such lexical items is 'good' which always means GOOD whatever it is that one may find good. Other such lexical items include 'enjoy', 'want', 'finish' and 'begin', which Pustejovsky treats as polysemous.

One of the reasons Pustejovsky has for treating 'enjoy', 'want', 'finish' and 'begin' as polysemous is, as briefly mentioned in the last section, the need to produce consistent readings of constructions of the form 'want NP' which would be consistent with the verb's full range of complementation (want S [+INF], want VP [+INF], want NP). The generative device producing interpretations for such expressions is called 'true complement coercion' and is intended to 'ensure that the semantic type of the verb is satisfied in all these cases, regardless of syntactic form' (Pustejovsky, 1995, p. 115). Lexical structures of these verbs specify that they take an event as their second argument, and an event reading is reconstructed from the qualia structure of the NP with which they combine. Thus, the telic role of CIGARETTE, for example, specifies that cigarettes are smoked and, as a result of the coercion operation, from 'Mary wants a cigarette' we receive the interpretation 'Mary wants to smoke a cigarette'. Another reason for treating these verbs as polysemous is the need to account for the semantic well-formedness of constructions of the form 'begin NP'. As Pustejovsky says, while 'Mary began the book' is semantically well-formed, 'Mary began the rock' is semantically odd (1995, p. 41), and the lexical semantic theory has to account for the difference in their semanticality.

As with the 'good' example, Fodor and Lepore note that Pustejovsky's lexicon is too restrictive and makes wrong predictions. Thus, there is nothing semantically odd with 'Mary began the rock' which can be interpreted as 'Mary began painting the rock'. However, this interpretation does not follow from the qualia structure of ROCK. Similarly, Pustejovsky's treatment of the 'want' examples produces interpretations which are not fully consistent with ordinary language use. 'Mary wants a cigarette' does not always mean 'Mary wants to smoke a cigarette', for Mary may want a cigarette for somebody else, or she may want it to add it to her collection of cigarettes, or for any other reason.

According to Fodor and Lepore, all that is needed to produce the interpretation of 'want a beer' is the notion of logical form. A logical form is the output of syntactic processes consisting of a disambiguated sequence of word types which is available for semantic interpretation. 'Want' denotes a relation between a creature and a state of affairs. Thus, the logical form of 'want an NP' is 'want to have an NP', and this way from 'want a beer' we receive 'want to have a beer'.[19] We can add to this that interpreting 'want an NP' as 'want to have an NP' rather than 'want to [event reading reconstructed from the telic role of the noun] an NP' produces correct readings in those cases where the generative lexicon fails. Thus, from 'John wants a car' we receive 'John wants to have a car' rather than 'John wants to drive a car'. Similarly, from 'John wants a rock' we receive 'John wants to have a rock', whereas the generative lexicon theory may well treat it as semantically odd, which it is not. (Note that the generative lexicon theory does not have the internal resources to predict when the 'have' reading has to be replaced by the event reading reconstructed from the noun's qualia structure.)

Now, let us turn to cases of nominal alternations considered by Pustejovsky as instances of logical polysemy (alternations involving no change in lexical category). Here are some examples: 'window' and 'door' are polysemous because each of them can denote the opening and what fills that opening; 'lamb' and 'chicken' are polysemous because each of them can denote an animal and meat of that animal;

'newspaper' is polysemous because it can denote the physical object, the information and the publishing organization. Whereas senses of these words are obviously related, only one of them is 'focused' in context or is available for interpretation (Pustejovsky, 1995, pp. 32, 156).[20] The generative lexicon captures these two observations by including all the senses of a logically polysemous word under a single entry (for NEWSPAPER: ARG1 = x:org ARG2 = y:info•physobj), and specifying information that is relevant for selecting one or the other sense in context in the qualia structures (for NEWSPAPER: TELIC = read(e2,w,y) AGENT = publish(e1,x,y); for DOOR: TELIC = walk_through(e,z,y)).

However, Fodor and Lepore object that Pustejovsky tries to offer unproductive generalizations:

> We suspect that there is nothing to say about such cases; the meanings of words can partially overlap in all sorts of ways in which polysemous terms can differ from mere homonyms. [continued from a footnote] There is a semiproductive generalization according to which terms for tastes double as terms for personalities: *sweet, bitter, sour, tart, acid, bland, salty*, and so on. Could anyone really suppose that lexical semantics should be required to capture this regularity? And if not, why should it be required to capture the polysemy of *window, door, newspaper*, and the like? (1998, p. 287)

We have seen that Pustejovsky's generative lexicon has to exclude cases of metaphorical polysemy, such as the polysemy of synaesthetic and double-function adjectives. The alternative meanings of metaphorically polysemous words cannot be accounted for by the generative powers of the lexicon where the interpretation of polysemous adjectives and verbs depends on the information specified in the qualia structures of nouns with which they combine. (For example, the lexicon cannot generate the meaning of 'sweet girl' because it is difficult to imagine what should be in the qualia structure of GIRL, if it were to contextually modify the meaning of 'sweet'.) For Fodor and Lepore, the whole story about polysemy is different. What they sell is the disquotational lexicon in which lexical items are atomic and specify only denotations and their contribution to the logical form of expressions where they occur. As such, they pick out only those sets of objects, properties or relations that a word/concept literally denotes. From this point of view, we may say that 'window' is simply homonymous because 'window' does not always refer to openings or those things that fill the openings.[21] Thus, for Fodor and Lepore, logical polysemy is simply not interesting.

However, besides cases of uninteresting polysemy, in Fodor and Lepore's story we also find presumably interesting cases of lexical ambiguity. Not only homonyms such as 'bank' which are represented in the mental lexicon as BANK$_1$ (financial institution) and BANK$_2$ (riverside), but also words that are considered to be polysemous by Pustejovsky. As we have seen, 'bake', which is ambiguous between warming something up by baking and creating something by baking, is one such word for them. Thus, 'bake' requires disambiguation in context. When you encounter 'Mary baked a cake', you have to map 'bake' onto BAKE$_1$ or BAKE$_2$ in your mental lexicon. (Note that in Fodor and Lepore's account, there is nothing to show that the two are connected in any other way apart from having the same name in the language.) However, this is somewhat inconsistent with Fodor and Lepore's general strategy of eliminating polysemy and maintaining that most concepts are univocal. As we have seen in section 9.2, Fodor (1998a) holds that there is no polysemy, that words which seem to be polysemous, such as 'keep', are univocal across semantic fields: thus, 'keep' always maps onto the same concept KEEP and always refers to instances of keeping.

So as we have seen, for Fodor, KEEP is an atom, and the reason we use 'keep' in a variety of contexts is that in all these contexts we depict the same relation that holds between things in the world, namely, the relation of keeping. Thus, Fodor rejects polysemy to make sure that concepts are not definitional or decompositional: 'keep' does not mean 'cause a state which endures over a period of time' and does not reduce to any primitives, being a primitive itself. However, Fodor and Lepore's treatment of 'bake' proves to be different. It is not the case that in 'Mary baked a cake' and 'Mary baked a potato' the word 'bake' means BAKE and refers in both cases to the same relation of baking. And from this, it is only a half-step away from saying that the meaning of 'bake' can be given by definition: the standard story that philosophers tell (see Fodor, 1998a:, pp. 69–87).

The only straw to keep Fodor and Lepore from slipping into meanings as definitions is to insist that the two meanings of 'bake' exhibit merely accidental overlaps. That is, to insist that the meaning of 'bake' in 'bake a cake' is BAKE$_1$ which denotes the activity of making something by baking, but which does not mean 'to make something by performing such and such operations with it to which we normally refer as "baking"'. Similarly, for 'bake' in 'bake a potato' and BAKE$_2$. Thus, in the case of such polysemous words as 'bake', one can avoid saying that meanings are definitions (that 'bake' means either 'create by baking' or 'warm up by baking') by claiming *a priori* that concepts are atomic, and that concepts which share a name do so only as a matter of chance.

However, this puts 'bake' on the same row with 'bank', blurring the distinction between homonymy and polysemy. And here is where the problem lies. 'Bank' as 'the bank of a river' and 'bank' as 'the place where one keeps money' have little in common. But the two activities of baking overlap in at least one aspect: when you bake something you normally shove this something into an oven (or other device that can be used for baking), no matter whether its origins are creative or non-creative. Thus, even though Fodor and Lepore want to keep polysemy and true homonymy apart (1998, p. 281), their assumption that meanings of polysemes are not related in any interesting way will not let them do so. Which is why they either have to deny polysemy ('good', 'want') or reduce it to a special case of homonymy (say that the word 'bake' expresses two different and unrelated concepts). What is being missed out, though, is the systematicity that is found in polysemy and lacking in homonymy (cf. Pustejovsky, 1998, p. 308).

But what is to prevent one from saying that 'bake' is not ambiguous, that 'bake' always means BAKE? There is nothing pleonastic in the sentences 'Mary baked a cake she made' and 'Mary baked a cake she bought'. In both sentences 'bake' means BAKE and refers not to a creative or a warming up activity, but rather to the activity of transforming an unbaked object into a baked one by placing it into devices designed for baking (ovens) and keeping it there for an amount of time. Fodor and Lepore accuse Pustejovsky of wanting to introduce ontological information into the lexicon without providing an argument for why it should be there (1998, p. 281). However, they are tripping over the same little problem: they introduce world knowledge about things that can be baked into the meaning of 'bake'. But even denotational semantics cannot require that concepts pick out all or some of the activity preceding an instance of a certain action-type (that BAKING should be about anything but shoving an object into a baking device and keeping it there for an amount of time).[22]

It thus appears that, in their critique of Pustejovsky's treatment of polysemy, Fodor and Lepore find themselves caught between atomism, which requires concept univocality, and 'enumerationalism' or strict compositionality, which requires that meanings of polysemes be kept apart unless they are completely context invariant. Unfortunately, the way out of this trap that Fodor and Lepore propose – to treat polysemy as a special case of homonymy – is the one that is not acceptable. The entire generative lexicon program was motivated precisely by the consideration that meanings of polysemes are related in some interesting ways while meanings of homonyms are not (and this has now been confirmed by psycholinguistic experiments; see Klepousniotou, 2002). It is probably also already clear that Fodor and Lepore's solution is not going to help us with understanding synaesthetic and double-function polysemy.

Their convictions prohibit introducing the polysemy of 'sweet', 'bitter', and so on into the lexicon but for reasons different from those of Pustejovsky. Their semantics requires that the meaning of a term (bar indexicals) be context invariant, that is, that 'sweet' always refer to the same property in the real world. Thus, 'sweet' in the context of cakes and cookies is only accidentally related to the meaning of 'sweet' in the context of auditory musical experience or in the context of personalities. If one wants these other meanings (if one considers them to be meanings at all) to be represented in the lexicon, we will have to say that there is SWEET$_1$, SWEET$_2$, and so on. The same also goes for 'sharp', 'soft', and other adjectives. However, if we leave aside the strict compositionality requirement,[23] what Fodor and Lepore's solution boils down to is that there are primary or basic meanings (however we happen to establish them), which are represented in the lexicon and their metaphorical extensions, which are most probably not a matter of semantics. However, this is the same position that is also taken by Pustejovsky, and that cannot be a correct position: alternative meanings of synaesthetic and double-function terms do seem to be part of the lexicon (even if one treats them as dead metaphors) and they are related in a different way than meanings of homonyms.

There does indeed seem to be something striking about these two types of polysemous adjectives: not only are they found cross-culturally and have fixed dictionary entries, but they are also univocally interpreted by people of different age and mental abilities. So, here is the rub. If one is doing some variety of abstract truth-conditional semantics, one may well be advised to keep apart different meanings of polysemes. However, if informational semantics of Fodor's type is supposed to be a theory of concepts (as mental entities), not a theory of how to compute meanings which are not attached to thought, then Fodor and Lepore's solution will not work. Criticizing definitional theories of concepts Fodor (1998a) himself pays attention to psychological research which shows that meanings are unlikely to be definitional (Carey, 1982). But as we have seen in the previous chapters, there is sufficient evidence showing that meanings of polysemes (in particular, of synaesthetic and double-function adjectives) are related in some unarbitrary way, and we should expect a theory of concepts to be able to explain that.

10
The No-Polysemy View: What It Is and What It Is Not

10.1 The one literal meaning assumption

In this chapter we shall see how the no-polysemy view of conceptual structure proposes to deal with adjectival polysemy of synaesthetic and double-function types. The no-polysemy view, according to which all meanings of a synaesthetic or double-function adjective map onto the same psychologically primitive concept, was mentioned quite early in the book and it is now time to see what precisely it amounts to.

I began the story by noticing that most metaphor researchers subscribe to the standard assumption according to which only one meaning of a polysemous adjective can be its literal or primary meaning, and that all its other meanings are secondary and metaphorically derivative. As it turned out, the notion of primary meaning depends heavily on the assumption of some conceptual primacy. This assumption, which was implicit in the classical theories of metaphor, received its full expression in the theory of conceptual metaphor proposed by cognitive semanticists. There, primary meanings are those that are closest to expressing directly experienced properties. However, when it comes to instances of physical-physical adjectival polysemy (including synaesthetic polysemy), it is not clear how the notion of conceptual primacy is to be cashed out.

Both classical and cognitive theories of metaphor assume that synaesthetic adjectives have only one literal or primary meaning, so that 'bright' is primarily (and/or exclusively) a term belonging to the visual modality, and 'soft' is primarily a term belonging to the tactile modality. Uses of these adjectives to refer to properties in other modalities are considered metaphorical, even though they may have been conventionalized and acquired their own dictionary entries. However, as we have seen in later discussions, what makes physical–physical polysemy so interesting is that transfers of predicates across modalities are both grounded in our perceptual functioning and go beyond merely perceptual associations. The same mechanisms underlie the detection of hot thermal and hot taste sensations, but we are able to distinguish the two and conceptualize the distinction. We can compare stimuli from different modalities by their intensity, but the meanings of adjectives used across modalities is not determined by correlations in stimuli intensity. Bright lights and loud sounds are correlated by stimuli intensity, but 'bright sound' is not synonymous with 'loud sound'. This is reflected in subjects' performance on rating tasks, and even young children are capable of cross-modal predicate transfers, which are neither semantically mediated nor confined to similarity in terms of stimuli intensity. (Recall that subjects can classify non-linguistic auditory stimuli by their brightness when prompted with the linguistic stimulus 'bright' and that brightness ratings are not identical with loudness ratings; Chapter 4). Recent experimental work by Gerald Winer and colleagues (2001) further suggests that people's understanding of predicate transfer across sensory domains is syncretic rather than metaphorical.

We have also seen that there are good reasons (supported by clinical evidence) to treat double-function adjectives alongside synaesthetic adjectives, and that the analogical similarity explanation that is not acceptable for synaesthetic adjectives is also unacceptable for double-function adjectives (Chapter 5). As we have further stipulated, the main question that has to be answered in connection with synaesthetic and double-function adjectives concerns their relation to the conceptual structure. What one's theory has to make sense of is how the different meanings of these polysemous adjectives are related in some unarbitrary way. Any theory which proposes to treat polysemy as a subtype of homonymy is doomed to fail as it cannot explain how we understand novel uses of polysemous adjectives. The visual synaesthetic meaning of 'cold' does not form a dictionary entry, but we can easily understand 'cold light' (as presumably also would people with reduced mental capacities). A theory equating homonymy with polysemy cannot explain how we do that. However, other theories that we have discussed (Chapters 8 and 9) and that do distinguish between polysemy and homonymy – theories proposed within cognitive linguistics and lexical semantics – for a number of reasons are similarly unsatisfactory as theories of concepts that would do justice to adjectival polysemy of synaesthetic and double-function types.

All the trouble, in my opinion, comes from the fact that most researchers accept without further question the standard assumption about the literal–metaphorical distinction. The assumption of one literal meaning stands in the way of making sense of our intuition that, for instance, 'sharp' in 'sharp sound' and 'sharp' in 'sharp knife', although not being the same, are somehow related in an unarbitrary non-metaphorical way. Besides, the standard assumption, in its various manifestations, commits one to an implausible view of the conceptual structure. It either makes one accept 'enumerationalism', or hold that 'sharp' in 'sharp sound' is understood through 'sharp' as in 'sharp knife'. But 'enumerationalism' is wrong, and nobody has so far made any sense of the idea that the understanding of 'sharp' in 'sharp sound' is secondary with respect to the understanding of 'sharp' in 'sharp knife'. 'Sharp sound' and 'sharp knife' are different from the well-familiar cases of metaphor ('My job is a jail'), where we can find a property shared by the topic and the vehicle ('confining'). They are also different from those cases of verbal polysemy that are treated by cognitive semanticists under the heading of conceptual metaphor (for example, 'take a paragraph out of the text'), where we might see how bodily simulation can contribute to the understanding of abstract meanings. The only property that is shared by sharp sounds and sharp knives is precisely the property of *being sharp*. No paraphrase would even approximately convey what is conveyed by 'sharp sound'. And even though we can presumably detect the similarity between the action of sharp cutting objects on our skin and the action of sharp sounds on our eardrums (with a good physiological reason; see Békésy, 1959), the evidence there is suggests that the transfer of adjectives across sensory modalities is not semantically mediated. Which suggests that the relation between 'sharp' in 'sharp sound' and 'sharp' in 'sharp knife' is not the relation between a literal and a metaphoric meanings. From the various issues that we have considered in the preceding chapters, at least one thing should be clear. Besides the standard assumption, there is no reason to think that 'sharp' has only one literal meaning.

10.2 The no-polysemy view

The no-polysemy view is what we get if we take away the one literal meaning assumption. The no-polysemy view says that the literal-metaphorical distinction does not apply to the conceptual structure. As a consequence of this, it denies the standard notion of the lit~ metaphorical distinction with respect to language (note moment I am restricting the discussion of the no-polysemy view to the two types of adjectival polysemy and corresponding concepts). Another claim that is important for the no-polysemy view is that a theory of concepts does not have to be at the same time a theory of meaning. Now, let us proceed.

According to the no-polysemy view, concepts BRIGHT, SHARP, COLD, and so on are psychologically primitive concepts spanning all domains of sensory experience. Their content cannot be further decomposed into features which would be more primitive than them. One may think of these psychologically primitive concepts as neuronal configurations responsive to certain ranges of stimuli. (If you find it hard to think of, say, BRIGHT as a primitive concept, try thinking of it as a primitive concept B, about which we know only that it becomes activated, or may become activated, in the presence of certain visual, auditory, and so on stimuli, and is necessarily activated when one is thinking about the property/properties denoted by it.)[1] Although psychologically primitive concepts are tied to perceptual functioning, their content is not exhausted by it (recall that similarity in stimuli intensity does not lead to the synonymy of corresponding expressions). They are primitives in the representational system, built-in devices for higher-level processing of stimuli coming from the environment through different modalities.

It has to be emphasized that the no-polysemy view should not be interpreted as a simple similarity view, according to which the perceptual ability to correlate stimuli across different modalities leads to conceptual overlaps. If anything, the no-polysemy view may be called the reversed similarity view: in some sense, concepts have to come before percepts. This does not mean that one can have the concept BRIGHT if there is nothing in the experienced world to cause it, but rather that the disposition to detect brightness in the environment has to be present before any interaction with it begins.[2] So, BRIGHT is understood here as a psychologically primitive concept, which we employ for organizing our thinking about perceptual stimuli (for example, for thinking about them as BRIGHT and NOT BRIGHT) whatever the source of perceptual information. The reason why sounds can be judged bright or thought of as bright is not because they remind one somehow of lights but because BRIGHT is a representational primitive.[3]

Now, it might be easier to accept SHARP as a psychologically primitive supramodal concept than BRIGHT. 'Sharp', one can say, sounds perfectly literal when predicated of knives, or sounds, or lights. 'Bright' seems to different: only objects in the visual modality can be properly labelled want to reiterate that the one literal meaning assumption is wrong. What one is doing when offering this kind of objection is confusing words with concepts. To a large extent, the question of proper use is a question of linguistic convention, and conventions are subject to change (we can see that from the etymology of synaesthetic adjectives, Chapter 8). Note also that this kind of objection places a lot of weight on the word 'properly' (you may have another look at Chapter 1 or the discussion of Marks *et al.*'s work in Chapter 4 to see how often the claim about the literal meaning of a polyseme reduces to the claim about its 'proper meaning').[4] This makes one wonder: how can the semi-technical word 'properly' impose any criteria for discriminating between meanings? Besides, if one leaves 'properly' out, the objection is hardly convincing: it is not even true that 'bright' denotes only a certain property in the visual modality. English speakers employ 'bright' to refer to properties in other modalities ('bright voice'). Unless one is prepared to say that they are not doing it 'properly', the objection hangs exclusively on an *a priori* assumption that 'bright' has only one literal meaning.

Even if one agrees that BRIGHT and SHARP are psychologically primitive concepts, one could still ask how the words 'bright' and 'sharp' relate to them. Namely, why some of their uses seem to be more literal than others. One answer to this is that the detection of some properties and informational exchanges about them are more important for our everyday purposes than the detection and informational exchanges about other properties. I believe that this is the reason why 'bright' seems to be more literal when predicated of objects in the visual modality than of objects in the auditory modality, whereas 'sharp' seems to be perfectly literal in both 'sharp knife' and 'sharp pain'. However, this does not show that we can establish *a priori* which are the literal and which are the metaphoric meanings of polysemous adjectives.[5] Neither the evidence from dictionaries, nor the evidence from language use support the standard assumption. If we have a fixed meaning for a polysemous adjective (for example, the auditory 'bright') whose first meaning we consider to be different, what does saying that this other meaning is not literal amount to? Since there is sufficient evidence of its use to make it into a dictionary entry, we may suspect that it is univocal across language speakers and causes no problem of interpretation. The assumption of one literal meaning appears to play no important role here.

In fact, I think that there can be only one serious objection to the view that the alternative meanings of synaesthetic adjectives are not their metaphoric meanings, and it comes from the causal theory of reference. The causal theory of reference appeared in the work of Saul Kripke (1972, 1980) and Hilary Putnam (1975), and one of its most important contributions to the philosophy of language concerns the meaning of natural kind terms.[6] I shall now briefly summarize its content and then show how it can be used against the view proposed here. After that, I shall argue that the no-polysemy view is perfectly consistent with the causal theory of reference, but that some assumptions about the relation between concepts and properties have to be reconsidered.

According to the causal theory, the meanings of natural kind terms cannot be given by descriptions we associate with them. Take the word 'water'. Roughly, the problem with holding that the meaning of 'water' is given by descriptions is that the descriptions people used some time ago to establish whether something is in the extension of 'water' have changed, but the meaning of 'water' has not. So, the causal theory dispenses with descriptions and says that we use the word 'water' to refer to water because of the causal connection that obtains between us and water exemplars in our world. 'Water' is a rigid designator, which means that it always denotes the same stuff: the stuff that we enter into causal interactions with in our world. The clear advantage of thinking about 'water' as a rigid designator is that it allows us to explain why the stuff that we referred to as 'water' many years ago, when we did not know that water is H_2O, and the stuff that we refer today as 'water', when we know that water is H_2O, is the same stuff. When we discovered that water is H_2O, the meaning of 'water' did not change. What we discovered was a necessary truth: it is metaphysically necessary that water is H_2O (and if some suspicious looking stuff is not H_2O then it is not water). However, even though we discovered a necessary truth, we discovered it *a posteriori*: we discovered that the stuff that we had been causally connected to is H_2O, but it is the same stuff that we had referred to and keep referring to as 'water'.

As I said above, one can use the causal theory to argue against the view that the alternative meanings of synaesthetic adjectives are not their literal meanings. Let us begin with the example of 'hot'. 'Hot' (of temperature) refers to certain kinetic energy of molecular motion. (We have discovered that increasing heat corresponds to increasing molecular motion; Kripke, 1972, p. 129.)[7] Therefore, when we want to establish whether 'This is hot' is true (ignore the problem of indexicals), we find out whether the object in question possesses the right kinetic energy of molecular motion (you can say that we have a mark on our hotness scale which tells us that everything above it qualifies as hot). And thus, 'hot' is used with its literal meaning only in those cases when it refers to certain kinetic energy of molecular motion. Things which do not possess kinetic energy (for example, temperaments) cannot literally be called 'hot'.

This is probably the best theory one can have about the meaning of 'hot' (of temperature). What some people find particularly appealing about it is its objective character. I also think that objectivity is a virtue. However, sometimes people are prone to forget the causal part itself. Here is what I have in mind. Leaving aside the questions of doing physics, how do you think it was possible to discover that heat is kinetic energy of molecular motion, or that being hot is possessing certain kinetic energy of molecular motion? Here is where the causal part comes in. Today we can define the property of being hot (of temperature) in non-psychological terms. But the discovery of what it is for a body to be hot had to begin with noticing that people exhibit a good deal of intersubjective agreement when calling bodies hot; in other words, that they are reliably causally connected to the property of being hot.

Now, one may say that when the word 'hot' is used to describe taste sensations, it is used metaphorically. But the story about 'hot' (of taste) is no different from the story about 'hot' (of temperature). Ignoring for the moment the fact that not all linguistic communities use the morpheme for 'hot' to describe taste sensations (see Chapter 3), we can say that people exhibit a good deal of intersubjective agreement in calling foods 'hot'; in other words, that they are reliably causally connected to some property possessed by hot foods. As it happens, it is possible to determine the hotness of foods in non-psychological terms: to be hot (of taste) is to have a certain vanilloid content which acts in a certain way on VR1. Just as we establish whether 'This is hot' (of temperature) is true by finding out whether the object in question possesses the right kinetic energy of molecular motion, we can establish whether 'This is hot' (of taste) is true by finding out whether the foodstuff in question (a pepper) possesses the right vanilloid content (we have a mark on our scale telling us how much vanilloid content is 'hot'). So, what is metaphorical about 'hot' (of taste)?

It looks like that we have to admit that these two meanings of 'hot' are its literal meanings. In other words, that 'hot' is ambiguous between 'hot' (of temperature) and 'hot' (of taste). But ambiguity encompasses both homonymy and polysemy. So, is 'hot' homonymous or polysemous? The proponents of standard denotational semantics will probably say that it is homonymous because different physical properties determine what is in the denotation of 'hot' (of temperature) and 'hot' (of taste). However, I am not sure that this would be the right answer. We proposed to talk here about concepts, which we understand not as abstract Fregean entities, but as mental entities (those 'things in the head' that, for example, can be lost following severe brain damage). In this respect, I find it completely unarbitrary that speakers of a language use the same words to refer to apparently different sensations, and I believe that a theory of concepts had better face that fact. The work on the 'hot' ion channel (see Chapter 3) was partly motivated by the observation that people refer to spicy foods as 'hot', and its discovery has undeniable effects for clinical practice. To treat the two meanings of 'hot' as unrelated, or as metaphorically related, is to turn one's back on how things really are.

The issue of how concepts relate to real world properties is terribly complicated. The simplest strategy is to assume that for every real world property that we can individuate there is a corresponding individual concept. But I doubt that this is an entirely correct strategy. The concept HOT spans two (or more) real world properties that resist reduction (at least, for all that we know now). Let me expand a little. It is traditionally stipulated that the meaning of 'hot' (of temperature) is constituted by the speakers' use of language (they are prone to call a certain state of things 'hot') and real world facts (heat is kinetic energy of molecular motion). It then presumably follows that only things possessing certain kinetic energy of molecular motion can reliably cause language speakers to call them 'hot' (and to have a corresponding concept HOT). However, this cannot be the full story. Sticking mustard plasters, that were once popular in treating chest colds, reliably produce the sensation of hotness among statistically large populations (the same as touching hot burners: the threshold of heat sensibility may differ among individuals), and language speakers thus have every reason to call them 'hot'. However, when a plaster comes into contact with the human skin, there is no change in its kinetic energy.[8] Similarly, with the action of vanilloids on VR1. As David Clapham put it: 'It is possible that the real purpose of the channel [VR1] is to sense noxious temperature, and that capsaicin is nature's low energy way of harnessing the sensor.' (1997, p. 784). So, I think that instead of thinking that mustard plasters or chilli peppers (in their 'active' state) are not properly called 'hot', it makes more sense to think that the concept HOT spans a number of sensory experiences caused by different real world properties.

I also think that 'hot' is not an exception. Here is a similar story about 'bright'. One may say that the difference between its literal (visual, as in 'bright light') and metaphoric (auditory, as in 'bright sound') meanings results from the difference in their denotational status: the application of 'bright' to visual objects seems to have the flavour of objectivity that its application to auditory objects lacks. But this is no longer true. Again, the causal part of the story about the visual 'bright' has to begin with intersubjective agreement as to what kind of light is reliably called by language speakers 'bright'. Today the brightness of light can be described in non-psychological vocabulary (in terms of luminance) but it all began with a highly subjective word 'bright'. It is exactly the same story with 'bright sound'. Music professionals noticed that there is a certain consistency in speakers' use of the word 'bright' in reference to sounds.[9] Instead of shrugging this observation off, they wondered whether they could find out what makes sounds bright. And indeed, today the brightness of sounds can be stated in non-psychological vocabulary (in terms of the 3d, 5th, and 7th even harmonics). So, I suspect that 'bright sound' is not a metaphor after all.[10]

The two examples we have considered above were examples of synaesthetic adjectives. And I think they suggest rather strongly that all meanings of synaesthetic adjectives are likely to be their literal meanings[11]. However, even if one is prepared to grant that all meanings of synaesthetic adjectives are their literal meanings, one may still hold to the comforting idea that the psychological meanings of double-function adjectives are their metaphoric meanings. Let us see what we can do about that. As the reasoning usually goes, 'hot' (of temper) is at best a metaphoric meaning of 'hot'. If it so happens that, for whatever reason, we need to establish whether 'He's got a hot temper' (ignoring the problem of indexicals again) is true, we have to translate the metaphorical 'hot temper' into, say, the literal 'violent temper', and then find out whether it is true or false. The standard assumption tells us that 'hot temper' is metaphorical, and although speakers and hearers may well understand this expression, tempers presumably have nothing to do with kinetic energy of molecular motion.

However, we have seen above that 'hot' (of taste) is just as literal as 'hot' (of temperature). There are precise ways of determining when a foodstuff is hot, such that we can know when someone is mistaken in his/her use of 'hot' (of taste). (Or else, we can know whether someone's detection of gustatory hotness is impaired.) The discovery of VR1, the molecular mechanism of transduction for hot thermal and hot gustatory stimuli, gives us good reasons to think that the use of the word 'hot' to refer to spicy foods is neither arbitrary nor metaphorical. But consider now the following story. A proponent of standard denotational semantics who has never heard of that discovery may hold that 'hot' has only one literal meaning and refers literally only to objects possessing certain kinetic energy of molecular motion. According to him or her, the meaning of 'hot' (of taste) cannot be more or less precisely given in terms of denotation, and for this reason 'hot' (of taste) is metaphorical and parasitic upon 'hot' (of temperature). However, when he or she hears about the discovery, he or she is prepared to reconsider and agree that 'hot' (of taste) is a literal meaning of 'hot'. But, we may ask, has the reference of 'hot' (of taste) changed since the mid-1990s? Presumably not: most people have no idea of what is happening in molecular chemistry, but just keep on calling capsicum peppers 'hot' as they did before. The causal theory is the best theory of meaning for natural kind terms because it can handle this (as well as 'water' and 'heat' cases).

Now, consider 'hot temper'. The causal part of the story about 'hot temper' is no different from the causal part of the story about 'hot burner' (and the like). 'Hot temper' has a fixed use and is found in historically and geographically unrelated languages.[12] The only thing that is lacking is a theory of what it is for a temperament to be 'hot'. But is that the reason to say that 'hot' (of temper) is a metaphoric meaning of 'hot'? I think there are two possible replies to that. One is to say that 'hot temper' has to be presently considered as a metaphorical expression, but may be transferred into the class of literal expressions should someone discover one day what is for a temperament to be 'hot' in non-psychological terms. The other is to say that no such theory is possible and that 'hot temper' is metaphorical and this is it. However, if one chooses the second reply, one comes close to saying that speakers' use of words is not a reliable indication of what words mean. But whereas this may be true with respect to their use of scientific terms, it is not clear how this view may be held with respect to their use of synaesthetic and double-function adjectives. If one chooses the first option, one says that the literal-metaphorical distinction is, in a sense, valid only retrospectively, for unconfirmed hypotheses.[13] But this does not contradict the no-polysemy view, since what the no-polysemy view denies is first of all is the literal-metaphorical distinction with respect to the conceptual structure.

The no-polysemy view makes its strongest claim with respect to synaesthetic adjectives (that, for example, all instances of 'sharp' map onto the same psychologically primitive concept SHARP), but I believe that this claim can be extended to include cases of physical–psychological polysemy. This move should not seem very surprising if one considers that the perception of other people (as different from other kinds of physical objects) may well form an individual module: 'other people module' (a more familiar term may be 'the theory of mind module' but I want to emphasize a different aspect of our perception of other people; on the theory of mind module see, for instance, Baron-Cohen, 1995; see also Byrne, 1995). Somehow, our emotional and dispositional evaluation of other people seems to work in the same mode as our perception of properties across sensory modalities rather than being a conscious inferential process. Here are just a few observations to this effect. Damasio describes a patient with a very severe learning and memory deficit who could neither recognize other people on photographs nor say anything about them, but who nonetheless exhibited surprising consistency in choosing or avoiding people for his company (1999, pp. 43–7). Patients with blindsight who report being unable to see visually presented objects, nonetheless are capable of correctly reporting other people's facial expressions/emotional states (de Gelder *et al.*, 1999, 2000, 2002; Heywood and Kentridge, 2000; Morris *et al.*, 1999). Ramachandran and Hubbard, who otherwise subscribe to the standard assumption, suggest that the use of the word 'disgusting' as an expression of social and moral disgust emerged because moral/social disgust is mediated by the orbito-frontal cortex which also mediates olfactory and gustatory disgust (2001b, p. 22). Although it may seem implausible at first, I believe that there is nothing impossible in the idea that the perception of other people as sharp or warm may be as direct as the perception of sounds as sharp or warm.[14]

At the beginning of this section I said that an important part of the no-polysemy view is that it does not propose to conflate meanings and concepts, and to this question we shall now turn. When I suggest that HOT is a psychologically primitive concept, I do not imply that we should not distinguish between the various meanings of 'hot'. Not only are the different meanings correlated with different real-world properties, language speakers do distinguish between them. 'The soup is hot' is ambiguous between 'The soup has been heated up to a high temperature' and 'The soup is spicy'. It is now an established fact that the mechanisms of transduction for noxious heat and vanilloid content largely overlap. However, when sensory information reaches higher-level processing centres and becomes translated into a representation of subjective experience, that representation presumably contains both the information about the quality of received stimulation which is decomposable into particular sensory characteristics and the information about the similarity of sensory experiences (Chapter 3). But whichever the route, we need to make sense of the fact that the two meanings of 'hot' are related in an unarbitrary way. The no-polysemy view suggests how we may do that.

I believe that we can hold both that, say, BRIGHT is a psychologically primitive concept and that the meaning of 'bright' in 'bright sound' is different from the meaning of 'bright' in 'bright light', if we distinguish between metaphysical and conceptual necessity. The reason why we need to distinguish between these two meanings of 'bright' is obvious: what makes sounds bright is different from what makes lights bright. Clearly, there is more to meanings than the disposition to detect brightness across sensory modalities. On the other hand, all the various meanings of 'bright' are related in an unarbitrary non-metaphorical way. The no-polysemy view says that BRIGHT is a psychologically primitive concept which allows one to entertain thoughts of certain type about various perceptual stimuli regardless of their source. But we do distinguish between vision and audition, we know that the information we receive about lights comes from vision, and that the information we receive about sounds comes from audition. There is no way we would confuse visual brightness with auditory brightness. Thus, in order to support the individuation of 'bright' all that we need is to have the conceptual structure that is reliably connected to our sensorium. Thus, whereas it is metaphysically necessary that 'bright' in 'bright sound' and 'bright' in 'bright light' are caused by different real-world properties (our physical theory of light is different from our physical theory of sound), it does not follow that we have two unrelated concepts BRIGHT. The no-polysemy view says that we do not; that there is only one concept BRIGHT, and that its possession is conceptually, although not metaphysically, independent of what science may tell us about what makes things bright. This, however, does not imply that the complex conepts BRIGHT SOUND and BRIGHT LIGHT are identical: they differ because sounds and lights differ, because our concepts SOUND and LIGHT differ, and because this difference is part of our conceptual make-up.

Since the concepts BRIGHT SOUND and BRIGHT LIGHT are different concepts, nothing prevents us from saying that the meaning of 'bright' in 'bright sound' is different from the meaning of 'bright' in 'bright light'. From the perspective of an individual language speaker, to know what either 'bright sound' or 'bright light' means all one needs is to have the concept BRIGHT (as well as the concepts SOUND and LIGHT). But 'bright' in 'bright sound' picks out a certain property with respect to sounds, and 'bright' in 'bright light' picks out a certain property with respect to lights. In this sense, the no-polysemy view is perfectly compatible with denotational semantics because the property of brightness is realized differently in the auditory and visual modalities. The purpose of the next section is thus to have a closer look at the relation between words, meanings, and concepts.

10.3 Words, meanings, concepts, and more

I said that the no-polysemy view is perfectly compatible with denotational semantics. Here is how it works. The adjective 'bright' can modify 'light' or 'sound' to give us 'bright light' or 'bright sound'. The corresponding concept BRIGHT is a supramodal atomic concept which spans both visual and auditory modalities. When you understand either 'bright light' or 'bright sound' the concept BRIGHT is activated. But note that when you understand 'bright light', what you understand is that some light is bright *as far as lights go*. Similarly, when you understand 'bright sound', what you understand is that some sound is bright *as far as sounds go*, not as far as lights go. For all intents and purposes, there is no reason to suppose that 'bright sound' should be understood as meaning that some sound is bright as far as lights go.[15]

A comparison with degree adjectives can help clarify the matters. Let us take 'big' as our example. 'Big' is not tied to any particular category of objects, the adjective 'big' can modify a very large number of nouns (on semantic dependency of adjectives on nouns they modify see, for instance, Dixon, 1982; Wierzbicka, 1986). Compare now the two sentences: 'It is a cat' and 'It is big'. The interpretation of both sentences is context-dependent, because they both contain the indexical element 'it' whose value has to be supplied by context. Still, there is also an important difference between them: to establish whether something is a cat all you need is to find out whether that something satisfies your best theory of what it is to be a cat. However, you cannot do that with 'big': to establish whether something is big you need to have a contextually relevant comparison class. As people noticed a long time ago, a big mouse is not really big when compared to a small elephant. The interpretation of 'big' depends on the relevant comparison class, and thus the relevant size standard, which has to be made salient by context. Recently, to account for this peculiar behaviour of degree adjectives, some semanticists have proposed that the adjective 'big' contains a hidden variable x whose value is the contextually relevant comparison class (Szabó, 2001; Stanley and Szabó, 2000). But how do you understand 'a big mouse' when no comparison class has been explicitly provided by context (for example, 'A big mouse is sitting on the rubbish bin')? Apparently, you understand it as saying that some mouse is big as far as mice go, not as far as elephants go (and not even as far as rubbish bins go).

Thus, in a sense, we should speak not of the meaning of 'big', but of the meaning of 'big (x)'. Following Fodor (1998b; see also section 9.4), we can say that 'a big NP' is 'an NP' that is big as far as NPs go'. Now, let us use square brackets for semantic representations of words to distinguish them from words of public language, on the one hand, and concepts, on the other hand. Why we may want to draw such a distinction will become clear in a moment. Let us also stipulate that what is specified at this level is a word's contribution to the logical form of sentences where it occurs. Thus, we can say that what enters the semantic interpretation of sentences containing the adjective 'big' is not the semantic representation [BIG], but the semantic representation [BIG (x)]. This will give us the reading that, unless overridden by context, 'a big NP' is 'an NP that is big for its own kind'. Since, in the absence of an explicitly supplied comparison class, we normally interpret 'a big mouse' as 'a mouse that is big for its own kind (mice)', the introduction of a hidden variable into the semantic representation of 'big' captures our intuitions pretty well.

On the other hand, we should be, and are, able to categorize objects as big or not-big when the context does not provide us with a comparison class, or when we do not know whether they are big for their own kind or not. One day you may happen to run into a Martian cat, is it big or not? What is the right comparison class for Martian cats if it is the only one you have ever seen? Or, take a different example. One day someone may rush into your house screaming: 'I've just seen something down the street. I don't know what it is, but it's big!'. Presumably, there is something that you understand about the size of that unclassified something. This suggests that we all have the primitive concept BIG through which we are causally connected to the property of being big. In other words, we can detect the bigness of objects by combining the egocentric and the allocentric perspectives (things can be big with respect to our body size and with respect to surrounding objects, including objects of the same kind)[16]. To think of something as big one needs the concept BIG. But what enters the interpretation of 'big'-expressions is [BIG (x)], where the default value of x is 'for its own kind'. This way we can draw a distinction between the level of concepts and the level of semantic representation or the level of meaning.[17]

Let us now return to synaesthetic adjectives such as 'bright' ('hot', 'sharp', and so on). I suggest that they are both similar and different from either 'big' or 'cat'. 'Bright' is more like 'big' in that the primitive concept BRIGHT causally connects us to the property of being bright which is realized differently in different modalities. But what enters the interpretation of 'bright'-expressions is [BRIGHT (x)], where the value of x is 'for its own kind', and where its domain comprises the sensory modalities and 'the other people module'.[18] But 'bright' is also unlike 'big', and like 'cat', because what counts as big depends on a perspective taken, whereas what counts as a cat depends on being a cat (cf. Kamp, 1975, on the distinctions between nouns and adjectives, and differences between classes of adjectives). Although 'bright' applies across modalities, what counts as bright with respect to any given modality has determinate (even if vague) boundaries. In this sense, we can say that the adjective 'bright' maps onto the concept BRIGHT but via the semantic representation [BRIGHT (x)]. The level of concepts is the one where we can talk about embodiment (not necessarily in cognitive semantics' sense)[19] or perceptual simulation (in the sense of Barsalou, 1999); but the level of meaning is the level of semantic representation.

Some of the issues touched on above have been at the centre of a continuing lively debate between more semantically and more pragmatically oriented theories of linguistic communication, and it is appropriate to mention them here. Unfortunately, I cannot discuss here all the terminological and conceptual issues that feature in this debate. For this reason, I first give its overall simplified picture and then consider some issues that are of relevance to the main ideas of this book.

In many ways following Grice (1989/1975), in their analysis of sentence meaning many philosophers distinguish between the following three levels: the level of logical form, the level of what is said, and the level of implicature.[20] We can see the difference between them by taking 'She bought a cat' as our example. Its logical form specifies that a female x at a past time y bought a cat. You cannot know whether the sentence is true or false unless you know who 'she' refers to. Thus, the further level is the level of what is said by the sentence in context, and at this level sentences can be evaluated as true or false. Our sentence, 'She bought a cat' may say that at some time in the past[21] Mary bought a cat (we assume that the name is not ambiguous). Finally, someone may say 'She bought a cat' to convey not only that Mary bought a cat but also that she finally got rid of her pet hamster. This level of sentence understanding where some additional information is inferred by the hearer (and is expected by the speaker to be recovered by the hearer) on the basis of what the sentence says is the level of implicature. The derivation of a sentence's logical form is based exclusively on one's semantic knowledge. But the understanding of what is said by a sentence requires some contextual information. According to the Griceans, two pragmatic processes are involved into the determination of what is said. One is saturation, or the assignment of contents to indexical expressions. And the other is disambiguation: if our example were 'She bought a plant', to understand what is said we would have not only to know who 'she' refers to, but also whether 'plant' denotes a factory or a vegetable organism. In short, what is said by a sentence is that sentence's logical form after the processes of saturation and disambiguation have been completed. Everything else belongs to the level of implicature.

However, for the last fifteen years or so a number of linguists and philosophers have been continuously challenging this picture. The main point of their disagreement with the Griceans is: either that the levels of what is said and implicature are insufficient to account for linguistic communication or that their notion of what is said is unrealistic. And although this disagreement has resulted in several different theories – the relevance theory of Dan Sperber and Deirdre Wilson (1986), the 'truth-conditional pragmatics' of François Récanati (1993), and the tripartite 'what is said/impliciture/implicature' theory of Kent Bach (1987) – for our purposes here we can consider them all under the general heading of pragmatically oriented theories of linguistic communication (cf. Carston, 2000, pp. 15–16). In what follows I mostly speak of the relevance theory, but the discussion applies to other pragmatically oriented theories as well.

According to the relevance theory, what the speaker says by uttering a sentence and what the hearer takes as the proposition explicitly communicated by the speaker goes well beyond the minimalist Gricean what is said. The proposition communicated by the speaker and recovered by the hearer is richer than what the sentence uttered by the speaker says. When somebody says to you 'I've had lunch', you understand her as saying that she has had lunch today, not that she has had lunch at some point during her lifetime (and this is what she most probably means). But 'today' is not a constituent in the sentence's logical form. 'Today' is an unarticulated constituent. The proposition that she (say, Mary) has had lunch today is an enriched proposition called 'explicature', and the process of deriving explicatures involves not only saturation and disambiguation, but also 'free (pragmatic) enrichment' (the addition of unarticulated constituents). Thus, explicatures have to be distinguished from what is said, but they also have to be distinguished from implicatures because they are, in a sense, ineliminable. The derivation of explicatures is considered as an important stage in understanding utterances because linguistic communication cannot be reduced to the decoding of linguistic information, but is largely inferential and guided by the principle of relevance. We can easily understand what people want to communicate to us by using incomplete sentences. And we can do so because in interpreting ostensive stimuli, including linguistic stimuli, we probably employ special pragmatic inferences, subserved by a specialized submodule of the 'theory of mind' module (Origgi and Sperber, 2000; Sperber, 1994; Sperber and Wilson, 2002; Wilson and Sperber, forthcoming). Unlike the level of what is said, the level of explicature is a psychologically realistic level corresponding to the representation of the propositional content of a sentence that arises in the hearer's mind. For this reason, explicatures can be considered as objects of truth-conditional evaluation (cf. Carston, 2000, p. 43).

The issue of unarticulated constituents is one of the issues on which the Griceans and relevance theorists strongly disagree. According to the Griceans, no pragmatic processes, except saturation and disambiguation, are involved into deriving the proposition expressed by a sentence relative to the context of utterance. According to the relevance theory, the pragmatic process of free constituent enrichment is essential for deriving the proposition expressed by a sentence relative to the context of utterance. The unarticulated constituents debate has largely concentrated on the topic of quantifier domain restriction, which we shall not discuss here (see Stanley, 2000, 2002 and Stanley and Szabó, 2000 for one position; see Bach, 2000 and Carston, 2000 for the other position). But what is of interest to us here is that the main weapon in the attack that the Griceans launched against unarticulated constituents is the notion of hidden variables that we have employed at the beginning of this section.

You may have already guessed that I am not siding with either party. The Griceans are not interested in questions of the conceptual structure, or generally, of what is going on in people's heads. From this point of view, I am entirely with the relevance theorists. But on the other hand, the brief discussion of degree adjectives at the beginning of this section has clearly revealed my sympathies to more semantically oriented theories. There I have suggested that it makes good sense to distinguish between the level of concepts and the level of semantic representation of words. Let us now apply this distinction to a consideration of two examples from the relevance-theoretical literature often quoted to support the notion of unarticulated constituents. What I am going to argue is that the question of whether hearers actually form representations of enriched propositions and reason on the basis of them (for example, in deriving implicatures) has to be distinguished from two further questions. One of these questions is the question whether the level of what is said as defined by the Griceans has any psychological reality. The other is the question of what propositional form ('enriched' vs. 'minimal') has to be the object of truth-conditional valuation.

Consider an utterance of the sentence 'He ran to edge of the cliff and jumped' which is a good candidate to support the notion of unarticulated constituents, since its interpretation in many, if not most, contexts of utterance 'will include the understanding that he jumped over the cliff although there's no linguistic expression there telling us this or requiring us to fill in a prepositional phrase' (Carston, 1988, p. 165). This example is reproduced by Récanati, who is even more persuasive about the presence of an unarticulated constituent 'over the cliff':

> It must be realized that non-minimalist pragmatic processes such as free enrichment are not contingent but essential to the constitution of what is said: although optional, unarticulated constituents of the sort I have just mentioned are *ineliminable* in some sense. When I say 'He went to the cliff and jumped', the situation I describe or refer to is a situation in which he jumped *over the cliff* even though nothing in my utterance indicated this particular feature of the situation referred to. The unarticulated feature is part of the truth-conditions of the utterance, part of the described situation. (1993, pp. 259–60)[22]

There are several points that have to be distinguished with respect to this example. First, note that whereas Carston explicitly says that the unarticulated constituent 'over the cliff' will be added to the interpretation of the sentence relative to most contexts of utterance, Récanati omits this seemingly minor detail. But it is not a minor detail. When you tell me about somebody's suicide and say 'He went to the cliff and jumped', you can reasonably expect me to infer that he jumped down, over the cliff (since this would be the best way of killing oneself when standing on the edge of a cliff). But if you just say 'He went to the cliff and jumped', as in the quote from Récanati above, your expectations are not justified. When I first read the sentence, the representation I formed was 'He went to the cliff and jumped (up, with joy)'. The view from a cliff can be fantastic, and some people (me) jump (up) when they experience pleasurable emotions[23]. Does it follow that my semantic abilities are impaired? In my view, to reply in the positive would be most counterintuitive, and I believe that a good way to prevent such a conclusion is to include a hidden variable into the semantic representation of 'jump'. Does it follow that my pragmatic abilities are impaired? Again, it seems that the answer is no: there is no law (most importantly, no natural law) saying that the only direction to jump when you are standing on the edge of a cliff is down, over the cliff.

According to the view I am advocating here, there is a primitive concept JUMP which incorporates the perceptual and embodied schematism of jumping. But there is no jumping, unless it is jumping in a certain direction. Thus, what enters the interpretation of 'jump'-expressions, or what 'jump' contributes to the logical form of sentences in which it occurs, is the semantic representation [JUMP (x)] where the value of x is a direction. From this point of view, a prepositional phrase is required by the sentence's logical form. When the value of x is not specified in the sentence's surface form, it has to be supplied by context. In many cases the context will favour 'over the cliff' as the value of x (when somebody is jumping to commit a suicide or is practicing hang-glider jumps). However, when the context does not make the value of x explicit (as in the quote above), x can take on any value from its range of possible values.

Of course, the notion of free enrichment does not require that 'over the cliff' be the only correct interpretation of the sentence relative to a context of utterance. On the contrary, any contextually felicitous interpretation can be considered as an instance of the pragmatic process of free enrichment. The question here is whether movement verbs come with a directional variable or whether directional elements, whenever necessary, are supplied by free enrichment on the basis of general world knowledge. Or in other words, the question is whether, relative to a context (for example, the suicide context), the hearer forms a mental representation of the sentence at the level of what is said (for example, 'John run to the edge of the cliff and jumped (x), x = over the cliff') or whether the decoded linguistic information has to be enriched by inferential pragmatic processes to obtain a complete representation (for example, what is said: 'John run to the cliff and jumped' → pragmatic enrichment: 'jumped over the cliff' → explicature: 'John run to the cliff and jumped over it').

I rather think that movement verbs do come with a direction variable in their semantic representations and that general world knowledge is not sufficient to account for the difference between movement and 'non-movement' verbs. Take 'jump' again. Presumably, you know what 'jump' means, even if you think that jumping always involves two legs. This would account for the differences in our world knowledge but not in our semantic knowledge. On the other hand, if you do not think that jumping always involves a directional movement (however small), it is highly possible that you do not know what 'jump' means (perhaps you think that 'jump' means EAT). But if you don't know what 'jump' means, your general world knowledge cannot supply this information.

Consider a similar example 'He saw a shark and swam faster'. Apparently, in the absence of further linguistic input, the interpretation concerning the direction of movement has to be supplied by pragmatic mechanisms on the basis of previous contextual information and general world knowledge (whether the person in question is an unfortunate tourist or a shark hunter). And this is what divides the two accounts: is supplying *a* direction of movement part of the linguistic decoding process or is it part of an inferential pragmatic process? Since every movement verb necessarily denotes a movement activity, I would think that in our example, supplying *a* direction of movement is part of the linguistic decoding process [SWIM (x)], whereas supplying *the* direction of movement is part of the pragmatic inferential process. However, variable saturation is allowed into the minimal notion of what is said, and therefore does not involve free pragmatic enrichment (adding constituents not specified in the sentence's logical form).

There is another point that we may consider with respect to an utterance of the sentence 'He run to the edge of the cliff and jumped'. It concerns the question of what constitutes a truth-evaluable entity. Suppose you say 'He went to the cliff and jumped' meaning 'He went to the cliff and jumped over it'. Suppose also I know who 'he' refers to. But even in that case I cannot be blamed for not guessing that you meant 'jumped over the cliff' in the absence of a more specific context. For this reason, the unarticulated constituent 'over the cliff' is not part of the sentence's truth-conditions (relative to the context of utterance). Whether the utterance is true depends on whether he jumped or not, in whichever direction the jumping took place. The fact (if it is a fact) that on hearing the word 'cliff' most people think of jumping down, over the cliff, has nothing to do with the truth-conditions of 'He went to the cliff and jumped' relative to the minimal context of utterance. (Where 'minimal context of utterance' can be understood as a situation of overhearing, somewhat similar to Katz's (1977, p. 14) 'anonymous letter criterion'). All this has to do with the point, emphasized by Grice (1989/1975) and many other theorists, that 'communication works by negotiation' (in the words of Fodor, 2001, p. 14). If I am not sure in which direction the jumping took place, I can (almost) always ask and you can tell me.

Now, for some complications. According to the relevance theory, 'over the cliff' is an unarticulated constituent which contributes to the proposition expressed by an utterance of the sentence 'He ran to the edge of the cliff and jumped'. The truth-evaluable entity in this case is the explicitly communicated proposition that, say, John ran to the edge of the cliff and jumped over it. However, as we saw above, the enriched proposition cannot be the truth-evaluable entity with respect to the minimal context of utterance. Above I proposed that the semantic representation corresponding to 'jump' is [JUMP (x)]. This may seem to suggest that the value of *x* has to be specified before an utterance of the sentence 'He ran to the edge of the cliff and jumped' can be said to express a proposition. But note a peculiar difference here. Whereas you just cannot know whether the proposition expressed by 'He ran to the edge of the cliff and jumped' relative to the context of utterance is true or false unless you know who 'he' refers to, you can know what kind of situations will make 'He ran to the edge of the cliff and jumped' true relative to the context of utterance when you know who 'he' refers to but do not know in which direction the jumping took place (namely, all you need to know is whether any kind of jumping took place at all). The story about 'jump' is, in my view, similar to the story about 'big'. There is something you understand about 'big' even in the absence of a comparison class. Similarly, there is something you understand about 'jump' even in the absence of a specified direction of jumping (as I like to put it, you have the concept JUMP). The difference between 'jump' and, for example, 'jump down' is that the latter depicts a unique kind of a jumping situation whereas the former does not depict any unique state of affairs. And in understanding 'He ran to the edge of the cliff and jumped' one can bypass saturating the variable *x* as long as one remains aware that there was some direction in which jumping took place (which one necessarily does if one knows what 'jump' means). Thus, I would think that we are dealing with two different kinds of variables: (a) variables corresponding to referring expressions, that have to be saturated before a sentence token can be said to express a proposition; and (b) variables forming part of the semantic representations of (a class of) denoting expressions, that can be left unsaturated. In this latter case a sentence token can be said to express a proposition, although a different one from a sentence token where the value of such a variable has been saturated. I think that this difference is pretty plausible intuitively, and that it is the non-existence of such a difference that requires an argument in its defence.[24]

Consider now another example (after Wilson and Sperber, 2000[25]; also discussed in Carston, 2000). I drop by your place at around eight in the evening when you are having supper with some friends. You ask: 'Do you want to join us for supper?' I reply: 'No, thanks. I've eaten'. Relying on the principle of relevance, you assume that I intended to express the proposition that I have eaten supper that evening and thus represent the propositional content of my utterance as something like

'MR has eaten supper this evening'. (For simplicity's sake, here and thereafter I talk of 'this evening', 'an hour ago', an so on as if they were part of the propositional content.) According to the relevance theory, a standard semantic analysis runs into trouble because it represents the propositional content of my utterance as 'MR has eaten something at some point in a time span whose endpoint is the time of utterance' (see Wilson and Sperber, 2000, p. 234). But this is clearly not what you understood from my utterance. You reasonably infer that eating took place on the evening of the day in question, and that I have eaten enough not to want supper when you offered it to me. Let us now ignore the complication provided by the use of the present perfect tense, and address the questions posed by the complement of 'eat'.

Let the reply now be 'I ate an hour ago'. Although the question of truth-valuation was not prominent in the discussion of the eating example by either Wilson and Sperber (2000) or Carston (2000), it seems safe to assume that from the relevance-theoretical perspective the truth-evaluable entity in this case is the propositional content 'MR ate supper an hour ago' recovered by you from my utterance. As it happens, I have peculiar sleeping habits and on some days go to bed at around nine in the morning, wake up at around six in the evening and eat breakfast at around seven in the evening (by 'breakfast' I understand here the meal one eats up to three hours after getting up). In our example, from 'I ate an hour ago' said at around eight in the evening you recover the propositional content 'MR ate supper an hour ago'. The proposition I had in mind when saying 'I ate an hour ago' is 'MR ate breakfast an hour ago' but I intentionally encoded it as 'I ate an hour ago' knowing that most people react strangely when they hear 'I had breakfast an hour ago' at around eight in the evening.

But which of the two 'enriched' propositions (the one that arises in your mind and the one that I have in my mind) has to be evaluated with respect to its truth or falsity? It seems that neither. The only truth-evaluable proposition in this case is the one expressed by the sentence 'I ate an hour ago' relative to the context of utterance. And this holds regardless of whether the proposition arising in your mind is that MR ate supper an hour ago or that MR ate something that cannot properly be described as 'supper' an hour ago (see Wilson and Sperber, 2000, p. 237). Even the enriched propositions 'MR ate enough an hour ago not to want supper now' or 'MR ate a meal an hour ago' can differ in truth-conditions from 'MR ate (something) an hour ago' because I may well be on a diet and hiding this fact (and thus starving but refusing the invitation to supper). What I communicate in this last case ('I ate an hour ago') is not necessarily equivalent to 'I ate a meal an hour ago' even if, guided by the considerations of relevance, you take my utterance to be providing a reason for not wanting a meal. Since, presumably, mind-reading can fail in many other cases as well (after all, you can ask: 'What did you eat?'), it is not clear how any unarticulated constituents may form part of the truth-conditions of a sentence relative to the (minimal) context of utterance. Obviously, some of them seem to be better candidates than others, but there is no way of telling which of them are more ineliminable than others.

The introduction of unarticulated constituents into the proposition expressed by a sentence in context works as an alternative to the introduction of hidden variables into the logical form of a sentence. Relevance theorists oppose the hidden variables view by saying that there is no way to put restrictions on the number of hidden constituents that the logical form of a sentence might contain. According to the hidden variables view, the logical form of 'I have eaten' contains two hidden constituents: x for the complement of 'eat' and t for the time span during which eating took place. As relevance theorists argue, from here on there is no stopping, because then one may expect the logical form of any 'eat'-sentence to contain hidden constituents for the location where eating took place, the manner in which eating took place, possibly the instrument with which eating took place, and so on. But none of these may be relevant to a conversational exchange as in the example above. This is 'a *reductio* argument' intended to eliminate the two hidden variables by making the pragmatic process do the job of supplying constituents in both cases (Wilson and Sperber, 2000, p. 239). Curiously, Searle (quoted in Récanati, 1993, p. 260) follows almost the same line of reasoning, although pursuing a somewhat different purpose. According to Searle, a lot more unarticulated constituents contribute to understanding the literal meaning of a sentence such as 'I have eaten' than philosophers have traditionally supposed. These constituents are background assumptions: when somebody says to us 'I have eaten', we understand that she has eaten by putting food in her mouth, and not by stuffing it into her left ear or digesting it through the soles of her shoes (on the notion of Background see Searle, 1983). But, as Searle says, 'there is nothing whatever in the semantic content of 'eat' that precludes these interpretations'.

I believe that here a number of issues have been confused again. Let us begin with the question of what contributes what to the logical form of a sentence. After presenting the *reductio* argument, Wilson and Sperber conclude that since 'eat' cannot contribute the variables for place, manner, or instrument, the present perfect tense similarly does not contribute the time variable. But one does not follow from the other. The logical form of 'I ate an hour ago' does not have a hidden time variable, even though one could still run a *reductio* argument with respect to the semantic contribution of 'eat'. Presumably, if there is a hidden time variable in the logical form of 'I have eaten', it is contributed by the present perfect tense and not by the verb 'eat' (and no other potential variable is contributed by the tense). Thus, for our present purposes we can ignore the complication connected with the present perfect tense and concentrate on the possible contribution of 'eat'. As Wilson and Sperber argue, since it would be strange to think that the logical form of 'eat'-sentences contains variables for location, manner, instrument, and so on, there is similarly no reason to think that the logical form of 'eat'-sentences contains the variable for the complement of 'eat', or the stuff that is the object of eating.

However, there is an important difference between the complement of 'eat' and the locative, manner or instrumental constituents as potential candidates to the status of hidden variables, and it has to do with the denotation of 'eat'. 'Eat' denotes the relation of eating that holds between an entity doing the eating and an entity being eaten. This is why you may eat in the bathroom standing on your head and using your toes to put the food in your mouth: as long as what you did was eating, nothing else matters for establishing the truth-conditions of 'I ate an hour ago' relative to the context of utterance. But if nothing gets eaten, there is no eating.[26] Thus, it seems justified to think that the semantic representation of 'eat' is [EAT (x)] (or rather [EAT (y,x)] since somebody has to do the eating).[27]

For the same reason I think that Searle is wrong about what constitutes the literal meaning of 'eat'-sentences. In many respects, 'eat' is like 'water'. Our criteria for finding out whether something is water have changed, but the denotation of 'water' has not. Similarly, our ways of eating (at least the manner of eating) have changed since the Stone Age, but presumably the denotation of 'eat' has not. However, following Searle's reasoning we may well say that what we understand when somebody says to us 'I have eaten' is that she has eaten using a fork and sitting at a table, and so on. And here indeed nothing is to stop us from adding more and more unarticulated constituents. However, the question of what stereotypes 'eat' evokes and what is the literal meaning of 'eat' are different questions. Even if one day we all start eating by stuffing food into our left ears, we need to be able to say that the denotation of 'eat' has not changed (as long as what we shall be doing is eating). But Searle's approach will not let us do that.[28]

None of the above means that I doubt the role of pragmatic processes in linguistic communication. On the contrary, I believe that pragmatic processes are essential for linguistic (as well as non-linguistic) communication.[29] We successfully communicate using incomplete or literally incorrect sentences all the time, and this certainly requires an explanation. However, in my view, semantic mechanisms do a bigger job than relevance theorists allow them to do. This is why I think that the semantic theory has to be combined with a theory of concepts and recent developments in cognitive science related to the notion of embodiment. The following example contributes to further illustrating why such a step may be necessary.

Apart from free enrichment, the relevance theory proposes another pragmatic process that is involved into utterance interpretation. It is discussed in the relevance–theoretical literature under the names of 'concept loosening and broadening', 'ad hoc concept construction', 'communication of unencoded meanings' or 'pragmatic adjustment of conceptual encodings' (for details see Carston, 1996, 2000, 2002; Sperber and Wilson, 1998; Wilson and Sperber, 2000). Since this pragmatic process has received little attention in the debate between the more semantically and the more pragmatically oriented theorists, and since it is not exactly clear how it contributes to truth values, I shall briefly consider only one pertinent example. Still, this example is worth considering here because the relevance theory treats metaphor as an instance of 'loose talk' (Sperber and Wilson, 1986), and it will help us connect the discussion in the first three sections of this chapter with the discussion in the next section, where I describe how the no-polysemy view of conceptual structure proposes to answer some traditional questions in metaphor research.

In a section called 'The explicit communication of unencoded meanings' Wilson and Sperber (2000) discuss loose uses of language, and one of their examples is the adjective 'flat'. In their scenario, Peter and Mary discuss going on a cycling trip. Peter says that he feels out of shape. Mary replies: 'We could go to Holland. Holland is flat'. According to Wilson and Sperber, Peter understands Mary as saying that Holland is FLAT*, 'where FLAT* is the meaning indicated by "flat", and is such that Holland's being FLAT* is relevant-as-expected in the context' (2000, p. 244). For Wilson and Sperber, to say that Holland is flat is to speak loosely. In understanding Mary's utterance Peter has to rely on the principle of relevance in order to infer the intended meaning of 'flat' that Mary wanted to convey. When, in a similar scenario, Mary replies: 'We could go to Holland. Holland is a picnic', the same pragmatic process is involved into determining the meaning that Mary intended to convey. But, according to Wilson and Sperber, whereas Mary's use of 'flat' is a case of loose talk (or hyperbole; 2000, p. 245), her use of 'picnic' is clearly metaphorical.

There are many issues interwoven in Wilson and Sperber's discussion of these two examples, and it would be best to consider them one by one. The first thing that strikes one is that Wilson and Sperber seem to identify concepts with meanings. On the same page (2000, p. 244) they say that FLAT* is the meaning indicated by 'flat' and that Mary's utterance indicates the concept FLAT*. But then it is not clear how they could deal with the polysemy of 'flat', since on their account every use of 'flat' indicates a different meaning and a different concept. Thus, one might think that they consider 'flat' to be homonymous. However, this is not so. Their solution is a typical standard assumption solution. According to them, 'flat' has only one encoded meaning (primary or literal meaning, to use the standard assumption vocabulary) which, presumably, has to do with ideally flat surfaces or something approaching the flatness of an ideally flat surface. This is clear from the following quote: 'Being FLAT* is quite compatible with small-scale unevenness' (2000, p. 244).

Unfortunately, they do not specify how much of small-scale unevenness is compatible with non-loose uses of 'flat'. In other words, they never say what the encoded meaning of 'flat' is. And we may want to know this for the following reasons. Since Holland[30] is not flat enough to be non-loosely called 'flat', something presumably is. Something that serves as a standard to which Holland's flatness can be compared. On the other hand, Holland is only loosely, but not metaphorically flat. Whereas Holland is only metaphorically a picnic. Since Wilson and Sperber draw this distinction, there must be a definite (even if vague) boundary after which something cannot be called 'flat' even loosely, but only metaphorically. I do not think that the answer that 'flat' refers strictly and literally only to ideally flat surfaces would be satisfactory. Because, if we follow Wilson and Sperber's reasoning, we would have to say that there are no ideally flat surfaces. The answer that the encoded meaning of 'flat' is, for instance, 'flat as a table surface' is going to be similarly unsatisfactory. Since Holland is not a table surface, and, besides being a surface, bears no literal similarity to table surfaces, one would have to say that Holland can be only metaphorically flat. But we have already decided that Holland is only loosely, not metaphorically flat. What is then the encoded meaning of 'flat' on the basis of which one can derive FLAT*? Since FLAT* is the meaning indicated by 'flat' to be relevant in the context, there must be some meaning FLAT that 'flat' indicates when it is not used loosely. But what is it?

What I think is wrong with this account is that, even though, Wilson and Sperber say that they consider 'flat' in 'Holland is flat' to be a loose literal use, they are in fact treating it as if it were a metaphor. According to them, 'Holland is flat' should be evaluated with respect to one of the following: 'flat as far as ideally flat surfaces go' or 'flat as far as table surfaces go'. Why not: 'flat as far as pancakes go'? But, on the other hand, what is wrong with 'flat as far as geographic terrains go'(cf. Lewis, 1979)? This seems to be the literal meaning of 'flat' in 'Holland is flat', and it is possible to establish with a good deal of precision what it is for a geographic terrain to be flat. The notion of compositionality, according to which the meaning of a phrase is a function of the meanings of its lexical constituents, is perfectly compatible with a word having more than one meaning. And as I have been arguing in this book, a word's having more than one meaning is perfectly compatible with there being only one primitive concept corresponding to that word. In this sense, 'flat' is like 'big'; and the semantic representation of 'flat' is [FLAT (x)], where the value of x is 'for its own kind'. This is the reason why we can produce and interpret novel 'flat'-expressions or sentences: 'These cigarettes are flat', 'This bottle is flat', and so on. Come to think of it, isn't FLAT* just a different notation for [FLAT (x)]?

10.4 Metaphors forever

In the previous section I described how the no-polysemy view of conceptual structure can be put into a broader perspective of the semantics–pragmatics debate. In this section I propose to broaden this perspective even more and describe the position of the no-polysemy view on a number of issues that are often discussed in metaphor (and polysemy) research. Note that I am not going to discuss these issues in detail in one short section, whose main purpose is to show how the no-polysemy view fits into a very general picture of metaphor research, what its logical consequences are, and how it can be developed in some further directions. Two remarks have to be made before I begin.

According to the no-polysemy view, polysemous adjectives map onto psychologically primitive concepts through which we are causally connected to the external world and which incorporate certain perceptual and embodied schematisms. However, since concepts are not linguistic entities, the mapping passes the level of semantic representation where the contribution of a word to the logical form of complex expressions is specified. The level of semantic representation is the level where meanings appear. Thus, the no-polysemy view consists of two parts which can be distinguished and discussed on their own. In what follows I shall begin with the second, semantic part. Still, I believe that both parts are necessary to form a complete picture of the relationship between linguistic polysemy and the conceptual structure. Thus, I shall make this connection by proposing a new typology of lexical-conceptual relatedness. The other remark is that in discussing metaphor it is important to distinguish, as has been emphasized by Ray Gibbs (1994), between the process and product perspectives. The process perspective deals with questions of how metaphors are processed in real time during language comprehension. Much of recent research on the understanding of figurative language has concentrated on this perspective and the question whether the figurative meaning of a sentence is accessed directly or via its literal meaning continues to provoke lively debates (for the recent state of affairs see Gibbs, 2002; Giora, 2002). The product perspective, on the other hand, deals with theoretical questions of what is literal and what is metaphorical. It is this perspective that will primarily concern us here.

Consider the following examples: 'Juliet is the sun', 'Harry is a bulldozer', 'Sam is a gorilla'. One may have heard or read them a thousand times, but still one clearly perceives them as metaphors. In Davidsonian terms (Davidson, 1978/1984a), what makes all these sentences metaphorical is that there are no interesting extensions that would include Juliet and the sun, Harry and bulldozers, Sam and gorillas. We can also put this in slightly different terms. You must have already understood that I identify meanings (literal meanings) with denotations. On my account, 'bright sound' is a literal expression because it has a fixed use, because language speakers have an intuitive grasp of how sounds can be distinguished by their brightness, and because we can establish, in terms other than 'brightness', what it is for a sound to possess the property of brightness (being bright). Manfred Pinkal (1983, p. 47) wrote: 'Knowing the meaning of an expression is knowing the ways the expression can be made more precise'. Paraphrasing him, we can say that an expression is a literal expression when we know that its denotation can be made precise. But, presumably, there is no way of knowing what it is for Harry to possess the property of bulldozerness (being a bulldozer), for Juliet to possess the property of sunness (being a/the sun), and for Sam to possess the property of gorillness (being a gorilla). Apparently, both ordinary speakers and metaphor researchers agree on that (for I have never heard anyone say that these examples are not metaphors).[31]

Since the causal theory of reference and denotational semantics are essential to the no-polysemy view, one logical consequence of it is that, although individual words can be used metaphorically, they do not have metaphoric *meanings*. When a word acquires a new fixed use such that its denotation can be made precise, a word acquires a new literal meaning. Note that this view is perfectly compatible with the fact that analogical (metaphorical) and metonymic reasoning are the two major sources of linguistic change (Apresjan, 1974). Since, besides the semantic part, the no-polysemy view also makes a claim about the existence of psychologically primitive concepts, the following typology of lexical–conceptual relatedness can be proposed: (1) one word – one meaning – one concept; (2) one word – several meanings – one concept; (3) one word – several meanings – several concepts (related); (4) one word – several meanings – several concepts (unrelated).

The first and the fourth categories are the clearest ones. The first category includes unambiguous words such as 'water', the fourth category includes obvious homonyms such as 'bank' or 'plant'. The second category is the one with which we have been concerned in this book using synaesthetic and double-function adjectives as our main example. In my view, the second category also includes many cases of verbal polysemy ('keep',[32] 'cut', 'open',[33] and so on) and probably some cases of nominal polysemy (for example, 'slice' as in 'a slice of bread' and 'time slice'). Finally, the third category includes cases that are somewhere in-between polysemy and homonymy. A relatively large number of nouns belong to that category (the metaphorically motivated polysemy of 'leg', 'mouth', and so on) and probably some verbs as well (for example, 'change').[34] New uses of words introduced into the language of science by linguistic baptism also belong here (cf. Pylyshyn, 1993; Quine, 1979; see also Black, 1993).[35] Cases of logical, or metonymically motivated, polysemy ('book', 'chicken') are probably best treated as a special subcategory within this category.[36] Words from one category can move onto another category, although it remains to be seen which movements are possible. From the perspective of the no-polysemy view, the second category should prove to be the most stable. Whereas the most frequent case of movement between categories is probably the movement of metaphorically motivated polysemes from the third into the fourth category with the historical development of language when two (or more) meanings of a word stop being perceived as related.

One of the reasons for proposing this typology of lexical–conceptual relatedness has to do with the consideration that language speakers generally seem to have a pretty good intuitive grasp of whether a new use of a familiar word is an instance of polysemy (the second category in the above typology), metaphor (as in 'Harry is a bulldozer'), or linguistic baptism (the third category in the above typology). Note also that this typology is not particularly new or original. John Lyons (1977) noticed that the two categories of polysemy and homonymy are not sufficient to cover all cases of meaning relatedness and suggested that there exists a continuum from pure polysemy to pure homonymy. Several studies (for example, Durkin and Manning, 1989) show that words whose meanings are historically related are perceived as pure homonyms ('port' as harbour and as an alcoholic drink). Finally, cognitive semanticists (Lakoff and Johnson, 1980, p. 54) emphasized the difference between conceptual metaphors and such expressions as 'the leg of a table' or 'a head of cabbage' (thus somewhat astonishing traditional metaphor researchers, see Kittay, 1987).

One may get the impression that the no-polysemy view is probably closely related to the monosemy theory (Ruhl, 1989; see also Frazier and Rayner, 1990; Pickering and Frisson, 2001). The monosemy theory says that meanings of polysemous words are represented as very abstract underspecified entities which acquire their specific meanings in context. This theory has been strongly criticized by cognitive semanticists precisely for the view that sometimes the abstract meaning underlying all other meanings of a polysemous word is so abstract that it cannot be specified semantically (Gibbs, 1994; Lakoff and Johnson, 1980). So, does the no-polysemy view say the same thing as the monosemy theory? The right answer is yes and no. What the no-polysemy view has in common with the monosemy theory is that it also postulates a certain level at which different meanings of a polyseme are related in a non-metaphorical way. But there are more differences than similarities between the two views. According to the no-polysemy view, this 'abstract' level is the level of psychologically primitive concepts, not the level of meanings. Further, whereas the monosemy theory seems to identify meanings with definitions, however abstract and inexpressible (cf. Caramazza and Grober, 1976), the no-polysemy view treats neither concepts nor meanings as definitional. According to the no-polysemy view, the content of concepts is constituted by the causal mind-world relations, and meanings are denotations.

A few paragraphs back I have proposed a typology of lexical–conceptual relatedness which distinguishes between three rather than two types of lexical ambiguity. Thus, I am not committed to the view that all instances of polysemy should be treated in the same way. I have also mentioned some examples of polysemous words that, in my opinion, belong either to the second (several meanings – one concept) or the third (several meanings – several related concepts) category. The main objective of this book was to argue that synaesthetic and double-function adjectives belong to the second category, and thus that their 'alternative' meanings are not their metaphoric meanings (either in the sense of being understood through something else or in the sense of being metaphorically motivated). However, the formulation of this proposal required an extensive consideration of a number of empirical and theoretical issues. In this connection, I do not think that it is possible to establish *a priori*, solely on the basis of one's own personal preferences, whether the different meanings of a polyseme are expressions of the same psychologically primitive concept, or whether they depend on that polyseme's primary meaning via metaphor, family resemblances, and so on.[37] Similarly, I think that a number of polysemes are best treated as belonging to the third category (one word – several meanings – several related concepts). Their 'new' meanings may have appeared as a result of an analogical (metaphorical) comparison or via some other route, but what matters is that all these meanings express different concepts, however related one may feel them to be. As far as the third category goes, I am ready to agree with Fodor and Lepore (1998) that meanings of words can overlap in all sorts of ways, but that this is not an interesting question for semntics.

Psycholinguistic study can probably show whether the typology of lexical–conceptual relatedness proposed above has any real psychological basis. However, it has to be emphasized that linguistic awareness of those who study language professionally should not be confused with linguistic awareness of ordinary speakers. Language professionals distinguish between different types of lexical relatedness, whereas it is perfectly possible for ordinary speakers to perceive the meanings of a polyseme, or even a monoseme, as totally unrelated (is a big mouse more like a big window or a big swimming pool?), as well as entertain together the meanings of a homonym, as often happens in puns and jokes (cf. Hayakawa, 1974; see also Giora, 2002; Nerlich and Clarke, 2001).[38] According to the no-polysemy view, all occurrences of a polysemous word (from the second category) map onto the same psychologically primitive concept. However, the mapping passes the intermediate stage of semantic representation. It follows that if a meaning of a polyseme is the most prominent on someone's mind, it will be the first to be activated. In this connection, I believe that Rachel Giora's (1997, 1998, 1999, 2002) graded salience hypothesis, according to which the first meaning that is activated is the most salient meaning, is probably the closest to truth. Still, I also believe that a more careful discrimination between types of lexical ambiguity (as well as between polysemes and metaphors, both novel and familiar) during psycholinguistic study can reveal different processing effects (cf. Klepousniotou, 2002).

So far we have stayed close to the level of individual words. Let us now move to the sentence level. According to the no-polysemy view, sentences (unlike words) can have a metaphoric meaning. And the reason they can have a metaphoric meaning is that metaphors can be used to express propositions. However, a metaphor does not express a unique proposition even relative to the context of utterance. It expresses an indefinite range of propositions. The story about metaphors is in many respects similar to the story about unarticulated constituents: you may stand a pretty good chance at guessing what somebody had in mind, but you may as easily be wrong. Just as with unarticulated constituents, the representation of some propositional content that you may form after hearing a metaphor could differ drastically from the proposition that somebody wanted to express with the help of that metaphor. Or else, you may not even form a single representation, but instead let your thoughts float freely. With metaphors, there is no way of telling. For this reason, even though metaphors express propositions, they do not express truth-evaluable propositions.

According to the no-polysemy view, the word 'bulldozer' does not have a metaphoric meaning. Still, I am saying that the sentence 'Harry is a bulldozer' does. How can these two views be reconciled? In fact, there is no contradiction between them. The no-polysemy view distinguishes between the level of meanings and the level of concepts. In this connection, I think that the greatest achievement of metaphor research was to stop talking about metaphor in terms of meaning transfer, and start talking about it in terms of *ad hoc* concept construction (as do Robyn Carston, Dan Sperber and Deirdre Wilson; see page 163), on-line concept construction (as do Sam Glucksberg and Boaz Keysar, see Glucksberg and Keysar, 1990, 1993; Glucksberg, 2001), or conceptual blending (as do Gilles Fauconnier and Mark Turner, see Fauconnier and Turner, 1996, 1998, 2002). I do not necessarily agree with everything in these theories (as they do not have to be in agreement on everything themselves), but the notion of on-line concept construction is perfectly consistent with the no-polysemy view. Since concepts are constituents of thoughts, you may entertain an indefinite number of thoughts in connection with Harry and bulldozers. The thoughts that come to your mind on encountering 'Harry is a bulldozer' may be evoked by some stereotypical properties associated with bulldozers or by your personal associations. When it comes to metaphor interpretation, no one is right and no one is wrong. This is what makes metaphors so attractive. And this is why you do not have to worry if, like me, you still do not know what 'Juliet is the sun' means.[39]

There are many other issues in metaphor research that I have not touched on here, but here is not the place to discuss them. Completing this section I would like to mention just one of them, the pragmatics of metaphor. Why do people speak metaphorically? There have been many answers to this question, and many of them are right answers (see Gibbs, 1994, and Stern, 2000 for a discussion of these issues). The only difference in answering this question that is an immediate consequence of the no-polysemy view is that pretty often they speak *literally*, not metaphorically.

11
A Very Short Conclusion

I have thrown into one melting pot informational atomism, the causal theory of reference, denotational semantics, and the theory of cognitive embodiment, but I hope that instead of getting a scary monster I have told you a story about the relationship between language and conceptual structure that may at least be partly true. The main objective of this book was to argue that there is a lot more literalness in language than has traditionally been supposed. I have argued this on the example of synaesthetic and double-function adjectives, and I hope to have eliminated them from the class of metaphors. In the course of this book I have also mentioned many other examples, but I am not as much committed to my treatment of them as I am to my treatment of synaesthetic and double-function adjectives.

This book is not against metaphor. And it is not against any particular theory. This book is about words, meanings and concepts. And the relationship between them. And synaesthetic and double-function adjectives. I have argued that all of their meanings are literal meanings. And this is so because they are all related at the level of psychologically primitive concepts. But concepts are not meanings, and the no-polysemy view will not get anyone into a muddle. Concepts are mental entities through which we are causally connected to the external world and which incorporate perceptual and embodied schematisms. Meanings are denotations, and, as I have argued, the no-polysemy view of conceptual structure does not contradict the causal theory of reference. On the contrary, it unifies the various notions of meaning that have been around for a long time: the philosophers' insight that meaning has to do with truth and reference, the linguists' notion of linguistic meaning (which I identify with semantic representation), and the psychologists' empirical observation that a word may have several different meanings that are stored differently in memory. Besides, the no-polysemy view agrees with a significant amount of empirical data across a number of research fields.

Interdisciplinary studies are important because they can reveal gaps in our understanding. Interdisciplinary studies provide new insights into the nature of our quests. In this respect, I find it hard to understand the antagonism with which philosophers often meet theories in linguistics and psychology and with which linguists and psychologists often speak of philosophical theories. This book is an attempt, for a narrowly defined topic, to fuse my fondness and respect for philosophy with evidence collected in empirical fields of study. Because of its novelty and, perhaps, eccentricity, it could not but be programmatic. Some doubts may have been resolved but other issues have to be clarified and refined, both in their empirical and theoretical aspects. Nevertheless, I hope that this book can serve as a launching pad for reconsidering some of our unjustified assumptions and for redirecting our inquiries to make different approaches to human language and cognition work for their mutual benefit. I have discussed many theories in this book and I strongly feel that all of them say something that is true. It may be time to bring all the best insights together.

Further research may confirm or disconfirm the no-polysemy view of conceptual structure. But it will have to be carried out with the global picture in mind, and include neurological, neurolinguistic, psychological, psychophysical, psycholinguistic, developmental, cross-linguistic and evolutionary data of the kind discussed here and probably covering an even broader area. It is also worth remembering that whatever evidence we discover, we also have to interpret it coherently. In this book I have presented a way to interpret the various data that bear on the question of synaesthetic and double-function polysemy. It may not be *the* right way, but the no-polysemy view can explain more than other interpretations which rely on the assumption that synaesthetic and double-function adjectives can have only one literal meaning. Since the standard assumption is wrong about synaesthetic and double-function adjectives, it may prove to be wrong about many other cases as well. The reinterpretation of data in the light of a new theory is the way in which science often proceeds. Whatever evidence we discover, our interpretation of it has to be consistent with other evidence and philosophically coherent. The best way is always in the middle, in trying to bring evidence and coherence as close as possible. This book is an attempt to do exactly that for the issues of metaphor, polysemy and the conceptual structure.

Notes

1 Introduction: On the Nature of the Literal–Metaphorical Distinction

1. Here and hereafter when I say 'polyseme' I primarily refer to polysemous adjectives of the synaesthetic and double-function types.
2. The story could become more complicated if one took into account that the requirement of finite vocabulary follows from Davidson's holistic approach to language. According to Davidson (1984b), semantic features of words are abstracted from semantic features of sentences. Which is to say that the meaning of a word is determined by the role it plays in sentences in which it occurs. The problem of abstracting meanings of words from meanings of sentences is greatly simplified if one assumes that words are not polysemous. However, since meaning holism is only one possible theoretical position, I do not discuss it here.

   We can discern another motivation behind the semantic normativity answer. It has to do with 'norm' as something that one ought to comply with. And this is precisely the approach to literal language that was criticized by I.A. Richards. If one's philosophy of language is reminiscent of books on good grammar and style which teach that one should not say 'strong' of lights (even though language speakers do it all the time), then it is probably bad philosophy.
3. There is another positive claim suggested by Davidson's essay. I am not sure that Davidson would agree with it (however, see Davidson, 1984c), but perhaps metaphors do reveal something about the world after all. It might be that never-dying metaphors ('Juliet is the sun', 'Christ was a chronometer', 'Tolstoy was an infant') reveal to us what categories we cannot form, and thus, what categories of things do not exist in the world.

2 Metaphor in Cognitive Linguistics

1. Later (Lakoff and Johnson, 1999) the name was changed to 'theory of embodied realism'. However, the content of the theory was not affected, and I use the terms 'experientialism' and 'theory of embodied realism' interchangeably.
2. Here are a few examples: 'not only language, but our cognition and hence our language, operates metaphorically' (Sweetser, 1990, p. 8); 'metaphor and the mental processes it entails are basic to language and cognition' (Goatly, 1997, p. 1). Sometimes such claims have clearly been exaggerated: 'metaphor neither pertains merely to phenomena occurring in the domain of poetic language nor is a linguistic phenomenon per se, but rather it is a much more widespread process...; ...recent psychological studies have *fully established* metaphoricality as a central cognitive mechanism' (Shen, 1992, p. 568, italics mine). To

have an idea of how deeply sceptical (justly, in my opinion) some psychologists are one may have a look at Murphy (1996) and Garnham (1989).

3   Lakoff (1990) describes two 'scientific commitments' of cognitive linguists: the generalization commitment and the cognitive commitment. The generalization commitment requires one to seek general principles by which human languages operate. The cognitive commitment requires that accounts of language be consistent with what we know about human cognition generally (p. 2). Lakoff and Johnson's theory of conceptual metaphor responds to these two requirements since an explanation for polysemy is given with reference to sensorimotor structuring of experience.

4   See Lakoff and Johnson (1980) for a critique of the 'strong' and 'weak' homonymy views. According to the strong homonymy view, the two meanings of 'attack' as in 'They attacked the fort' and 'They attacked my argument' are different and unrelated. According to the weak homonymy view, 'attack' has two different meanings that are related through similarity of meaning. Lakoff and Johnson argue that since nobody has shown what this similarity of meaning is, 'in practice there seem to be only strong homonymy theories' (p. 114). But the strong homonymy view is not psychologically plausible because the two meanings of 'attack' are related in our understanding, unlike the two meanings of 'bank' as in 'The Bank of England' and 'the bank of the river'.

5   It has to be remarked that although Gibbs says that '[t]he problem of polysemy cannot be solved by simply distinguishing between a primary, or literal, and a derived meaning' (1994, p. 43), he has no such doubts about synaesthetic and double-function terms. For him 'sharp' has only one literal meaning, and applies properly and non-metaphorically only to cutting instruments (Gibbs, 1999b). The assumption that polysemous adjectives have only one literal meaning is in fact shared by cognitive linguists and 'objectivists' (those who, according to Lakoff and Johnson (1999), hold that concepts have to fit the world uniquely).

6   It must be clear why I say here 'metaphor and polysemy'. Cognitive semanticists talk about 'conceptual metaphor', but the examples they mostly deal with would be considered by many researchers as examples of polysemy (cf. Jackendoff and Aaron, 1991). According to cognitive semantics, conceptual metaphor operates in thought, and polysemy is its manifestation at the linguistic level.

7   Gibbs (1994, 1996) is probably the only cognitive linguist who admits being aware of criticisms. Unlike him, Lakoff and Johnson (see, for example, Lakoff and Johnson, 1999) seem to be unaware of any critical literature.

8   Johnson and Lakoff (2002) deny being empiricists and thus say that my critique does not apply to them. However, they miss the point. Whatever label they choose for their views, the point remains: the theory of conceptual metaphor is only consistent with an empiricist position.

9   Mandler (1994) presents her account as an alternative to Piaget's idea of developmental stages with its emphasis on parallel development of sensorimotor and cognitive functions (Piaget, 1947). There are indeed striking similarities between Piaget's developmental theory and Lakoff and Johnson's experientialism in that both connect intelligence with sensorimotor functioning. However, Piaget never endorsed a clearly empiricist

position (for Piaget's own comments on the issue see Piatelli-Palmarini, 1980, pp. 150, 157). Besides, since Mandler's early visual schemas are supposed to give rise to concepts that ground linguistic meaning (Mandler, 1992b), her theory is subject to the critique that Chomsky directed a long time ago against Piaget: linguistic development of blind children is not retarded by their blindness but, on the contrary, accelerated (Piaget, 1980b, pp. 170–1).

The similarity between Piaget's views on human conceptual development and experientialism and was also noticed by Jackendoff (1992): '...an extension of spatial concepts to this new domain [the domain of ownership] cannot take place unless some aspects of the domain are already made available by the primitives of conceptual structure, that is, unless they are innate. Therefore, even if Piaget and Lakoff and correct in thinking that abstract concepts are built by extending perceptual concepts, they are not correct in claiming that the abstract concepts therefore need no innate basis' (p. 60).

10 Not all cognitive linguists share Lakoff and Johnson's philosophical views. Thus, Steen believes that the experientialist stand is 'immaterial' to the work on metaphor (1994, p. 9). Steen and Gibbs make a similar disclaimer:

> children may acquire conceptual metaphors wholesale from their learning language without necessarily having to re-experience all the cultural and embodied events that originally gave rise to these conceptual metaphors, events that also keep these alive in human conceptual systems. It is not necessary for every adult to have undergone the same set of cultural experiences motivating the bulk of conventional conceptual metaphors for these metaphors to be a significant part of people's personal conceptual and linguistic repertoires. Adults may have simply learned how to use particular words in a conventionally metaphorical fashion on suitable occasions. (1999, p. 4)

Unfortunately, one cannot have it both ways – one cannot claim that conceptual metaphors are constitutive of our conceptual structure *and* that conceptual metaphors are acquired after language has been learned. For if we grant that concepts exist prior to language and are created not by language, but by our interaction with physical and social environments (this assumption is widely shared by cognitive linguists; see Gibbs, 1999a, p. 148), then it is not clear how the acquisition of conceptual metaphors from conventionalized linguistic expressions could produce changes in conceptual organization (as opposed to the way we talk about things). In Lakoff and Johnson's theory the dependence of abstract concepts on directly meaningful concepts is explained through pre-conceptual schemas which determine the parameters of human experience. This is why Lakoff says that experientialist cognition is the most promising approach to cognitive semantics (1988, p. 120). If the experientialist stand is removed from the theory of conceptual metaphor, the idea of metaphor as a fundamental cognitive process stops being exploited in any interesting sense.

Gibbs (1999a) claims that metaphors are conceptual (for example, ANGER IS FLUID IN A HEATED CONTAINER) because they belong to the cultural world. There is, as it were, a large network of culturally shared conceptual metaphors of which individual speakers partake to a greater or smaller extent. However, this claim does not validate the view that conceptual metaphors are concept constitutive. In any naturalistic account (and this is what cognitive linguistics claims to be) if you have the concept ANGER, it is you who has it, not the culture to which you belong (although of course you share this concept with other speakers of your linguistic community; cf. Marconi, 1997: Chapter 5). Besides, it has to be remarked that from the perspective of embodied cognition, this conceptual metaphor for anger is a bit suspicious: if conceptual primacy is determined in terms of the phenomenological experience of the body, the concept of anger cannot depend on any concepts from the field of fluid dynamics (see Barsalou, 1999 for the evidence that the concept of anger is acquired directly rather than metaphorically). Thus, it appears that outside the experientialist framework no serious claim can be made about the constitutive role of metaphor in conceptualization.

11 Experientialists talk of abstract concepts as 'skeletal' and abstract domains as 'inferentially poor', and claim that, because of this, our understanding of abstract domains, such as love, has to be structured by our understanding of some concrete and directly meaningful domains, such as journeys. However, experimental studies do not confirm this claim (Glucksberg and McGlone, 1999). Besides, if experientialists were right, then eating should also be travelling ('half-way through steaks'). But it is doubtful that in an *experientialist* story travelling can be more primary than eating.

As has been noted many times, cognitive linguists often overdo their rhetoric (cf. Stern, 2000). Thus, Lakoff and Turner write: 'As a consequence, the understanding of life as a journey permits not just a single simpleminded conceptualization of life but rather a rich and varied one' (1989, p. 61). Try as I might, I have no idea what a 'simpleminded conceptualization of life' might be.

12 Lawrence Barsalou (1999) proposed a theory of perceptual symbol systems which is similar to experientialism in that it considers perceptual simulation as a basis of conceptual structure. As will become clear later, I agree with Barsalou about the importance of perceptual simulation in conceptual organization. However, his treatment of abstract concepts suffers from the same problems as experientialism because abstract concepts are supposed to be understood through the activation of perceptual simulators. Thus, according to Barsalou, we understand the expression 'the end of time'

> by simulating the ends of known processes, such as *the end of growth* and *the end of walking*.... Applying the same schematic simulation to *time* yields an interpretation of *the end of time*, even though we have not experienced it. Simple-mindedly, we might imagine all the clocks stop running – and imagine what it would be like. With a little more sophistication, we might imagine all change in the world ending, with everything freezing in place. Or, we might simply imagine all matter disappearing into nothing. (p. 647)

The problem with this, as with all imagistic accounts of how we understand abstract concepts, is that one does not need to experience images in order to understand linguistic expressions or think. Imagining all the clocks stop running can go together with entertaining the complex concept of all the clocks stop running. However, imagining it till you drop will not give you the concept of the end of time. There is a very simple example which shows that thought is not imagery-dependent. I can think of my cat having sixty legs, but I cannot imagine him with sixty legs.

13   One also gets the impression that Lakoff and Johnson tend to oversimplify the matters. Thus, they refer to artificial neural modelling research to claim that perceptual mechanisms 'can actually do *conceptual* work in language learning and reasoning' (Lakoff and Johnson, 1999, p. 38). Although it is a popular and to some extent justified view, one has to tread carefully around the issue of perceptual-cognitive continuity. Unfortunately, Lakoff and Johnson's approach is simplistic because it presupposes that exactly the same neural structures can be employed by the brain for tasks of differing complexity. Thus, for instance, they say that 'the neural structure of motor control must already have all the capacities necessary to characterize aspect...and its logic' (p. 43).

Evidently, having brain programs for initiating, continuing and completing actions is a prerequisite for having conceptual structure able to support the logic of aspect, but this alone does not amount to having conceptual structure from which an aspect-expressing language could develop (on the notion of brain programs see Young, 1987). No serious account of human cognition can be derived from artificial models if the representational complexity of real brains is ignored. Even contemporary *empiricist* theories view cognitive development not as a matter of the same neural configurations and pathways being employed for novel tasks, but as a hierarchical construction of increasingly complex representations (Quartz, 1999, Quartz and Sejnowsky, 1997, 2000).

14   On the whole, some semblance of plausibility in Grady's account comes from the fact that he selectively restricts the range of meanings of the polysemes he discusses. One could presumably invent a story why HEAVY correlates with DIFFICULT in early experience thus giving rise to 'heavy problem'. However, early experiential correlations that would underlie 'heavy music' or 'heavy smell' are not so easy to find.

15   In responding to my critical comments Johnson and Lakoff (2002) refer to fMRI and ERP data showing that the part of the motor cortex connected to the hands is activated not only during hand experience, but also in understanding sentences about the hands. However, this is something I have never argued against. My critique was directed against the theory of primary metaphors which is *falsified* by neural evidence (Johnson and Lakoff leave it without any comment). As to the data they cite, it perfectly fits the view I develop in this book. Moreover, there are good reasons to expect this part of the motor cortex to be activated in understanding sentences about pens, hammers, and other objects that we manipulate (see, for example, Gainotti *et al.*, 1995; Martin *et al.*, 1995, 1996; Warrington and Shallice, 1984). However, nobody quite knows how to individuate HAND, PEN and HAMMER in terms of the patterns of neural activation.

There is another comment that I cannot help making. Johnson and Lakoff (2002) accuse me of not understanding their theory and say that in my critique they 'can spot a great deal of Anglo-American analytic philosophy...as well as some flashes of Plato, Aristotle, Descartes, and Kant'. Since this is a book about metaphor I hope I may be allowed a metaphorical comparison. If I were a composer and somebody said to me in an accusatory tone that they could spot in my work flashes of Bach, Mozart, Beethoven and Rachmaninov, and that I failed to understand country music, I must say that this would have left me totally unimpressed.

3 The 'Hot' Polysemy

1. Of course, since then vision and colour naming research have changed. For a critique of Berlin and Kay's hypothesis see Van Brakel (1993) and Saunders and Van Brakel (1997). However, as powerful critique of Van Brakel (1993) by Hardin (1993), and multiple peer reviews of Saunders and Van Brakel (1997) show, the assumption that there are nontrivial constraints on colour categorization, and that the opponent theory can help us specify these constraints, remain the main working hypotheses of vision and colour naming research.
2. What makes capsaicin particularly interesting for pain researchers is that it is a noxious (pain-producing) chemical stimulus which, nonetheless, does not mimic the action of known chemical modulators of nociceptor function (nociceptors are receptors for painful stimuli). The action of capsaicin on nociceptors is however similar to that of its analogue, resiniferatoxin, from the flowering cactus *Euphorbia resinifera* (Caterina *et al.*, 1997, p. 819).
3. The receptor is called vanilloid receptor because vanilloid moiety constitutes an essential chemical component of capsaicin and resiniferatoxin structures. According to Liu *et al.* (1998), its existence was first postulated in 1975 from the structure–activity analyses of a number of capsaicin analogues.
4. Recently Julius and colleagues have also identified the COOL channel that responds to cold stimuli and menthol (McKenny *et al.*, 2002; Zuker, 2002). Although hot and cold seem to go together in our experience, it is interesting to note that noxious cold and heat are detected by different mechanisms.
5. Chaucer: 'On this roote [contrition] eek spryngeth a seed of grace...and this seed is egre and hoot' ('hoot' = 'hŏt').
6. Ancient Greek: *English–Greek Dictionary* and *Greek–English Lexicon*; Latin: *Smith's Smaller English–Latin Dictionary* and *Oxford Latin Dictionary*; Italian: *Sansoni-Harrap Standard Italian and English Dictionary* and *The Collins Italian Dictionary* (wordreference.com); Spanish: *Collins Spanish–English English–Spanish Dictionary*; French: *Collins and Robert French–English English–French Dictionary*, *Harrap's Standard French and English Dictionary* and *Harrap's New Standard French and English Dictionary*; German: *Collins German–English English–German Dictionary*; Dutch: *Cassell's Dutch Dictionary*; Russian: *Modern English–Russian Dictionary* and *The Oxford Russian Dictionary*.

    It is curious to note that dictionaries are sometimes inconsistent in their translations. Thus, for French, *Collins* and *Robert* does not translate 'hot' as 'piquant', but translates 'piquant' as 'hot' or 'pungent'. Similarly, *Harrap's* translates 'hot' as 'piquant', but does not translate 'piquant' as 'hot'.
7. 'Piquant' came into English through French 'piquer', which means 'prick, irritate' (COED). *Le Robert Quotidien* defines one of the meanings of 'piquant' as 'Qui présente une or plusieurs pointes acérées capables de piquer, de percer ⇒ pointu'.

8 The material in the body text of this section mostly comes from Fields (1987).
9 Although visceral pain is different, and there are specific visceral nociceptors, it may also be relevant to mention that several studies have shown the activation of Aδ nociceptors by capsaicin in viscera (Sann, 1998).
10 Some evidence suggests that in the CNS there is not only differentiation, but further integration of stimuli from different modalities. Defrin *et al.* (2002) tested subjects with spinal cord injury who suffered from loss of thermal sensibility, and discovered that in areas with no thermal sensibility the application of warm and cold stimuli produced a sensation of pricking pain.
11 It is interesting to note that the 9th edition of COED does not mark 'hot' in the sense of 'pungent' *figurative*.
12 The sample in the body text includes only those languages with which I can claim at least some personal acquaintance. Finnish, for example, follows the spicy-hot association: 'hot' (of taste) is 'tulinen' which translates into English as 'firesome' (the word for hot temperature is 'kuuma'; I am grateful to Jussi Tuovinen for the information on Finnish).
13 Note that, unlike English, Russian has only one word for 'spicy' or 'hot' ('ostryj').

4 Across Sensory Modalities

1 The title of this section alludes to Lawrence Marks's article 'Bright sneezes and dark coughs, loud sunlight and soft moonlight' (1982a).
2 Jakobson (1968) remarks on the existence of phenomenal similarity between sound and colour systems, noting the tendency of the vowels *o* and *u* to be associated with dark colours, and the vowels *e* and *i* with light colours. However, Cytowic's (1989a) reports on synaesthetes' systems of colour associations show that such generalizations may be problematic. Whether there are any important analogies between the development and pathologies of the colour and the phonological systems (Jakobson, 1968, p. 84) still remains to be ascertained as this issue has not been raised in recent discussions of synaesthesia.
3 The emphasis that Cytowic places on the involuntary character of synaesthetic perception may suggest that cross-modal associations made by non-synaesthetes are 'voluntary' – a view that is not entirely justified in view of the evidence collected by Marks *et al.* I return to this question later.
4 Nonethless, elsewhere Cytowic quotes a synaesthete's report which shows that the induced sensations may sometimes have a strong negative effect: 'The only real problem is that when I am driving and a very loud sound comes on...it is hard to see. The image intensity is directly proportional to the sound level. People laugh when I say "turn that down, I can't see where I'm driving."' (1989a, p. 51).
5 The relevance of this discussion will become clear later in the chapter. Here I would like to remark that Cytowic would most probably disagree with the understanding of synaesthesia as a compensatory mechanism. However, this view does not contradict his understanding of synaesthesia as a normal brain process which, in most individuals, does not arise to consciousness (Cytowic,

1995). The view of synaesthesia as a mechanism of compensation for symbolization deficits is also consistent with both cortical disinhibition (Grossenbacher and Lovelace, 1999) and cross-wiring (Ramachandran and Hubbard, 2001b) models of the neural basis of synaesthesia.

6 According to most accounts of multisensory integration, input from vision dominates input from other modalities (for example, in the ventriloquism effect; Stein and Meredith, 1993, p. 3). However, recent work by Shams *et al.* (2000) suggests that auditory information can also alter visual perception (for further evidence see Shimojo and Shams, 2001).

7 Note, however, that the fact that hallucinogenic drugs such as LSD can induce synaesthetic experiences in non-synaesthetes may speak in favour of normal neural connectivity in synaesthetes (Grossenbacher and Lovelace, 2001, p. 40).

8 Note that what I propose to take for granted are *perceptual* similarities, not corresponding linguistic expressions.

9 It has to be remarked that in the later work the holistic account of meaning is rejected: 'Unlike percepts, words are defined absolutely, meaningfully, and discretely in their own right, and thus do not have to be defined in comparison to another word' (Martino and Marks, 1999, p. 920).

10 Note, however, that it is not entirely clear what 'synaesthesia' means in this quotation since Marks *et al.* do not draw a distinction between synaesthetic perception and the ability to form cross-modal matches.

11 Marks *et al.* also found that adjectives are easier to translate across modalities than nouns. It is possible that the translation of adjectives across modalities ('high-pitched' is judged brighter than 'low-pitched') has to do with perceptual correspondences (for instance, the perception of intensity in different modalities). On the other hand, the translation of nouns ('sunlight' is not so readily judged to be higher in pitch than 'moonlight') is may be more difficult because perceptual attributes are not part of their denotations (for instance, pitch has little relevance for establishing the meaning of 'sunlight' or 'moonlight').

12 I do not mean that it is impossible to describe sneezes. For example, they may be loud. What I mean is that we dot not normally assign much importance to the description of sneezes. On the contrary, certain sound qualities of voices enter into the interpretation of utterances as paralinguistic cues. For example, Morton and Trehub write: 'speech marked by high pitch, rapid tempo, large pitch range, and bright voice quality signals happiness' (2001, p. 834; note that the expression 'bright voice' does not appear in quotes thus suggesting that the authors do not take it to be a metaphorical description of some voice quality).

13 As Martino and Marks themselves note, different effects were observed for perceptual and linguistic stimuli. Thus, Garner interference was diminished or even absent from interactions with linguistic stimuli (1999, pp. 918–20).

14 I discuss the cognitive semantics treatment of synaesthetic adjectives in Chapter 8. For the moment it will suffice to say that according to the experientialist explanation (see Chapter 2), adjectives acquire alternative meanings through associations made between co-occurring properties in an individual's early experience (primary metaphors). Such possibility has

been considered by Marks *et al.* (1987; see section 4. 3), but rejected on the grounds that many cross-modal associations (such as the association between loudness and brightness) cannot be derived from experience because their presence had been documented at early infancy. Besides, the co-occurrence of brightness and loudness is not experientially salient even at later stages of development. Some of the data discussed in this chapter is also discussed by Gibbs (1994, pp. 413–17) as a manifestation of metaphorical ability in infants. But since he does not provide any independent argument for his view (that is, why the ability to make cross-modal associations is a *metaphorical* ability) and does not address alternative explanations, the considerations offered in section 4.4 apply to his view as well.

15 In her commentary on Marks *et al.* (1987) Smith writes:

> The central contribution of this work is the specification of a perceptual basis for certain metaphors. The developmental story about metaphors offered in the *Monograph* rings true to me. The authors suggest that metaphors such as 'loud lights' might not actually be metaphors early in development. Instead, 'loud lights' may simply be a statement concerning a directly perceived similarity. Perceptual 'metaphors' may become metaphors only with development and with the organization of specific sensory dimensions as dimensions. Not until loudness and brightness are organized distinctly can one be used to illuminate the other metaphorically. (1987, p. 98)

Note that Smith has to put one of her 'metaphors' in quotes. It is obvious that the expression 'perceptual metaphor' strikes her as a contradiction in terms. However, as long as one accepts the standard assumption, one would struggle forever trying to show how and why statements about directly perceived similarities become metaphors.

16 There are cases even more interesting and puzzling than 'bright' – they are adjectives that do not clearly belong to only one sensory modality, for instance, 'dry' or 'soft'. While one might argue that 'bright' is primarily about vision, it is not clear that this could be done for these two examples.

17 Although Cytowic and Marks are on the opposite poles of the debate concerning the relation between synaesthetic perception and non-synaesthetic cross-modal associations, Marks once expressed a similar view: 'Metaphoric expressions of the unity of the sense evolved in part from fundamental synesthetic relationships but owe their creative impulse to the mind's ability to transcend these intrinsic correspondences and forge new multisensory meanings. Intrinsic, synesthetic relations express the correspondences that are, extrinsic relations assert the correspondences that can be' (1978, p. 103).

18 As Dingwall (1995) notes in his commentary, in Wilkins and Wakefield's hypothesis the parieto-occipito-temporal junction includes the angular gyrus, the supramarginal gyrus and Wernicke's area. It is interesting to note that Ramachandran and Hubbard (2001b) identify the angular gyrus as the structure crucially involved in cross-modal linguistic associations, and also

speculate on the possible connection between the evolution of language and synaesthesia. (Although as their discussion suggests, what they have in mind is not true synaesthetic perception, but rather the more general ability to form cross-modal associations.)

19 The ability to transfer the recognition of properties from one modality to another is often referred to as metaphorical mapping. However, since this terminology may imply in the context of the overall discussion that chimpanzees may be able to distinguish between the literal and the metaphorical I avoid using it in the body text.

20 In this chapter I do not discuss cross-linguistic data. However, at least two more languages from different groups – Russian and Spanish – have the same synaesthetic adjectives as English.

21 Of course, this is only a speculation. Perhaps future research will show whether the reorganization in the processing of perceptual information and the emergence of human conceptual structure had any connection between them. The no-polysemy view of conceptual structure does not depend on this particular evolutionary scenario. Note also that in accepting Wilkins and Wakefield's scenario I do not necessarily accept their view of the neuroanatomical basis for conceptual structure. Such elusive entities as concepts may be widely distributed in the brain (Damasio and Tranel, 1993), and any attempt at localization in one neural site may fail.

Perhaps a better candidate for a neural structure whose reorganization resulted in the emergence of specifically human conceptual capacities is the prefrontal cortex. The prefrontal cortex is implicated in a large number of cognitive tasks, some of which have been said to be crucial for supporting human-like conceptual structure. They include: high-level integration of sensory and limbic inputs (see Jacobs and Horner, 1995); the ability to go beyond here and now aspects of perceptual experience (see in Wilkins and Wakefield, 1995, p. 175); the ability to switch between different perceptual dimensions, such as switching from selectively attending to colours to selectively attending to shapes (Brodal, 1992; de Oliveira-Souza *et al.*, 2001); and the ability to form specific semantic categories or 'manipulate semantic codes' (as in semantic generation tasks; see Fox, 1995 for references; for a comprehensive review of the functions of the prefrontal cortex see Stuss and Levine, 2002; for an impressively argued view connecting the emergence of human cognitive capacities with the expansion of the prefrontal cortex see Deacon, 1997).

Since the no-polysemy view of conceptual structure postulates the existence of 'supramodal' concepts corresponding to synaesthetic adjectives, the role that the prefrontal cortex plays in the integration of sensory information *and* the ability to switch between domains or features of experience indicates it as a structure that may have been crucially involved in the formation of such concepts. (Or, in the ability to entertain the concept SOFT in connection with different sensory modalities *and* the ability to distinguish that what makes pillows soft is not what makes voices soft. In this respect, it is interesting to note that patients with damage to the prefrontal cortex exhibit a certain 'concreteness' or 'literalness' in their interpretation of sentences, see Deacon, 1997, p. 267; see also Chapter 6.)

5 Double-Function Terms

1. Although, Li draws the analogy between language and other biological systems such as eukaryotic cell division to show that Chomsky and Lasnik's (1993) principles and parameters model is not a biologically viable theory, I believe it is appropriate to use it in semantic contexts too.
2. For simplicity sake I use the word 'adjective', even though a language may express the same meanings without having the lexical category of adjectives (cf. 'shapeless' and 'out of shape').
3. Even 'straight' and 'crooked' that seem to embody an ethical judgement can express different evaluation in different contexts: 'a bit crooked' may express admiration in a society prohibiting private initiative, and 'straight' may be a negative evaluative judgement when uttered by a crook.
4. I have deliberately broken OED entries into a larger number of psychological meanings to make clearer the point I want to make and to avoid the problem of explaining synonymy, that is, a lexicographer's reasons for classifying 'cold-bloodedness' and 'lack of emotions' as instances of one psychological meaning, and 'indifference' as an instance of another psychological meaning, of 'cold'.
5. Hintikka and Sandu's argument against semantic fields theory of meaning is of the same nature as the one I employ against Marks et al.'s (1987) discussion of sensory meanings in the last chapter: although perceptual properties are continuous, meanings are not (for example, you can arrange temperature sensations from colder to warmer on a scale, but the meanings of 'cold' and 'warm' are distinct and discrete).
6. But see note 4 to Chapter 3.
7. Children's understanding of psychological meanings of double-function adjectives in Asch and Nerlove's experiments can be subdivided into three general stages. Stage one (children aged from three years and one month to aproximately six years and one month) is characterized by an indignant reaction to the experimenters' suggestion that physical adjectives can describe persons (or more precisely, their psychological properties). At stage two (from seven years and six months to eight years) children understand both meanings as equally acceptable but unrelated (as in the example in the body text). Finally, at stage three (from nine years and three months to twelve years and one month) children are able to understand the two meanings as related.

    Note, however, that explanations of the similarity between the two meanings of a polysemous adjective given by older children employed terms which themselves have a dual function, as in '*Hard* things and *hard* people are alike in that neither of them break' (Asch and Nerlove, 1960, p. 50). And such explanation already presupposes the knowledge of the two (or more) meanings of 'break'. For this reason, it would be unjustifiable to conclude that at stage three the understanding of the psychological meanings of double-function adjectives finally becomes influenced by the understanding of their physical meanings.
8. Winner and Gardner consider the psychological meanings of double-function adjectives as instances of relational metaphor because preschoolers mostly fail to grasp the psychological meanings of such adjectives as 'hard'.

However, they do not say what this possible nonperceptual similarity between physical hardness and emotional hardness could be. Standardly, the notion of nonperceptual/structural similarity is illustrated with the help of such examples as 'Plant stems are drinking straws' (Gentner and Stuart, 1983; see also Gentner, 1988, 1989), where the structural similarity is between people using straws for drinking water and plants drawing water from the ground. It is not clear that the same structural similarity underlies the understanding of such expressions as 'a hard person'.

Besides, one could question some of the examples used in Winner *et al.*'s (1976) study and quoted by Winner and Gardner (1993). Thus, in Winner *et al.*'s (1976) study, six-year-olds interpreted such examples as 'After many years of working in jail, the prison guard had become a hard rock' to mean that the prison guard had strong muscles rather than was unfeeling. This was taken to show children's difficulty with understanding the psychological meaning of 'hard'. However, the test sentence favours both physical and psychological interpretations, and it is possible that the use of the compound 'hard rock' rather than the adjective alone biased children towards seeking an interpretation in terms of physical similarity.

9 A lack of knowledge about personality traits (as seems to be suggested by Winner and Gardner, 1993; but see Heyman and Gelman, 1998, 1999) may also affect children's understanding of double-function terms. Although at the age of four to five children normally acquire an understanding of the mental world (Flavell and Miller, 1998; Wellman and Gelman, 1998), it is still different from that of adults. Flavell *et al.* (2001) show that at that age children have difficulty understanding other people's mental states if those are not caused by an external stimulus. The understanding of the psychological meanings of double-function adjectives may similarly require a greater degree of abstraction than the understanding of non-ambiguous trait adjectives. It is also possible that this comprehension difficulty is caused by both their polysemous character and young children's general difficulties in the acquisition of adjectival meanings (for a recent review see Graham *et al.*, 2003, pp. 17–19).

6 Double-Function Terms Again

1 For one example the non-central target produced 59 per cent of *yes* responses: 'The engineer explained to his apprentice how to make a very smooth surface – SLICK' (Williams, 1992, p. 216).
2 This and other sets come from the appendix to Williams (1992).
3 Here and in the rest of this section I rely on meaning definitions found in the *Concise Oxford English Dictionary*.
4 One may object that 'mighty' cannot be substituted for 'strong' in the first sentence. However, the point I am making is not about substitution in sentence contexts, but about the availability of contextually relevant meanings in the mental representations of target words.
5 I have been making quite a point out of the tendency to overinterpretation in connection with Williams' study that I might have appeared to be stretching its importance (as Williams says, some subjects use all sources they can

to come up with an interpretation). However, there may be reasons to believe that this problem is not something merely accidental to psychological research, but that it may bear strongly on the problems of language psychology and metaphor understanding, in particular.

At a RAAM III session, J. Hoorn (1999), who tested among others the anomaly theory of metaphor, expressed surprise at subjects' tendency to interpret anomalies as metaphors. Some other researchers have also reported subjects' ability (Pavio and Walsh, 1993, p. 322) or tendency to interpret anomalies metaphorically ('striving after meaning', Margalit and Goldblum, 1994, pp. 225, 229; see also Gibbs et al., 1991).

In this connection I think that if the question of overinterpretation arises persistently in experimental work, it may be misleading to consider the 'unreliability' of subjects' interpretations as an impediment to getting clearer results. In my view, it may be more productive to consider the tendency to overinterpretation as an indication of what is going on in subjects' heads during the processes of language understanding. Given this 'presumption of meaningfulness', even famous Black's 'a chair is a syllogism' (1993, p. 23) can receive a meaningful interpretation.

6 Rachel Giora has argued that certain meanings are always accessed first. She uses the term 'salient meaning', which is not necessarily the literal meaning of a word or expression (idioms). In commenting on Williams' (1992) experiments she writes that the fact that both meanings of an adjective were activated initially, regardless of context, can be explained in terms of their equal salience (2002, p. 495). Since Giora further notes that her graded salience hypothesis is consistent with the underspecification model (Groefsema, 1995; Ruhl, 1989; Frazier and Rayner, 1990; see Chapter 10), it is safe to assume that it also consistent with the no-polysemy view. Thus, one prediction that follows from the no-polysemy view (and that presumably can be explained in terms of the graded salience hypothesis) is that if the psychological meaning of 'strong' were made more salient to subjects than the physical meaning of 'strong' prior to an experiment, the priming effects would be greater for the psychological than the physical meaning.

7 However, Brownell et al. (1990) did not consider the possibility that homonyms (non-metaphoric alternative meanings of nouns in their study) and polysemes generally (rather than metaphoric meanings of words) may be represented in the brain differently (cf. Klepousniotou, 2002).

8 Unfortunately, Chobor and Schweiger are not very explicit about their criteria for distinguishing between the three types of ambiguity. However, examples included under the rubric of metaphor, such as 'fresh' (new), can be considered relevant to the present discussion. Note also that examples included under the rubric of polysemy may be more appropriately described as instances of homonymy, for example, 'trip' (journey/fall).

9 It has to be remarked that Zaidel et al. (2002) did not confirm Chobor and Schweiger's (1998) suggestion about the involvement of the frontal lobes (but see Bottini et al., 1994, whose PET study showed the activation of the right frontal lobe in metaphor processing). However, Zaidel et al.'s results do not support the old view either. As they say, language functions that are tapped by RHCB most likely require interhemispheric integration rather than 'modularized' representations in the two hemispheres. Overall, even if

the difficulty with related alternative word meanings is not associated with the proper functioning of the frontal lobes, it still remains a strong posibility that this difficulty has to be characterized as a deficit of retrieval (the blocking of alternative interpretations or the persistence of the initial interpretation) rather than a destruction of corresponding semantic representations.

10 One cannot conclude to the literal–metaphorical distinction from the studies of differential semantic representation in the cerebral hemispheres of normal subjects either. Thus, although Anaki *et al.* who studied differential hemispheric processing of polysemous adjectives ('feeble') in normal subjects interpret their findings as supporting the idea of 'an enhanced role of the RH in metaphoric comprehension of single word metaphors' (1998, p. 698), their study does not show that subordinate meanings of polysemous adjectives are metaphoric meanings.

The reason that the conclusion about the literal–metaphorical distinction cannot be drawn from such studies is that exactly the same patterns of meaning activation in the two hemispheres were obtained in the study of homonyms, showing an enhanced role of the right hemisphere in the processing of their subordinate meanings (Burgess and Simpson, 1988; the similarity between the two studies is noticed by Anaki and colleagues themselves). However, one would certainly want to avoid the conclusion that 'bank' (riverside) is the metaphoric meaning of 'bank' (financial institution).

To the best of my knowledge, so far there have been no studies that would throw light on how differential semantic processing in the cerebral hemispheres relates to the differences in types of lexical ambiguity. Besides, some studies obtained priming effects in the RH, but not the LH, for non-associated words from the same semantic fields (for example, 'king'–'duke'; Chiarello, 1985; Chiarello *et al.*, 1990), which is clearly a different type of meaning relation than polysemy or metaphor. Thus, whereas the model according to which the RH activates a broader range of semantic representations (Beeman *et al.*, 1994; Chiarello, 1991; Chiarello *et al.*, 1995) is generally supported by the data, these data do not support the literal–metaphorical distinction as drawn by the standard assumption theorists.

7 Words and Concepts

1 I use here Fodor's terminology which some people may disapprove of. Philosophers in the Fregean tradition in particular would disagree with the formulation that 'words are names for concepts': in Fregean terms, concepts are the senses rather than the referents of words. However, we can make use of the formulation 'words are names for concepts' in the following way: 'cat' (the word) is the name for CAT (the concept) in the sense that whenever 'cat' is encountered, CAT becomes activated. CAT is a shorthand for whatever it is that connects us to both 'cats' and cats. The peculiarity of Fodor's use of 'name' stems from his being unhappy with the Fregean tradition of thinking about concepts: he wants to avoid senses so as to avoid meaning holism. That is, to avoid the possession of CAT depending on the possession of ANIMAL (as it is in the neo-Fregean position of Peacocke, 1992).

Another instance of Fodor's peculiar use of words is 'particular'. On the standard conception of particulars, if concepts are mental particulars, there arises the problem of sharing them. However, in Fodor's philosophy the solipsism is avoided since concepts are nomological connections to the world, and are as such atomic and innate. Thus, for example, the mental state one is in when thinking about triangles does not differ across individuals because having the concept TRIANGLE is being nomologically connected to the property of being a triangle. As long as humans are similar with respect to their perceptual processing mechanisms and their conceptual endowment, the concept TRIANGLE will be shared by them. Presumably, Fodor calls concepts 'particulars' because they are 'about' particular entities: TRIANGLE is about triangles and nothing else. Such are the idiosyncrasies of Fodor's terminology, and although I largely share Fodor's views about concepts, I use 'mental entities' instead of 'mental particulars'.
2 It is curious to note that Tranel and Damasio (1999) also talk of words being names for concepts.
3 In an inquiry into concepts, part-of-speech distinctions may be of some significance: nouns pick out entities or groups of entities, verbs and adjectives are predicates, picking out relations and properties in the external world. To a certain extent they are probably processed differently as well: verbs and nouns (perhaps, adjectives too) are possibly 'orchestrated' by separate neuronal networks (see Damasio and Tranel, 1993).
4 The choice of the example was completely arbitrary.
5 I am told that sounds that appear sharp to the human ear (presumably with an abrupt or sudden onset) have a visually sharp-edged form on the oscillograph. English is a bit confusing in this respect because 'sharp' in music refers to a semitone higher in pitch than the intended pitch (as in 'A' and 'A-sharp'). However, it is curious to note that in natural scales sharp notes do indeed produce an impression of auditory sharpness (for example, A-sharp in A-minor or C-major).

8 Back to Cognitive Semantics

1 Especially since a number of researchers connect the evolution of specifically human cognitive abilities, and linguistic abilities in particular, with the evolution of social organization and/or social cognition ('gossip', Dunbar, 1998; see also Humphrey, 1976; Ulbaek, 1998).
2 A similar objection is raised by Stern with respect to Lakoff's analysis of 'My job is a jail' in terms of the conceptual metaphor PSYCHOLOGICAL FORCE IS PHYSICAL FORCE: 'But this metaphor enters into the story only because Lakoff *begins* by assuming that our "knowledge schema" about jails specifically includes *only* the "knowledge that a jail imposes extreme *physical* constraints on a prisoner's movements"....Why couldn't the ur-schema equally well include the knowledge that a jail imposes extreme *psychological* constraints (social isolation, limited access to family and outsiders) on a prisoner? Once we include that information in our initial knowledge-schema there is no work left to be done by the PSYCHOLOGICAL FORCE IS PHYSICAL FORCE metaphor' (2000, p. 186).

3 Lass's, of course, is not the most widespread view. Most historical linguists are in favour of unidirectionality in grammaticalization (Traugott and Heine, 1991; Traugott and Knig, 1991), and perhaps they are right, at least on force of statistical evidence. However, I believe that the situation is different with semantic change. Metaphor as the main mechanism in semantic change soon becomes extended to the main mechanism in conceptual change, and this is what I disagree with. It is plausible, for example, that spatials developed into temporals in English and other languages, but it is much less plausible that there was a process of conceptualization (developing concepts for a domain) keeping pace with grammatical-semantic changes as some authors seem to suggest (Claudi and Heine, 1986). We are not only spatial but also temporal beings (with probably innate spatio-temporal maps of experience; see Young, 1987, p. 167). What presumably developed was not our ability to perceive time but the ability to express sequentiality in discourse. In short, I argue that language does not restrict thought.
4 Murphy writes: 'Although Sweetser (1990) shows convincingly that current words that have meanings related to vision also tend to have meanings related to abstract mental activity, she presents less evidence that their historical predecessors were not polysemous in the same way. Thus, it is not always clear where the historical progression is.' (Murphy, 1996, p. 198).
5 Besides, if one checks the tables Williams (1976) provides at the end of his article, it will be clear that etymological explanations are no help to cognitive semantics' approach. That is, since the primary (etymologically primary) meaning of 'bitter' is tactile, then to say that its primary meaning is gustatory and that its tactile meaning is a metaphorical extension of the gustatory meaning will be contradictory.
6 A number of authors tried to provide an ordering of sensory modalities in which those inform one another and serve as sources of metaphorical transfers. Shen's ordering in close to that of Ullmann (1964). However, Day (1996) provides a different ordering, which is, in its turn, questioned by Bretones Callejas (2001). In any case, even if one eventually settles on some particular ordering, this will not make it any clearer why and how terms that presumably belong to one sensory modality are transferred onto the other sensory modalities, and, further, how their meanings are derived in those sensory domians where they presumably do not belong.
7 For the critique of an alternative cognitive semantics approach to adjectival polysemy developed by Joseph Grady see Chapter 2.
8 Cf. Murphy: 'metaphors arise out of the similarity of pre-existing conceptual structures' (1996, p. 179). Similarly, see Murphy's argument that 'Inflation is rising' is not a metaphor because 'rise' has both physical and abstract meanings, and underlying them is the abstraction of undergoing a change such that the value of an entity on a dimension increases (1996, p. 190).
9 Blackburn's comment deserves being reproduced in full:

> Consider the way in which we use terms which also describe physical affairs to describe psychological affairs. We think of matches in boxes, and thoughts in the head; of being pulled by ropes, or being pulled by desires; of jumping to attention, or jumping to a conclusion. Metaphorical, of course. Or is it? We most probably cannot cash the metaphors, either by giving a single literal

way of saying something which they yield or even by indicating a range of comparisons which they suggest. On the other hand we should not be happy with just postulating two different senses of the terms: it is not pure accident that we talk of thoughts in the heads, for instance. If it were simply a case of the word 'in' being ambiguous we might just as well have planted the ambiguity on some other term, and talked of terms being *on* the head, for instance. Yet we should also be unhappy with the idea that there is a smooth or natural extension of the terms from the physical to the mental. Someone who understands what it is for one thing to be in another physically has a definite range of capacities: he can find things, obey instructions, perform a range of tasks which exhibit or exercise this understanding. These tasks are not the same as any (whichever they might be!) which exercise an understanding of thoughts being in the head. (1984, p. 178)

10 Johnson and Lakoff (2002) say that representations are not inner mental entities, but 'flexible patterns of organism–environment interactions'. However, this hardly works even for the examples thay traditionally deal with. If one wants to know what constitutes the content of such concepts as LIFE (so that on encountering 'life' the coresponding concept LIFE is activated), one cannot simply claim that life-representation is a flexible pattern of organism–environment interactions with whatever it is that constitutes its content, since all living organisms interact with their environments, but none of them presumably represent life the way we do (cf. Allen and Houser, 1991). Besides, there are lots of things that fall into the category of patterns of organism-environment interactions, but not all of them are intentional entities (cf. Fodor, 1990).

9 Polysemy in Lexical Semantics

1 To this one can also add that analyzing transitive sentences as causative ones does not work for all languages: 'More surprisingly, perhaps, in Classical Greek "to die" functions as the passive of "to kill". (One can "die BY someone".) Formally, at least, Greek treats "to kill", not "to die", as the more basic.' (Palmer, 1976, p. 133).
2 Another reason for introducing systems of lexical composition, which I do not discuss here, concerns questions of inference and the purported inability of meaning postulates theories to account for them (see Jackendoff, 1992, pp. 48–52).
3 One can easily notice the similarity between the Thematic Relations Hypothesis (TRH) and approaches developed in cognitive linguistics. However, even in 1983 Jackendoff emphasized that the TRH is not a theory of metaphor systems in language and thought. Thematic structure is the only means that we have for coherent conceptual organization of semantic fields, and for that reason cannot be a metaphorical application of the analysis within the spatial field to all other fields. In Jackendoff's words: 'the theory of thematic relations claims not just that some fields are structured in terms of other fields, but that all fields have essentially the *same* structure....I am inclined to think of thematic structure not as spatial metaphor but as an abstract organization

that can be applied with suitable specialization to any field' (1983, pp. 209–10). As Jackendoff further notes, it is possible to think of the thematic structure developing from spatial cognition long before language in evolutionary time, but these evolutionary considerations are 'beside the point' for questions of individul conceptual development. This line of thought, explicitly contrasting the TRH and cognitive linguistics approaches, is further developed in Jackendoff and Aaron (1991). Note also, however, that both cognitive linguists and Jackendoff 'regard semantics as rooted in psychology' (Jackendoff, 1998b).

4 This account may need further modification to incorporate the ontological category [ACTIONS], and such modified representations are also discussed by Jackendoff (1983, section 9.4). Since these modifications do not affect the content of the discussion in the body text I do not mention them any further. For the same reason, I do not mention the ways in which the conceptual structure is 'carved up' into lexical items (for example, the difference in representations for 'go into' and 'enter').

5 As Fodor says, his arguments against Jackendoff 'apply without alteration to Lakoff as well' (1998a, p. 50, f. 8).

6 Note that Fodor (1998a) discusses only those instances of 'keep' that have CAUSE in their conceptual representation.

7 As it happens, since Jackendoff is talking about the conceptual structure, which is a level of representation where periferal and linguistic information converge, he has no independent reason for treating CAUSE and STAY as primitive concepts, and KEEP as a complex concept. As he writes: 'The different uses of the words *go, change, be, keep*... are distinguished only by the semantic field feature, despite the radically different sorts of real-world events and states they pick out. However, the precise values of the field feature that a particular verb or preposition may carry is a lexical fact that must be learned. Thus *be* and *keep* are unrestricted...' (1992, p. 38). However, since both 'be' and 'keep' have an unrestricted application across semantic fields, why does an atomic concept correspond to 'be' and not to 'keep'?

8 What is important for the discussion in the body text is that decompositional accounts in fact lead to an anti-polysemy view. However, there are some interesting details that have to be mentioned here. According to Fodor, the difference that one feels between the meanings of 'keep' in 'Susan kept the money' and 'Sam kept the crowd happy' is not due to 'keep' being polysemous (having several different but related meanings), but to the fact that in one case the relation is between the NP and the money, and in the other between the NP and the crowd's being happy. Since the money and the crowd's being happy are different things, the relation of keeping will be different too. Fodor gives a parallel example: 'chairs exist' and 'numbers exist'. Here one also feels a difference in meaning, so that one may be tempted to treat 'exist' as polysemous. But:

> [a] familiar reply goes: the difference between the existence of chairs and the existence of numbers seems, on reflection, strikingly like the difference between numbers and chairs. Since you have the latter to explain the former, you don't also need 'exist' to be polysemic. (1998a, pp. 53–4)

Let us return now to the 'keep' examples. Fodor considers one objection to the view that 'keep' is univocal because it always means KEEP. As the objection goes, the important difference between the two sentences is that 'keep' implies possession in 'Susan kept the money' but not in 'Sam kept the crowd happy'. But as Fodor notes, this difference may not be due to the polysemy in 'keep'. It might be that these 'keep' sentence contain underlying complements such that 'Susan kept the money' can be rendered as 'Susan kept having the money', and 'Sam kept the crowd happy' as 'Sam kept the crowd being happy' (1998a, p. 54). This way the implication of possession would derive not from the polysemy in 'keep' but from underlying complement clauses.

However, although Fodor's proposal may account for some differences, I do not find it entirely compelling because it seems to leave out a large number of examples, which, intuitively, also have to be accounted for by the univocality of KEEP. According to Fodor, sentences of the form 'NP keep NP' become transformed into 'NP keep having NP'. But consider the following examples:

1. John kept the money.
2. John kept the accountant.
3. John kept the promise.
4. John kept the secret.
5. John kept the score.
6. John kept the distance.

Whereas in (1) 'keep' clearly implies possession, it does so less clearly in (2), and it is doubtful that possession is implied at all in (3–6), unless one chooses to talk about metaphorical possession (but see Fodor's own doubts concerning the notion of metaphorical possession in 1998a, p. 60; note also that I ignore here the difference in interpretation depending on whether the definite or indefinite article precedes the second NP, as in 'John kept a dog' vs. 'John kept the dog').

One may say that in sentences (3–6) 'keep' forms part of idiomatic expressions (those that exhibit some degree of non-compositionality (see Moon, 1998, Chapter 1) and have to be learned independently of the usual meaning of 'keep'), and as such these expressions have to be excluded from the analysis. However, this approach would not let one make sense of the curious fact that languages different from English employ the same verb for practically the same range of expressions. Thus, for instance, English and Russian have the following parallels: 'to keep books on the shelf' = 'deržat' knigi na polke', 'to keep a mistress' = 'deržat' lubovnitsu', 'to keep someone's attention' = 'deržat' čjo-libo vnimanie'; 'to keep a promise' = 'deržat' obeshchanie', 'to keep a secret' = 'deržat' sekret', 'to keep the score' = 'deržat' sčjot', 'to keep the distance' = 'deržat' rasstojanie' (and even in 'the cake will keep till Monday' = 'tort proderžitsja do ponedel'nika', and 'the dollar kept its value' = 'dollar uderžal svou pozitsiu'). Finally, although the possessive 'to keep the money' would standardly be translated with a different verb: 'ostavit' den'gi (sebe)', we find that the same morpheme is used in Russian for temporal possession: 'prideržčat' den'gi' (to keep the money after the time when it had to be returned) and 'Mogu ya poderžat' tvoi den'gi?' = 'Can I keep your money for some more time?'. I believe that a semantic theory has to take such cross-linguistic data into account, and that perhaps it is not the existence of such examples as 'to keep a promise' that spoils the picture, but the notion of the semantic field of possession. After all, why does one feel that possession is implied in the spatial 'Harry kept the bird in the cage' but not in the circumstantial 'Louise kept Fred in the attic' (assuming that Fred is a man; see Jackendoff, 1983, p. 198) which have the same syntactic structure?

9 I write BOOK in capitals because it is a semantic representation corresponding to the word 'book'. I propose to treat here Pustejovsky's semantic representations for lexical items as if they were concepts to make the discussion consistent with the previous discussions. I hope that adopting this notation here will not be too confusing, and that this way we can better capture the idea that a single (although complex) representation corresponds to the different meanings of a polyseme. Some justification for using this notation here also comes from the fact that in the generative lexicon theory semantic representations are 'enriched' representations and include information that would otherwise be considered as part of the world or conceptual knowledge (see also Pustejovsky, 2001).

10 For reasons of simplicity I reproduce here only some of Pustejovsky's formalisms (for details see Pustejovsky, 1995, 1998).

11 The same is also true for adjectives in predicative position. In 'This pen is good', the meaning of 'good' depends on the meaning of 'pen'. For simplicity I hereafter say that an adjective is predicated of a noun or modifies a noun regardless of whether it is in attributive or predicative position.

12 There are other related problems which, I think, may count against the generative lexicon approach to adjectival polysemy. One concerns the productive use of polysemous adjectives in context and the information specified in the qualia structures of nouns. Thus, consider the scenario in which someone buys a do-it-yourself bookcase. After reading the instruction, he says: 'Good, this is a fast bookcase'. The hearer can easily understand 'a fast bookcase' as 'a bookcase that can be assembled in a short amount of time'. However, 'to be assembled' is not the telic role for BOOKCASE (and it is not clear whether it is its agentive role, which may well be 'to be made'; however in our context 'a fast bookcase' does not mean 'a bookcase that can be made in a short amount of time').

Here is how the assumption of primary meanings shows up in Pustejovsky's treatment of adjectival polysemy. Pustejovsky says that 'fast', 'long' and 'bright' can be considered as event predication. Adjectives of this type modify an event predicate associated with the head, and this event predicate is specified as the telic role in the qualia structure of the head. This distinguishes them from such adjectives as 'expensive' or 'opaque' which select the formal role and such adjectives as 'good' which can select any role (1995, pp. 130, 254). However, tying up the interpretation of adjectives in context with the information specfied in the qualia structure of nouns with which they combine leads to the state of affairs when either appropriate senses cannot be generated at all or senses that are generated require further disambiguation. 'Fast bookcase' is an example of the situation when the appropriate sense is not generated by Pustejovky's lexicon. As an example of sense generation requiring further disambiguation we can take 'a fast ball'. 'A fast ball' can denote in context a ball that is moving fast or a ball that is inherently fast (think of tennis balls). However, the information in the qualia structure of BALL is not sufficient to distinguish between the two senses (presuming that the telic role of BALL specifies some kind of movement). Perhaps, after all, we do not need qualia structures to account for the interpretation of 'fast' in context: 'fast' always means FAST whatever the activity that is selected by the context.

13 Another reason to distrust metaphor is the intention to maintain the distinction between lexically and non-lexically based inferences (Pustejovsky, 1995, p. 268). But consider the expression 'a sharp knife'. According to Pustejovsky, its interpretation is generated via 'sharp' selectively binding the telic role of KNIFE, which is cutting (1995, p. 100). Thus, 'a sharp knife' should always receive the same interpretation across contexts: a knife that is sharp for the purpose of cutting. However, it is perfectly possible to say 'This knife is sharp on the other side as well'. Here 'sharp' is not predicated of that part of the knife that is designed for cutting, but the sentence can nonetheless be easily understood. Does this suggest that the entry SHARP should specify all the parts that knives are made of in the constitutive role? Or is the understanding of 'sharp' in 'This knife is sharp on the other side as well' mediated by general world knowledge, whereas the understanding of 'This knife is sharp' is mediated by lexical knowledge? It appears that once one admits complex concepts into the picture, the distinction between lexical and general world knowledge is so not easy to maintain.

14 In fact, Fodor and Lepore's critique of Pustejovsky is a continuation of their wide-scale attack (Fodor and Lepore, 1992) on inferential role semantics, according to which lexical entries are typically complex and specify meaning constitutive inferences. Since we are mostly interested here in the issue of polysemy, the details of this attack need not concern us, as long as we keep in mind that, as Fodor and Lepore show, having complex lexical entries is not a solution to the problem of polysemy.

15 It is probably worth keeping in mind that there is an important difference between computational (in the sense of machine translation) and conceptual (in the sense of human conceptual representation) problems. For computational purposes, where lexical knowledge representation systems are hard to separate from general knowledge representation systems, the introduction of structured entries may be the best solution. However, whether entries in the mental lexicon are complex is a different question. Fodor and Lepore's critique addresses the conceptual, not the computational, problem (note that the two are easily confused, as, for example, in Wilks, 2001).

16 Fodor and Lepore's formulation is somewhat curious since, like Pustejovsky, they seem to assume that all objects and entities referred to by nouns have functions: '"good" quantifies over the function of the NP it modifies' (1998, p. 286). But does 'good' (always) mean 'good for'? Whereas one can easily imagine contexts where 'good weather' means 'weather that is good for something' (going for a walk, sunbathing, sailing, and so on), I find it hard to think of a context where 'good children' would mean 'children that are good *for* something' (I exclude here such odd contexts as cannibalism, and so on).

17 It seems that, on the whole, natural kind terms pose a lot more problems for the generative lexicon theory than artefacts. Take the expression 'a bright bulb'. Modification by 'bright' is, according to Pustejovsky, event predication, such that 'bright' selectively binds the telic role of BULB, which is illuminating. This way we arrive at the interpretation of 'a bright bulb' as

'a bulb which shines brightly when illuminated' (Pustejovsky, 1995, p. 130). However, I find it utterly counterintuitive to say that 'bright sun' is 'the sun which shines brightly when illuminated (???) or 'the sun which shines brightly when in the sky' (?); rather, 'bright sun' is just 'the sun which shines brightly', but can we say that shining is the function or the purpose of the sun's existence?

Even with terms for artefacts not everything is simple. According to Pustejovsky, 'a good knife' means 'a knife good for cutting' because 'good' selects for the telic role of KNIFE (unless context favours the interpretation following from its agentive role). However, 'a good knife' can perfectly well mean 'a knife good for stabbing' (or 'a knife good for throwing into trees', and so on). Stabbing is an activity, and as such can only be specified in the telic role of a noun. Perhaps the telic role of KNIFE could specify all activities that involve knives (probably ordering them by their prototypicality); perhaps the entry STAB could specify its relation to cutting. But those seem to be dubious solutions. It thus appears that making the interpretation of 'good' depend on the telic roles of nouns, Pustejovsky incorporates world knowledge into semantic representations rather them keeping them separate as was his intention.

18 It has to be remarked that Fodor and Lepore's use of the words 'ambiguity', 'homonymy', and 'polysemy' is not exactly clear. Often the impression is that they do not really distinguish between homonymy and polysemy, and that when they say that a word is ambiguous or polysemous, they mean that a word has two (or more) meanings regardless of whether these meanings are related or not. As we shall see later, this disregard of the homonymy-polysemy distinction does not let them offer a psychologically realistic theory of concepts. And as we have also seen in Chapter 1, the same indiscriminatory approach to polysemy and homonymy (both instances of lexical ambiguity) makes Davidson (1978/1984a) say somewhat contradictory things (that is, he treats most uses of 'strong' as metaphorical, but 'mouth' as homonymous).

19 For this reason, what the lexicon has to specify is not only denotation, but also a rule of composition that 'want' contributes to the logical form of the phrases where it is a constituent.

20 Being relevant for interpretation in context but not 'focused' (Pustejovsky, 1995, p. 32) and not being available for interpretation (1995, p. 156) are quite different things. Pustejovsky seems to contradict himself when he applies the first description to all cases of logical polysemy, and using the second description in his discussion of the 'newspaper' example. However, both senses of 'newspaper' can be available for interpretation within a single sentence as in 'The newspaper has decided to change its format' (Nunberg, 1979, p. 150). The same goes for other cases of logical polysemy: 'John's dissertation, which weighs five pounds, has been refuted', 'The window was broken so many times that it had to be boarded up' (Nunberg, 1979, p. 150), 'The book, which weighs ten pounds, ended sadly', 'The university, which was built in 1896, has a left-wing orientation' (Jackendoff, 1983, p. 147).

21 'Door' can be treated as polysemous because 'John broke the door' and 'John walked through the door' seem to refer to different 'aspects' of the door. 'Wall' does not exhibit the 'door'-like polysemy. But semantically there seems to be nothing wrong with the sentence 'John walked through the

196 *Notes*

wall' just as with 'John broke the wall'. For example, 'to walk through a wall' can be literally and unambiguously used in a story about aliens or David Copperfield. Besides, in such stories 'to walk through a door' may be ambiguous between walking through an aperture and walking through the thing that fills the aperture. However, it is doubtful that the entries for 'door' or 'wall' should specify all imaginable ways of walking through them. Which suggests that 'door' has two different, although tightly interconnected, meanings rather than one meaning with two 'aspects'.

22 I believe that the difference between 'bake a cake' and 'bake a trolley' is not a difference that should be specified in the lexicon – it is supplied by our world knowledge. Although it may be reflected grammatically in the difference between the perfective and the imperfective. There is nothing wrong semantically with 'I am baking a trolley' (as said, for instance, by a mentally disturbed person who managed to get a trolley into a device designed for baking and switch the latter on) – it refers to a particular activity in the real world, however nonsensical this activity may appear to us. And the reason it appears nonsensical to us is that on the basis of our world knowledge we realize that 'I have baked a trolley' may never come true (or we may never know what it is for a trolley to have been baked). However, I would like to emphasize again that semantics cannot be confined only to those instances of language use which we judge to be describing normal states of affairs. What makes language so interesting is that it seems to be just as suited for describing situations that are atypical or abnormal from the point of view of our everyday life (and this is why 'a good knife' can mean 'a knife good for stabbing').

As it happens, artefacts can be created by a process that is no different from baking; the technical term for it in powder metallurgy is 'sintering', but informally it can be referred to as 'baking'.

23 In fact, Fodor and Lepore conclude that the entirely rigorous notion of compositionality (full context-independence) cannot be had since the lexicon has to specify not only denotations, but also contributions to the logical form (1998, p. 287).

10 The No-Polysemy View: What It Is and What It Is Not

1 Only for simplicity sake do I say that BRIGHT is the primitive concept expressed by the adjective 'bright'. In no way do I propose to confuse words with conceptes. Although I have followed Fodor (1975, 1998a) in assuming that there is a pretty close fit between words and concepts (cf. Sperber and Wilson, 1998, p. 187), I am perfectly aware that different languages may have two words where English has one, or one word where English has two. But something similar is found within one and the same language. The phenomenon of collocations is most probably not a conceptual phenomenon. And a language can have a number of words that have the same denotation and differ only in the social context with which they are associated ('girl' vs. 'chick' vs.'young lady').

Still, as Fodor says, questions about meaning have to be distinguished from questions about possession conditions. 'Spoiled' and 'addled' are synonymous, but their possession conditions differ (you have to know that 'addled' can be said only about eggs or brains). And this works across languages as well: 'Suppose English has two words, "spoiled" and "addled", both of which mean *spoiled*, but one of which is used only of eggs. Suppose also that there is some other language which has a word "spoilissimoed" which means *spoiled* and is used both of spoiled eggs and of other spoiled things.... The difference between the languages is that one, but not the other, has a word that means *spoiled* whose possession condition includes having the concept EGG.' (1998a, p. 55). I have used this line of reasoning in Chapter 3 when discussing Russian words 'rezkij' and 'ostryj' which are both translated into English as 'sharp', but which differ in their collocations. 'Rezkij nož' would mean the same as 'ostryj nož' ('sharp knife'), if anybody had used 'rezkij' with 'nož' ('knife'). From the perspective of the no-polysemy view, violations of collocational restrictions are not instances of speaking metaphorically.

2 This is clearly a nativist view of conceptual structure, but given the data we discussed in Chapter 4 there seems to be nothing wrong with being a nativist about concepts corresponding to polysemous adjectives. In very broad terms, what I mean is that these concepts are not formed in the course of individual development but are part of the overall human conceptual make-up; and that possibly they appeared at whatever time it was when human conceptual abilities could be separated from non-human conceptual abilities (see section 4.7).

3 If anyone had known exactly what kind of things concepts are and how to individuate them, I could have been a lot more specific about why I believe SOFT, SHARP, BRIGHT, and so on to be psychologically primitive concepts. However, nobody quite knows the answers to these questions (cf. Braisby, 1999). The view that SOFT, SHARP, BRIGHT, and so on are psychologically primitive concepts was suggested to me by a careful consideration of the data on cross-modal integration and cross-modal transfers discussed in Chapter 4 (see also Chapter 3). The considerations that there are no adequate, even approximately adequate, paraphrases for synaesthetic uses of 'soft', 'sharp', 'bright', and so on; that their synaesthetic meanings cannot be further decomposed; and that their denotations can be established with a good deal of precision (as I discuss later in this section) seem to lend futher support to the no-polysemy view. Additionally, there is some indication that a disruption of the ability to detect a property in one modality may affect the ability to detect that (or corresponding) property in other modalities. I was told (private communication with Dr Josef Merilashvili, Senior Research Fellow at the Bekhterev Psychoneurological Research Institute) that people with reduced thermal sensibility (who may suffer severe tissue damage because of this) practically never use the word for 'hot' in describing their experiences in any of the modalities and also seem to have an 'impaired' understanding of this word (in such expressions as 'hot temperament'). If things are indeed this way, in my view, this would rule all standard assumption explanations. However, presently it is hard to be any more specific than that.

4 See Stern (2000) for a discussion of the medieval roots of understanding literal meaning as 'proper' meaning.

5 *Nature*'s Milestones issue on cell division (2001, Nature Publishing Group) contains an article 'Polar expedition' next to which there is a pretty photo of a white polar bear. The meaning of 'polar' that is activated in the reader's

mind once her gaze falls on the page is the one that has to with polar bears. However, the first words of the article reveal that it is not about polar bears, but meiosis. A certain journalistic effect is achieved by making the reader entertain two different meanings of 'polar' at the same time; but would anyone say that the meaning of 'polar' in 'polar bodies' depends on the meaning of 'polar' in 'polar bear'?

6   Of course, the causal theory of reference is not without its own problems and complexities. However, those can be ignored for the purposes of the discussion in the body text. The issue whether a purely causal theory of reference is possible or whether a hybrid causal-descriptive theory should be preferred to it is discussed, for instance, in Devitt and Sterelny (1987) and Miller (1992; see also Putnam, 1992). Linguists and psychologists may find interesting the articles by Malt (1994), Chomsky (1995), and Braisby et al. (1996) which question the adequacy of metaphysical essentialism as an explanation of natural language use. Philosophical discussions of this issue can be found in Abbott (1997) and Soames (2002).

7   As Kripke says, his treatment of natural kind terms applies not only to nouns but to adjectives as well: '...my argument implicitly concludes that certain general terms, those for natural kinds, have a greater kinship with proper names than is generally realized. This conclusion holds for certain for various species names, whether they are count nouns, such as "cat", "tiger", "chunk of gold", or mass terms such as "gold", "water", "iron pyrites". It also applies to certain terms for natural phenomena, such as "heat", "light", "sound", "lightning", and, presumably, suitably elaborated, to corresponding adjectives – "hot", "loud", "red"' (1980, p. 134).

8   Nor are there any chemical reactions apart from those that take place inside the body (the nerve endings).

9   English: 'bright light' – 'bright sound'; Russian: 'jarkij svet' – 'jarkij zvuk'; Mexican Spanish: 'luz brillante' – 'sonido brillante' (more frequently encountered: 'suene brillante' – 'sounds bright').

10 The following is a technical description from the Laney LC15 guitar amplifier User Manual: 'BRIGHT SWITCH: Adds brightness and sparkle to the upper frequencies of the amplifier.' Clearly, it was not intended as a metaphorical instruction. Such examples are legion in musical and sound engineering literature: 'There are a few slightly-varied substitutes for the 12AX7, such as the Russian 12AXR, which is somewhat *brighter*, with quicker compression and lower gain' (*Guitar Shop*, October 1996, p. 84; my italics); 'The perfectly tuned sound chamber and Duncan Seth Lover pickups offer up many of the inspiring tonal characteristics of a vintage 335 without the bulky body. Its clean tone is best described as *bright* and rich' (*Guitar Player*, October 1996, p. 57, my italics). I believe that the authors of these articles knew perfectly well what they were talking about when using the word 'bright' (to the extent that they could be accused of misinforming the reader).

11 I want to emphasize that I do not include colour adjectives into the category of synaesthetic adjectives. While non-colour associations made by synaesthetes and non-synaesthetes seem to follow the same pattern, colour associations vary even among synaesthetic individuals (Chapter 4).

12 Cf. Brown: 'No case was discovered in which the morpheme for *hot* named a remote, calm (in fact, *cool*) manner' (1958, p. 146).

13 If I read Kripke (1980) and Putnam (1975) correctly, they both allow that even if 'hot temper' is not yet literal it may become so.
14 Perhaps we judge people to be warm or hard by the introspectable effect they have on us. Somehow other people form a special category of objects, and whole cell populations preferentially respond to faces and facial expressions (Gauthier and Logothetis, 2000). It turned out that there is a good physiological reason for calling chilli peppers 'hot'. Perhaps there are also good physiological reasons for calling people 'warm' or 'hard'.
15 I am stealing the way of putting it from Fodor: 'Consider RED HAIR, which, I will suppose, is compositional (that is, not idiomatic) and applies to *hair that is red as far as hair goes*. The view of its semantics explains why, though red hair is arguably not literally red, still somebody who has RED and has HAIR and who understands the semantic implications of the syntactic structure AND, can figure out what 'red hair' means. So, *prima facie*, RED HAIR is compositional and the demands of productivity are satisfied according to the present analysis' (1998b, p. 41). The only difference is that I think that 'bright' in 'bright light' is literally bright.

Still, I suspect that Professor Fodor will not agree with the view I am putting forward here. For, in response to my question why KEEP can be a univocal concept but SWEET cannot (see section 9.4) he kindly replied that 'keep' in 'Sam kept the crowd happy' is literal, but 'sweet' in 'sweet girl' or 'sweet music' is not (e-mail communication, August 1999). The metaphoric use of 'sweet' has to do with praising, but not its literal meaning. I wonder whether this is true at all. You may love Wagner, but you will not say that his music is sweet. And you may hate Saint-Saens, but his music is most certainly sweet. Is the use of 'sweet' in talking about music a negative evaluation? On the other hand, cold thin sopranos are excellent for singing Wagner, but not much good for singing Verdi. Is 'cold thin soprano' a positive or a negative evaluation?
16 For some predicates another perceptual perspective can be added to these two. Thus, something can be tall not only with respect to our body size or surrounding objects, but also with respect to its own proportions (due to the difference in its dimensions along the vertical and the horizontal axes).
17 I doubt that anyone would want to say that 'big' is ambiguous and maps onto one of the following four concepts: (a) BIG FOR THINGS OF ITS KIND; (b) BIG WITH RESPECT TO A CONTEXTUALLY SALIENT COMPARISON CLASS; (c) BIG WITH RESPECT TO OUR BODY SIZE; and (d) BIG WITH RESPECT TO SURROUNDING OBJECTS. Introducing the hidden variable x into the semantic representation of 'big' stops this unnecessary proliferation of concepts.

In my story, the interpretation 'for its own kind' can be either contextually overridden when a different comparison class is made salient by the context, or bypassed, thus evoking the corresponding primitive concept, when the relevant comparison class is hard to find. Both problems were noticed by Ludlow (1989), who remarks with respect to the latter that 'No flea is large' cannot have the absurd interpretation that no flea is large relative to the class of fleas. His solution to this puzzle is 'to suppose that ... language users assume the speaker intended some more general c-class, which is something like objects generally, or perhaps mid-sized earth-bound objects' (p. 530).

Why do I not want to say that the relevant comparison class is supplied by the context in *every* case, as do Szabó (2001) and Stanley and Szabó (2000)?

One reason for this is that no contextual information seems to be required in order to understand 'a big mouse': understanding it as 'a mouse that is big as far as mice go' seems to be part of one's context-independent semantic knowledge. (Another reason is that contextual information is too 'coarse-grained' to fix the comparison class by itself; Ludlow, 1989, p. 531.) Consider also the example 'John is tall'. As Stanley and Szabó say, '[w]ithout contextual background we only have a vague sense of what this sentence might say – whether John is tall with respect to basketball players or his colleagues (2000, p. 233). However, they give no reason why, without contextual information, 'John is tall' says something only vaguely rather than saying that John is tall as far as human adult males go (that John is a human adult male is obvious in their discussion of the example). If the interpretation 'for its own kind' were not available to language users, how would they understand 'I am tall' when said to them on the phone by a person they had never met before?

18 John Searle shows that double-function adjectives are equally fatal for simile and 'associationist' theories of metaphor, saying that they are 'a matter of perceptions' (1993, pp. 97–8). I.A. Richards discusses the following extract from Denham's lines on the River Thames: 'O, could I flow like thee and make thy stream / My great exemplar as it is my theme! / Though deep, yet clear; though gentle yet not dull: / Strong without rage, without o'erflowing, full' (1936, p. 121) by sorting the words as literally or metaphorically descriptive. However, one page later he remarks that on a careful analysis there is no similarity between deep rivers and deep minds: '[w]hat the lines say of the mind is something that does not come from the river', even though the vehicle somehow 'controls' the tenor. These two authors felt that there was something wrong about the transfer of meaning explanation for double-function adjectives. The no-polysemy view attempts to take away that feeling of something having gone wrong.

In this book I have discussed a significant amount of experimental data that, in my view, supports the no-polysemy view. There are some other data that can be reinterpreted in this light. Thus, in Gildea and Glucksberg's (1983) study subjects were asked to judge whether sentences presented to them were true or false. The sentence 'Some marriages are iceboxes' was presented after two primes: 'Some summers are cold' and 'Some people are cold'. Curiously, in both prime conditions their subjects had difficulty saying that the sentence was literally false, whereas no such effect was observed for neutral primes. The metaphor 'Some marriages are iceboxes' is neither highly familiar, nor very apt for the priming effects to be explained in these terms (cf. Blasko and Connine, 1993). But an explanation in terms of similarity (either simple or analogical) would be equally bad, as Searle (1993) has convincingly argued.

In my view, such metaphors are interpreted via a lexical association route. 'Cold' applies literally both to iceboxes and to people, but to make a stronger impact on one's listeners one may convert a literal statement into a metaphor by using as that metaphor's vehicle a prototypically cold physical object. Another example of this would be 'Arctic was coming out of his eyes'. I believe that the no-polysemy view of double-function adjectives may include not only personalities, but also certain products of human intentionality, as in 'cold reply'. However, this does not mean that the same explanation should be available for all cases. 'Hot news' and 'hot trail' would be two exceptions, where one is metaphorically, and the other metonymically motivated. On the other hand, as I have argued in this book, metaphoric and metonymic (or associationist) explanations do not work for other cases.

19 I agree with cognitive linguists that polysemy has to be dealt with at the level of conceptual structure, and that the level of conceptual structure has important connections with the sensorium and kinaesthesia. Regrettably, those cognitive linguists who employ the notion of embodiment usually forget about other issues that are important for theories of concepts and theories of meaning. (But see Gibbs (2003) who says that the theory of embodiment is not entirely incompatible with traditional approaches to linguistic meaning.)

20 A clarification is in order. Grice himself never spoke of a level of logical form, distinguishing only between the levels of what is said and what is implicated (see, for instance, 1989/1975, p. 33), and characterizing what is said as 'the conventional commitment of an utterance' (ibid., p. 39). The level of logical form is a later addition to the debate between more semantically and more pragmatically oriented theorists (for a number of problems related to the question of how to draw a line between different levels see Récanati, 2001). Note also that in the body text I reserve the term 'Gricean' for those semanticists (e.g., Stanley, Szabó, Ludlow) who defend the notion of hidden variables. My reasons for giving them this somewhat idiosyncratic label are explained by the consideration that by introducing the notion of hidden variables they are carrying out one part of the Gircean programme, namely reducing the gap between sentence meaning and speaker's meaning.

21 It is very probable that the temporal span in 'what is said' is more narrowly fixed than 'at some time in the past'. That is, at the very least, it has to be restricted by the life-time of the individual. However, the question of how this fixation is achieved should not worry us here.

22 Note that Récanati's notion of what is said is closer to the notion of explicature than the Gricean notion of what is said (see Bach, 1994, for a critique).

23 I do not know what the physiology of this is, but it seems that some people cannot help jumping when they are pleased. During the England vs. Sweden game of World Cup 2002 the Swedish-born coach of the English team, Sven Goran Eriksson, actually jumped when the Swedish team scored. Then, remembering that he was supposed to be upset, he lowered his back and put on a sad face, but the first reaction unmistakeably revealed his joy.

24 Note that I do not restrict the role of pragmatics solely to reference assignment. The core of my objection to the more pragmatically oriented theories, and in particular to the notion of free pragmatic enrichment, is that the issue of context individuation remains largely ignored. Given a rich preceding context, it is often (although not always) the pragmatic mechanism alone that supplies the value 'over the cliff' for the semantically specified slot x in 'He ran to the edge of the cliff and jumped (x)'. However, the question of how previous contextual information selects the unique or the correct completion is not normally addressed in the discussions of free pragmatic enrichment. (Cf. the striking difference in how the acceptable interpretations become limited when we move from 'The policeman stopped the car' to 'The policeman was driving the car. Then he stopped it'.)

In a recent article, of which I unfortunately became aware only when the manuscript had been completed, Récanati (2002) provides a detailed argument in defence of unarticulated constituents. Here is not the place to discuss it to a significant extent but one point has to be mentioned. It is interesting to note that by employing practically the same considerations Récanati arrives to the conclusion opposite to the one I propose in the body text. Thus, he writes: 'This, then, is the criterion we must use when testing for (genuine) unarticulatedness: Can we imagine a context in which the same words are used normally, and a truth-evaluable statement is made, yet no such constituent is provided? If we can imagine such a context, then the relevant constituent is indeed unarticulated (in the strong sense); if we cannot, it is articulated, at some level of linguistic analysis' (p. 316, see also the Optimality Criterion on p. 323). And later in the article: 'On this [Récanati's] view, each *utterance* has two sets of truth-conditions. First, there are the truth-conditions of the sentence, obtained by submitting the LF-representation to semantic interpretation (in context). Second, there are the truth-conditions of the richer representation resulting from the interplay of linguistic and pragmatic factors' (pp. 341–2, my italics). From this Récanati concludes to the existence of unarticulated constituents which affect the second set of truth-conditions. On the contrary, from very similar considerations (although not given such a detailed treatment as by Récanati) I conclude to the existence of two types of variables and the non-existence of unarticulated constituents. (Note, however, that I associate the two different types of variables not with 'bindability' but with expression types and the existence of different representational levels; relevant pages in Récanati's article are 326–8 and 339–42. Note also that Récanati distinguishes between two varieties of unarticulatedness and does not consider unarticulatedness in connection with degree adjectives, which are of primary interest to us here, as an instance of strong or true unarticulatedness, see pp. 305–13.)

25   A slightly revised version of this article can be found in *Mind*, 111 (2002) 583–632.

26   Part of Wilson and Sperber's *reductio* argument is that in some situations 'what the speaker means by saying that she has or hasn't eaten might also involve a specification of the place of eating, some manner of eating, etc.' (2002, p. 239), where such specification is part of the explicature but not of what the sentence says. One example of this is 'I must wash my hands: I've eaten' where 'using my hands' is the unarticulated constituent. In my view, 'using my hands' belongs to the level of implicature rather than explicature; that is, it may not be part of the truth-evaluable proposition expressed by the sentence relative to the context of utterance. The speaker may have the habit of washing hands after every meal regardless of whether she uses her hands for eating. Compare this example to: 'I must wash my hands: I've been to the bathroom' or 'I must wash my hands: I've just returned home'. Presumably, in neither of these parallel examples does an unarticulated constituent involving using one's hands form part of the proposition expressed. On the other hand, the example 'I've often been to their parties, but I've never eaten anything' seems to require the unarticulated constituent 'there' as part of the proposition expressed by the sentence. It would be interesting to know where exactly this difference between the two sentences comes from.

27   One may think it counterintuitive that 'eat' only contains a hidden variable for the complement and not, for example, for the location. After all, one may say, a location is also crucial to the act of eating: if there is no place of

eating, there is no eating. Perhaps, one could appeal to metaphysical necessity to support this claim: every instance of eating must take place at some location or other (cf. Récanati, 2002, who argues along these lines contra hidden variables and in favour of unarticulated constituents, especially p. 320). I have to say that I have a different view of metaphysical necessity. For instance, if you could eat a hamburger inside a black hole, you would be eating a hamburger but the instance of eating would not be taking place at a (certain) location (this is what makes black holes so funny). However, without a hamburger there would be no eating.

28 For a detailed discussion of radical pragmatics (Searle) and its overlaps with moderate pragmatics (relevance theory, Récanati) see Cappelen and Lepore (2001). For more on radical pragmatics see Bezuidenhout (2002). For a discussion of radical pragmatics and adjectival interpretation see Szabó (2001).

29 For instance, when figuring out whether 'a good knife' is 'a knife good for cutting' or 'a knife good for stabbing'.

30 For simplicity's sake I assume that 'Holland' denotes a geographically (geopolitically) delineated terrain.

31 Here I am expressing a position that is close to the theory of psychological essentialism (Keil, 1989; Medin and Ortony, 1989), according to which people are prone to think that things that have the same name share some essential property. Whether and how language speakers employ such considerations in deciding whether something is a metaphor is, of course, a different question. (For some recent discussions of psychological essentialism see Malt (1994) and Braisby *et al.* (1996). Note, however, that neither of the articles concludes that psychological essentialism is false but rather that both essentialist and non-essentialist considerations underlie human thinking and language use.)

32 As one can see, the reason why my account of polysemy and the conceptual structure diverges from Fodor's (1998a), with whom I am otherwise largely in agreement, is that I understand concepts differently. For Fodor, the sameness of concepts implies the sameness of meanings (KEEP is a univocal concept because 'keep' always means the same). This is the standard assumption all over again, but the standard assumption is wrong when it comes to synaesthetic adjectives. Thus, I suspect that it may be generally wrong. Unlike Fodor, I believe that polysemy is a real phenomenon, and emphasize that a theory of meaning does not have to be at the same time a theory of concepts. 'Keep' always expresses the same univocal atomic concept KEEP, but the meaning of 'keep' in 'keep'-phrases depends on what it is that is being kept. That is, what makes 'He kept the money in the wallet' and 'He kept the promise' true is whether he kept the money in the wallet and whether he kept the promise; but keeping money in a wallet and keeping promises differ inasmuch as money and promises differ.

Fodor considers the possibility that 'keep' may be ambiguous (read: homonymous; 1998a, p. 50, f. 7) as there is something zeugmatic about 'He kept his promises and his snowshoes in the cellar'. But there is something similarly zeugmatic about 'He kept the crowd happy and his snowshoes in the cellar', even though, according to Fodor, 'keep' means the same in 'He kept the crowd happy' and 'He kept his snowshoes in the cellar'. (Consider also 'After the deal he kept the snowshoes and the money in the wallet'.) In any case, since verbal polysemy is not a concern of this book, and since a detailed consideration of it would require several pages of text, I do not discuss this example any further.

33 Polysemous verbs such as 'open' have always puzzled those who study language (see, for example, Carston, 1996; Searle, 1983, pp. 145–8). Curiously, it is one of the cases of polysemy that, as far as I know, has been ignored by cognitive semanticists. But perhaps this is not surprising, since it would be very hard to say which of the meanings of 'open' is the experientially primary meaning: does one model one's understanding of 'open the mouth' on the understanding of 'open the door', or are things the other way round? When I say that psychologically primitive concepts incorporate perceptual or embodied schematisms I do not intend it in the cognitive semantics sense. 'Open' always expresses the concept OPEN which allows us to detect the relation of opening in its various realizations. The perceptual schematism that the concept OPEN incorporates is probably something like 'make the contents of something accessible by opening it whichever way it can be best opened' (this is not the definition of 'open'). Perhaps this is the reason why young Russian children often say 'open the TV' when they mean 'switch on the TV'. As far as I can see, whether language speakers possess any such primitive concept OPEN can be tested by asking them to carry out 'open'-requests on those objects for which they are not likely to have 'open'-stereotypes (cf. Searle, 1983, p. 147). I would expect that lighters (the cheapest kind that are not supposed to be opened) will prove amenable to such requests whereas drinking glasses (without packaging) will not. (The protest 'How do you think I am going to open it?' will be voiced at different delays.) An interesting question for the semantics-pragmatics debate is wheher such metonymic expressions as 'open tomatoes' are processed pragmatically, or whether a number of short-cuts exist at the semantic level.

34 I think it is not surprising that the second category includes mostly verbs and adjectives, whereas the third category consists mostly of nouns. As Bickerton (1990, pp. 96–8) notes, verbs are a lot more abstract than nouns, and the same, presumably, goes for adjectives as well.

35 Scientific discoveries are often considered as examples of global metaphoric thinking and metaphoric 'enrichment' of new theories. Elsewhere (Rakova, forthcoming) I argue that such claims have been exaggerated. In particular, I discuss the emergence of Bohr's atomic theory which is often cited as an example of discovery through metaphor (Gentner, 1983; Gentner and Jeziorski, 1993; Nersessian, 1992), and show that this view can be held only by those who have a very superficial knowledge of physics.

36 Logical polysemy certainly deserves a discussion of its own, but here is not the place to do that. As Apresjan (1974) noted, the difference between metaphorically and metonymically motivated polysemy is that metaphorically motivated polysemy is relatively unconstrained, whereas metonymically motivated polysemy is systematic or 'regular'. The connection between the meanings of a word in the cases of metonymically motivated polysemy also seems to be stronger than in the cases of metaphorically motivated polysemy. Still, I think that in the cases of logical polysemy we also have the one word – several meanings – several related concepts pattern. Let me explain why.

'Book' is a case of logical polysemy because it can refer to a physical object and a certain type of information. The two meanings are clearly interconnected in our thought: books as a certain type of information are normally contained within books as physical objects. So, it might appear that there is just one concept BOOK, different 'aspects' of which can be focused whenever necessary. However, books as physical objects and books as a certain type of information do not have to come together. On the one hand, today a good number of books appear on CDs or are published on the Internet: they do not stop being books because of that. On the other hand, 'book' refers to a certain type of binding, and thus there can be books of reproductions or comics books which do not contain the right type of information to be called 'books'. Thus, it seems that although the connection between the two meanings/concepts is very strong, it is not a necessary connection. The same is probably true of 'chicken' as well. Even though 'chicken' as meat comes from 'chicken' as a bird, it is possible that one could have the concept $CHICKEN_1$ (meat) but not the concept $CHICKEN_2$ (bird). Some recent evidence also suggests that the meanings of logical polysemes are represented separately (see Klein and Murphy, 2001, 2002).

37 Here is one example of wishful thinking about metaphoric motivation: 'It is especially risky to speculate on the basis of surface "appearance" whether a given expression is a *dead* metaphor. Kronfeld [1980/81] cites Alston's [1964] use of "fork in the road" as a nice example of fallacious armchair theorizing. Although Alston tells a *prima facie* plausible story of how the phrase came to be metaphorical, in actual fact it did not historically originate as metaphor but rather as a literal application of "fork" meaning "that which branches or divides"' (Stern, 2000, p. 324, f. 38; this example is also discussed in Gibbs, 1994, p. 275).

38 Some people hate it when jokes and puns are only alluded to. Here is a very old one: 'I've just bought my wife a bottle of toilet water for 100 pounds' – 'You could have had some from my loo for nothing'. Or, as an unfortunate advertisement said: 'This is your new XYZ vacuum-cleaner! It really sucks!'. Dascal (1987) uses jokes as evidence that the literal meaning of sentences is processed even though it may not be the final product of understanding. Given the evidence from differential hemispheric language processing (see Chapter 6) this seems to be a correct view, although it equally concerns polysemes and homonyms.

39 Dictionaries may specify standard figurative *uses* for some words. However, this does not make them metaphoric *meanings* (cf. Pynte et al., 1996). 'These fighters are lions' which has the standard interpretation 'These fighters are courageous' (or something like it, if you think that metaphors cannot be paraphrased) can be easily understood as 'These fighters are blonde and hairy' or as 'These fighters are violent'. One cannot argue over metaphor interpretation.

References

Abbott, B., 'A Note on the Nature of "Water"', *Mind*, 106 (1997), 311–19.
Allen, C. and M. Hauser, 'Concept Attribution in Nonhuman Animals: Theoretical and Methodological Problems in Ascribing Complex Mental Processes', *Philosophy of Science*, 58 (1991), 221–40.
Alston, W.P., *Philosophy of Language* (Englewood Cliffs, NJ: Prentice Hall, 1964).
Anaki, D., M. Faust and S. Kravetz, 'Cerebral Hemispheric Asymmetries in Processing Lexical Metaphors', *Neuropsychologia*, 36 (1998), 691–700.
Apresjan, J., 'Regular Polysemy', *Linguistics*, 142 (1974), 5–32.
Asch, S.E., 'On the Use of Metaphor in the Description of Persons', in H. Werner, ed., *On Expressive Language: Papers Presented at Clark University Conference on Expressive Language Behavior* (Worcester, MA.: Clark University Press, 1955), pp. 29–38.
Asch, S.E., 'The Metaphor: A Psychological Inquiry', in R. Tagiuri and L. Petrullo, eds, *Person Perception and Interpersonal Behavior* (Stanford, CA: Stanford University Press, 1958), pp. 80–94.
Asch, S.E. and H. Nerlove, 'The Development of Double Function Terms in Children', in B. Kaplan and S. Wapner, eds, *Perspectives in Psychological Theory* (New York: International Universities Press, 1960), pp. 47–60.
Bach, K., *Thought and Reference* (Oxford: Oxford University Press, 1987).
Bach, K., 'Conversational Implication', *Mind and Language*, 9 (1994), 124–62.
Bach, K., 'Quantification, Qualification and Context. A Reply to Stanley and Szabó', *Journal of Pragmatics*, 15 (2000), 262–83.
Badecker, B. and A. Caramazza, 'On Considerations of Method and Theory Governing the Use of Clinical Categories in Neurolinguistics and Cognitive Neuropsychology: the Case against Agrammatism', *Cognition*, 20 (1985), 97–125.
Bailey, M.E.S. and K.J. Johnson, 'Synaesthesia: is a Genetic Analysis Feasible?', in S. Baron-Cohen and J.E. Harrison, eds, *Synaesthesia: Classic and Contemporary Readings* (Oxford: Blackwell, 1997), pp.182–207.
Ballard, D.H., 'Animate Vision', *Artificial Intelligence*, 48 (1992), 57–86.
Ballard, D.H., M.M. Hayhoe, P.K. Pook and R.P.N. Rao, 'Diectic Codes for the Embodiment of Cognition', *Behavioral and Brain Sciences*, 20 (1997), 723–61.
Barkow, J., L. Cosmides, and J. Tooby, eds, *The Adapted Mind* (Oxford: Oxford University Press, 1992).
Baron-Cohen, S., *Mindblindness: an Essay on Autism and Theory of Mind* (Cambridge, MA: MIT Press, 1995).
Baron-Cohen, S., 'Is There a Normal Phase of Synaesthesia in Development?', *Psyche*, 2 (1996), http://psyche.cs.monash.edu.au/v2/psyche-2-27-baron_cohen.html.
Baron-Cohen, S., J. Harrison, L. Goldstein and M.A. Wyke, 'Coloured Speech Perception: Is Synaesthesia what Happens when Modularity Breaks Down?', *Perception*, 22 (1993), 419–26.
Baron-Cohen, S., L. Burt, F. Smith-Laittan, *et al.*, 'Synaesthesia: Prevalence and Familiarity', *Perception*, 25 (1996), 1073–9.

Barsalou, L.W., 'Perceptual Symbol Systems', *Behavioral and Brain Sciences*, 22 (1999), 577–633.
Baynes, K. and C. Iven, 'Access to the Phonological Lexicon in an Aphasic Patient', Paper Presented to the Annual Meeting of the Academy of Aphasia (1991).
Beardsley, M., 'Metaphorical Twist', *Philosophy and Phenomenological Research*, 22 (1962), 293–307.
Beardsley, M., 'Metaphorical Senses', *Nous*, 12 (1978), 3–16.
Beeman, M., R.B. Friedman, J. Grafman, *et al.*, 'Summation Priming and Coarse Semantic Coding in the Right Hemisphere', *Journal of Cognitive Neuroscience*, 6 (1994), 26–45.
Békésy, G. von, 'Similarities Between Hearing and Skin Sensations', *Psychological Review*, 66 (1959), 1–22.
Berlin, B. and P. Kay, *Basic Colour Terms: Their Understanding and Evolution* (Berkeley, CA: University of California Press, 1969).
Bezuidenhout, A., 'Truth-Conditional Pragmatics', *Nous*, supp. 16 (2002), 105–34.
Bialystok, E., 'Metalinguistic Awareness: The Development of Children's Representations of Language', in C. Pratt and A.F. Garton, eds, *Systems of Representation in Children: Development and Use* (Chichester: Wiley, 1993), pp. 211–33.
Bickerton, D., *Language and Species* (Chicago, IL: University of Chicago Press, 1990).
Black, M., 'Metaphor', in his *Models and Metaphors* (Ithaca, NY: Cornell University Press, 1962), pp. 25–47.
Black, M., 'More About Metaphor', in A. Ortony, ed., *Metaphor and Thought*, 2nd edn (Cambridge: Cambridge University Press, 1993), pp. 19–41.
Blackburn, S., *Spreading the Word: Groundings in the Philosophy of Language* (Oxford: Clarendon Press, 1984).
Blasko, D.G. and C.M. Connine, 'Effects of Familiarity and Aptness in the Processing of Metaphor', *Journal of Experimental Psychology: Learning, Memory and Cognition*, 19 (1993), 295–308.
Bottini, G., R. Corcoran, R. Sterzi, *et al.*, 'The Role of the Right Hemisphere in the Interpretation of Figurative Aspects of Language. A Positron Emission Tomography Activation Study', *Brain*, 117 (1994), 1241–53.
Bower, T.G.R., *A Primer of Infant Development* (San Francisco: W.H. Freeman, 1977).
Boynton, R.M. and C.X. Olson, 'Locating Basic Colour Terms in the OSA Space', *Color Research and Application*, 12 (1987), 107–23.
Braak, H., U. Rub, D. Sandmann-Keil, *et al.*, 'Parkinson's Disease: Affection of Brain Stem Nuclei Controlling Premotor and Motor Neurons of the Somatomotor System', *Acta Neuropathologica*, 99 (2000), 489–95.
Braisby, N., 'When are Concepts One or Many?', *Trends in Cognitive Sciences*, 3 (1999), 321.
Braisby, N., B. Franks and J. Hampton, 'Essentialism, Word Use, and Concepts. *Cognition*, 59 (1996), 247–74.
Bretones Callejas, C., 'Synaesthetic Metaphors in English' (On-line Publication, 2001) http://www.icsi.berkeley.edu/ftp/pub/techreports/2001/tr-01-008.pdf.
Brodal, P., *The Central Nervous System. Structure and Function* (Oxford: Oxford University Press, 1992).
Brown, R., *Words and Things* (New York: The Free Press, 1958).

Brown, A.L., 'Analogical Learning and Transfer: what Develops?', in S. Vosniadou and A. Ortony, eds, *Similarity and Analogical Reasoning* (Cambridge: Cambridge University Press, 1989), pp. 369–412.
Brownell, H.H., H.H. Potter, D. Michelow and H. Gardner, 'Sensitivity to Lexical Denotation and Connotation in Brain Damaged Patients: a Double Dissociation?', *Brain and Language*, 100 (1984), 717–29.
Brownell, H.H., T.L. Simpson, A.M. Bihrle, *et al.*, 'Appreciation of Metaphoric Alternative Word Meanings by Left and Right Brain Damaged Patients', *Neuropsychologia*, 28 (1990), 375–83.
Burgess, C. and G.B. Simpson, 'Cerebral Hemispheric Mechanism in the Retrieval of Ambiguous Word Meanings', *Brain and Language*, 33 (1988), 86–103.
Burgess, C. and C. Chiarello, 'Neurocognitive Mechanisms Underlying Metaphor Comprehension and other Figurative Language', *Metaphor and Symbolic Activity*, 11 (1996), 67–84.
Bush, G., P. Luu and M.I. Posner, 'Cognitive and Emotional Influences in Anterior Cingulate Cortex', *Trends in Cognitive Sciences*, 4 (2000), 215–22.
Byrne, R., *The Thinking Ape* (Oxford: Oxford University Press, 1995).
Caplan, D., *Neurolinguistics and Linguistic Aphasiology* (Cambridge: Cambridge University Press, 1987).
Cappelen, H. and E. Lepore, 'Radical and Moderate Pragmatics: Does Meaning Determine Truth Conditions?', unpublished manuscript, 2001.
Caramazza, A. and E. Grober, 'Polysemy and the Structure of the Subjective Lexicon', in C. Rameh, ed., *Semantics: Theory and Application* (Washington, DC: Georgetown University Press, 1976), pp. 181–206.
Carey, S., 'Semantic Development: the State of the Art', in L. Gleitman and E. Wanner, eds, *Language Acquisition: the State of the Art* (New York: Cambridge University Press, 1982).
Carston, R., 'Implicature, Explicature and Truth-Theoretic Semantics', in R. Kempson, ed., *Mental Representations: the Interface between Language and Reality* (Cambridge: Cambridge University Press, 1988), pp. 155–81.
Carston, R., 'Enrichment and Loosening: Complementary Processes in Deriving the Proposition Expressed?', *UCL Working Papers in Linguistics*, 8 (1996), 61–88.
Carston, R., 'Explicature and Semantics', *UCL Working Papers in Linguistics*, 12 (2000), 1–46.
Carston, R., 'Linguistic Meaning, Communicated Meaning and Cognitive Pragmatics', *Mind and Language*, 17 (2002), 127–48.
Cassell's *English–Dutch, Dutch–English Dictionary*, completely revised by J.A. Jockin-La Bastide, G. van Kooten and J. Kramers (London: Cassel, 1980).
Cassirer, E., *Language and Myth* (New York: Dover, 1946).
Caterina, M.J., M.A. Schumacher, M. Tominaga, *et al.*, 'The Capsaicin Receptor: A Heat-Activated Ion Channel in the Pain Pathway', *Nature*, 389 (1997), 816–24.
Caterina, M.J., A. Leffler, A.B. Malmberg, *et al.*, 'Impaired Nociception and Pain Sensation in Mice Lacking the Capsaicin Receptor', *Science*, 288 (2000), 306–13.
Chiarello, C., 'Hemisphere Dynamics in Lexical Access: Automatic and Controlled Priming', *Brain and Language*, 26 (1985), 146–72.
Chiarello, C., 'Meanings by Cerebral Hemispheres: One is Not Enough', in P.J. Schwanenflugel, ed., *The Psychology of Words Meanings* (Hillsdale, NJ: Lawrence Erlbaum, 1991), pp. 251–78.

Chiarello, C., C. Burgess, L. Richards and A. Pollock, 'Semantic and Associative Priming in the Cerebral Hemispheres: Some Words Do, Some Words Don't...Sometimes, Some Places', *Brain and Language*, 38 (1990), 75–104.

Chiarello, C., L. Maxfield and T. Kahan, 'Initial Right Hemisphere Activation of Subordinate Word Meanings is Not Due to Homotopic Callosal Inhibition', *Psychonomic Bulletin and Review*, 2 (1995), 375–80.

Chobor, K.L. and A. Schweiger, 'Processing of Lexical Ambiguity in Patients with Traumatic Brain Injury', *Journal of Neurolinguistics*, 11 (1998), 119–36.

Chomsky, N., 'Language and Nature', *Mind*, 104 (1995), 1–61.

Chomsky, N. and H. Lasnik, 'The Theory of Principles and Parameters', in J. Jacobs, A. von Stechow, W. Sternefeld and T. Vennemann, eds, *Syntax: an International Handbook of Contemporary Research* (Berlin: Walter de Gruyter, 1993), pp. 506–69.

Churchland, P.M., *A Neurocomputational Perspective: the Nature of Mind and the Structure of Science* (Cambridge, MA: MIT Press, 1991).

Clapham, D.E., 'Some Like it Hot: Spicing up Ion Channels', *Nature*, 389 (1997), 783–4.

Clark, A., 'Reasons, Robots, and the Extended Mind', *Mind and Language*, 16 (2001), 121–45.

Claudi, U. and B. Heine, 'On the Metaphorical Basis of Grammar', *Studies in Language*, 10 (1986), 297–335.

Cohen, J., 'The Semantics of Metaphor', in A. Ortony, ed., *Metaphor and Thought*, 2nd edn (Cambridge: Cambridge University Press, 1993), pp. 58–70.

Cohen, T., 'Metaphor, Feeling, and Narrative', *Philosophy and Literature*, 21 (1997), 223–44.

Collins Concise Spanish–English English–Spanish Dictionary, ed. by M. Gonzalez (London: Collins, 1985).

Collins German–English English–German Dictionary, ed. by P. Terrell (Glasgow: Harper Collins, 1993).

Collins and Robert French–English English–French Dictionary, ed. by B.T. Atkins (Glasgow: HarperCollins, Paris: Le Robert, 1987).

Concise Oxford Dictionary, The, ed. by D. Thompson (Oxford: Clarendon Press, 1995).

Cooper, D., *Metaphor* (Oxford: Oxford University Press, 1986).

Costall, A., G. Parovel and M. Sinico, 'Getting Real About Invariants', *Behavioral and Brain Sciences*, 24 (2001), 219–20.

Cramer, P., 'Homonym Understanding and Conversation', *Journal of Experimental Child Psychology*, 36 (1983), 179–95.

Curtis, M., 'Children's Understanding of Polysemous Terms', Abstract of the Talk Presented at Developmental Psychology Section Conference, 14–17 September 1984, Lancaster University, *Bulletin of the British Psychological Society*, 38 (1985), A17.

Cytowic, R.E., *Synesthesia: a Union of the Senses* (New York: Springer-Verlag, 1989a).

Cytowic, R.E., 'Synesthesia and Mapping of Subjective Sensory Dimensions', *Neurology*, 39 (1989b), 849–50.

Cytowic, R.E., *The Man Who Tasted Shapes* (New York: Warner Books, 1993).

Cytowic, R.E., 'Synesthesia: Phenomenology and Neuropsychology. A Review of Current Knowledge', *Psyche*, 2 (1995), http://psyche.cs.monash.edu.au/v2/psyche-2-10-cytowic.html.

Dahl, O., 'Women, Fire and Dangerous Things: What Categories Reveal about the Mind – Lakoff, G' (Book Review), *Linguistics*, 21 (1989), 1143–52.
Dailey, A., C. Martindale and J. Borkum, 'Creativity, Synaesthesia and Physiognomic Perception', *Creativity Research Journal*, 10 (1997), 1–8.
Damasio, A.R., *The Feeling of What Happens: Body and Emotion in the Making of Consciousness* (New York: Harcourt Brace, 1999).
Damasio, A.R. and D. Tranel, 'Nouns and Verbs are Retrieved with Differently Distributed Neural Systems', *Proceedings of the National Academy of Sciences of the United States of America*, 90 (1993), 4957–60.
Dann, K.T., *Bright Colours Falsely Seen* (New Haven, CT: Yale University Press, 1998).
Dascal, M., 'Defending Literal Meaning', *Cognitive Science*, 11 (1987), 259–81.
Davidson, D., 'What Metaphors Mean', in his *Inquiries into Truth and Interpretation* (Oxford: Clarendon Press, 1978/1984a), pp. 245–64.
Davidson, D., 'Reality Without Reference', in his *Inquiries into Truth and Interpretation* (Oxford: Clarendon Press, 1984b), pp. 215–25.
Davidson, D., 'The Method of Truth in Metaphysics', in his *Inquiries into Truth and Interpretation* (Oxford: Clarendon Press, 1984c), pp. 199–214.
Davis, J.B., J. Gray, M.J. Gunthorpe, *et al.*, 'Vanilloid Receptor-1 is Essential for Inflammatory Thermal Hyperalgesia', *Nature*, 405 (2000), 183–7.
Day, S., 'Synaesthesia and Synaesthetic Metaphors', *Psyche*, 2 (1996), http://psyche.cs.monash.edu.au/v2/psyche-2-32-day.html.
Deacon, T.W., *The Symbolic Species: The Co-Evolution of Language and the Bran* (New York: W.W. Norton, 1997).
Defrin, R., A. Ohry, N. Blumen and G. Urca, 'Sensory Determinants of Thermal Pain', *Brain*, 125 (2002), 501–10.
de Gelder, B., J. Vroomen, G. Pourtois and L. Weiskrantz, 'Non-Conscious Recognition of Affect in the Absence of Striate Cortex', *NeuroReport*, 10 (1999), 3759–63.
de Gelder, B., J. Vroomen, G. Pourtois and L. Weiskrantz, 'Affective Blindsight: Are We Blindly Led by Emotions?', *Trends in Cognitive Sciences*, 4 (2000), 126–7.
de Gelder, B., G. Pourtois and L. Weiskrantz, 'Fear Recognition in the Voice is Modulated by Unconsciously Recognized Facial Expressions but Not by Unconsciously Recognized Affective Pictures', *Proceedings of the National Academy of Sciences of the United States of America*, 99 (2002), 4121–6.
de Oliveira-Souza, R., J. Moll, F.T. Moll and D.L.G. de Oliveira, 'Executive Amnesia in a Patient with Pre-Frontal Damage due to a Gunshot Wound', *Neurocase*, 7 (2001), 383–9.
Devitt, M. and K. Sterelny, *Language and Reality* (Oxford: Blackwell, 1987).
Dingwall, W.O., 'Complex Behaviors: Evolution and the Brain', *Behavioral and Brain Sciences*, 18 (1995), 186–8.
Dixon, R.M.W., *Where Have All Adjectives Gone? and Other Essays in Semantics and Syntax* (New York: Mouton de Gruyter, 1982).
Dixon, M.J., D. Smilek, C. Cudahy and P.M. Merikle, 'Five Plus Two Equals Yellow', *Nature*, 406 (2000), 365.
Dretske, F., *Naturalizing the Mind* (Cambridge, MA: The MIT Press, 1995).
Dummett, M., *Frege: Philosophy of Language* (New York: Harper & Row, 1973).
Dunbar, R., 'Theory of Mind and the Evolution of Language', in J.R. Hurford, M. Studdert-Kennedy and C. Knight, eds, *Approaches to the Evolution of Language* (Cambridge: Cambridge University Press, 1998), pp. 92–110.

Durkin, K. and J. Manning, 'Polysemy and the Subjective Lexicon: Semantic Relatedness and the Salience of Intraword Senses', *Journal of Psycholinguistic Research*, 18 (1989), 577–612.
Edelman, G.M., *Bright Air, Brilliant Fire: On the Matter of the Mind* (New York: Basic Books, 1992).
Eimas, P., 'Categorization in Early Infancy and the Continuity of Development', *Cognition*, 50 (1994), 83–93.
English–Greek Dictionary: a vocabulary of the Attic language, ed. by S.C. Woodhouse (London: G. Routledge and Sons, 1932).
Ettlinger, G., 'The Relationship Between Metaphorical and Cross-Modal Abilities: Failure to Demonstrate Metaphorical Recognition in Chimpanzees Capable of Cross-Modal Recognition', *Neuropsychologia*, 19 (1981), 583–6.
Ettlinger, G. and W.A. Wilson, 'Cross-Modal Performance: Behavioural Process, Phylogenetic Considerations and Neural Mechanisms', *Behavioural Brain Research*, 40 (1990), 169–92.
Fauconnier, G. and M. Turner, 'Blending as a Central Process of Grammar', in A. Goldberg, ed., *Conceptual Structure, Discourse, and Language* (Stanford, CA: CSLI, 1996), pp. 183–203.
Fauconnier, G. and M. Turner, 'Conceptual Integration Networks', *Cognitive Science*, 22 (1998), 133–87.
Fauconnier, G. and M. Turner, *The Way We Think: Conceptual Blending and the Mind's Hidden Complexities* (New York: Basic Books, 2002).
Fields, H.L., *Pain* (New York: McGraw-Hill, 1987).
Flavell, J.H., 'The Development of Children's Knowledge about the Mind: From Cognitive Connections to Mental Representations', in J. Astington, P. Harris and D. Olson, eds, *Developing Theories of Mind* (New York: Cambridge University Press, 1988), pp. 244–67.
Flavell, J.H. and P.H. Miller, 'Social Cognition', in D. Kuhn and R.S. Siegler, eds, *Handbook of Child Psychology: Vol. 2 Cognition, Perception, and Language*, 5th edn (New York: Wiley, 1998), pp. 851–98.
Flavell, J.H., E.R. Flavell, and F.L. Green, 'Development of Children's Understanding of Connections Between Thinking and Feeling', *Psychological Science*, 12 (2001), 430–32.
Fodor, J.A., 'Three Reasons for Not Deriving "Kill" from "Cause to Die"', *Linguistic Inquiry*, 1 (1970), 429–38.
Fodor, J.A., *The Language of Thought* (New York: Crowell, 1975).
Fodor, J.A., *The Modularity of Mind: an Essay on Faculty Psychology* (Cambridge, MA: MIT Press, 1983).
Fodor, J.A., 'A Theory of Content, I: The problem', in his *A Theory of Content and Other Essays* (Cambridge, MA: MIT Press, 1990), pp. 51–87.
Fodor, J.A., *Concepts: Where Cognitive Science Went Wrong* (Oxford: Clarendon Press, 1998a).
Fodor, J.A., 'There are No Recognitional Concepts – Not Even RED', in his *In Critical Condition: Polemical Essays on Cognitive Science and the Philosophy of Mind* (Cambridge, MA: MIT Press, 1998b), pp. 35–47.
Fodor, J.A., 'Language, Thought and Compositionality', *Mind and Language*, 16 (2001), 1–15.
Fodor, J.A. and E. Lepore, *Holism: a Shopper's Guide* (Oxford: Blackwell, 1992).

Fodor, J.A. and E. Lepore, 'The Emptiness of the Lexicon: Reflections on James Pustejovsky's The Generative Lexicon', *Linguistic Inquiry*, 29 (1998), 269–88.
Fodor, J.D., J.A. Fodor, and M. Garrett, 'The Psychological Unreality of Semantic Representations', *Linguistic Inquiry*, 6 (1975), 515–32.
Fogelin, R., *Figuratively Speaking* (New Haven, CT: Yale University Press, 1988).
Fox, P.T., 'Broca's Area: Motor Encoding in Somatic Space', *Behavioral and Brain Sciences*, 18 (1995), 344–5.
Frazier, L. and K. Rayner, 'Taking on Semantic Commitments: Processing Multiple Meanings vs. Multiple Senses', *Journal of Memory and Language*, 29 (1990), 181–200.
Frith, C.D. and E. Paulesu, 'The Physiological Basis of Synaesthesia', in S. Baron-Cohen and J. Harrison, eds, *Synaesthesia: Classic and Contemporary Readings* (Oxford: Blackwell, 1997), pp. 123–47.
Fuster, J.M., M. Bodner and J.K. Kroger, 'Cross-Modal and Cross-Temporal Association in Neurons of Frontal Cortex', *Nature*, 405 (2000), 347–51.
Gainotti, G., M.C. Silveri, A. Daniele and L. Giustolisi, 'Neuroanatomical Correlates of Category-Specific Semantic Disorders: A Critical Survey', *Memory*, 3 (1995), 247–64.
Gardner, H., 'Metaphors and Modalities: How Children Project Polar Adjectives onto Diverse Domains', *Child Development*, 45 (1974), 84–91.
Gardner, H. and H.H. Brownell, *Right Hemisphere Communication Battery* (Boston: Psychology Service, VAMC 1986).
Garnham, A., 'Women, Fire and Dangerous Things: What Categories Reveal about the Mind – Lakoff, G.' (Book Review), *Quarterly Journal of Experimental Psychology*, 41 (1989), 415–7.
Garrett, M.F., 'The Analysis of Sentence Production' in G.H. Bower, ed., *Psychology of Learning and Motivation*, Vol. 9. (New York: Academic Press, 1975), pp. 133–77.
Garrett, M.F., 'Syntactic Processes in Sentence Production', in R. Wales and E. Walker, eds, *New Approaches to Language Mechanisms* (Amsterdam: North-Holland, 1976), pp. 231–56.
Garrett, M.F., 'Production of Speech: Observations from Normal and Pathological Language Use', in A. Ellis, ed., *Normality and Pathology in Cognitive Functions* (London: Academic Press, 1982), pp. 19–76.
Garrett, M.F., 'The Organization of Processing Structure for Language Production: Applications to Aphasic Speech', in D. Caplan, A.R. Lecours and A. Smith, eds, *Biological Perspectives on Language* (Cambridge, MA: MIT Press, 1984), pp. 172–93.
Gauthier, I. and N.K. Logothetis, 'Is Face Recognition not so Unique After All?', *Cognitive Neuropsychology*, 17 (2000), 125–42.
Gazzaniga, M.S., R.B. Ivry and G.R. Magnum, *Cognitive Neuroscience: The Biology of the Mind* (New York: W.W. Norton, 1998).
Gentner, D., 'Structure-Mapping: A Theoretical Framework for Analogy', *Cognitive Science*, 7 (1983), 155–70.
Gentner, D., 'Metaphor as Structure-Mapping: The Relational Shift' *Child Development*, 59 (1988), 47–59.
Gentner, D., 'The Mechanisms of Analogical Learning', in S. Vosniadou and A. Ortony, eds, *Similarity and Analogical Reasoning* (Cambridge: Cambridge University Press, 1989), pp. 199–241.

Gentner, D. and M. Jeziorski, 'The Shift from Metaphor to Analogy in Western Science', in A. Ortony, ed., *Metaphor and Thought*, 2nd edn (Cambridge: Cambridge University Press 1993), pp. 447–80.

Gentner, D. and P. Stuart, *Metaphor as Structure-Mapping: What Develops*, Tech. Rep. 5479 (Cambridge, MA: Bolt, Beranek & Newman, 1983).

Geschwind, N., 'The Development of the Brain and the Evolution of Language', in C.J.J.M. Stuart, ed., *Monograph Series on Language and Linguistics, Vol. 17* (Washington, DC: Georgetown University, 1964).

Geschwind, N., 'Disconnexion Syndromes in Animals and Man', *Brain*, 88 (1965), 237–94, 585–644.

Gibbs, R.W., 'Process and Products in Making Sense of Tropes', in A. Ortony, ed., *Metaphor and Thought*, 2nd edn (Cambridge: Cambridge University Press, 1993), pp. 252–76.

Gibbs, R.W., *The Poetics of Mind: Figurative Thought, Language, and Understanding*. (Cambridge: Cambridge University Press, 1994).

Gibbs, R.W., 'Why Many Concepts are Metaphorical', *Cognition*, 61 (1996), 309–19.

Gibbs, R.W., 'Taking Metaphor out of our Heads and Putting it into the Cultural World', in G. Steen and R.W. Gibbs, eds, *Metaphor in Cognitive Linguistics* (Amsterdam: John Benjamins, 1999a), pp. 145–66.

Gibbs, R.W., 'Interpreting what Speakers Say and Implicate', *Brain and Language*, 68 (1999b), 466–85.

Gibbs, R.W., 'A New Look at Literal Meaning in Understanding what is Said and Implicated', *Journal of Pragmatics*, 34 (2002), 457–86.

Gibbs, R.W., 'Embodied Experience and Linguistic Meaning', in *Brain and Language*, 84 (2003), 1–15.

Gibbs, R.W., J. Kushner, and R. Mills, 'Authorial Intentions and Metaphor Comprehension', *Journal of Psycholinguistic Research*, 20 (1991), 11–30.

Gibbs, R.W., D.L. Buchalter, J.F. Moise and W.T. Farrar, 'Literal Meaning and Figurative Language', *Discourse Processes*, 16 (1993), 387–403.

Gibson, J.J., *The Senses Considered as Perceptual Systems* (Boston: Houghton Mifflin, 1966).

Gilbert, A.N., R. Martin and S.E. Kemp, 'Cross-Modal Correspondences Between Vision and Olfaction: The Colour of Smells', *American Journal of Psychology*, 109 (1996), 335–51.

Gildea, P. and S. Glucksberg, 'On Understanding Metaphor: the Role of Context', *Journal of Verbal Learning and Verbal Behavior*, 22 (1983), 577–90.

Giora, R., 'Understanding Figurative and Literal Language: The Graded Salience Hypothesis', *Cognitive Linguistics*, 7 (1997), 183–206.

Giora, R., 'When is Relevance? On the Role of Salience in Utterance Interpretation', *Revista Alicantina de Estudios Ingleses*, 11 (1998), 85–94.

Giora, R., 'On the Priority of Salient Meanings: Studies of Literal and Figurative Language', *Journal of Pragmatics*, 31 (1999), 919–29.

Giora, R., 'Literal vs. Figurative Language: Different or Equal?', *Journal of Pragmatics*, 34 (2002), 487–506.

Giora, R., E. Zaidel, N. Soroker, *et al.*, 'Differential Effect of Right and Left Hemispheric Damage on Understanding Sarcasm and Metaphor' (Unpublished Manuscript, 1997).

Glenberg, A.M., 'What Memory is For', *Behavioral and Brain Sciences*, 20 (1997), 1–19.

Glenberg, A.M., and D.A. Robertson, 'Symbol Grounding and Meaning: a Comparison of High-Dimensional and Embodied Theory of Meaning', *Journal of Memory and Language*, 43 (2000), 379–401.
Glucksberg, S. and B. Keysar, 'Understanding Metaphorical Comparisons: Beyond Similarity', *Psychological Review*, 97 (1990), 3–18.
Glucksberg, S. and B. Keysar, 'How Metaphors Work', in A. Ortony, ed., *Metaphor and Thought*, 2nd edn (Cambridge: Cambridge University Press, 1993), pp. 401–24.
Glucksberg, S. and M.S. McGlone, 'When Love is Not a Journey: What Metaphors Mean', *Journal of Pragmatics*, 31 (1999), 1541–58.
Glucksberg, S., *Understanding Figurative Language: From Metaphors to Idioms* (Oxford: Oxford University Press, 2001).
Goatly, A., *The Language of Metaphors* (London: Routledge, 1997).
Goldstein, K., *Language and Language Disturbances* (New York: Grune and Stratton, 1948).
Goodman, N., *Languages of Art* (Indianapolis, IN: Hackett, 1968).
Goswami, U., *Analogical Reasoning in Children* (Hillsdale, NJ: Lawrence Erlbaum, 1992).
Grady, J.E., 'A Typology of Motivation for Conceptual Metaphor: Correlation vs. Resemblance', in G. Steen and R.W. Gibbs, eds, *Metaphor in Cognitive Linguistics* (Amsterdam: John Benjamins, 1999), pp. 79–100.
Grady, J.E., S. Taub and P. Morgan, 'Primitive and Compound Metaphors', in A. Goldberg, ed., *Conceptual Structure, Discourse and Language* (Stanford: CSLI/Cambridge, 1996), pp. 177–87.
Graham, S.A., A.N. Welder and A.W. McCrimmon, 'Hot Dogs and Zavy Cats: Preschoolers and Adults' Expectations about Familiar and Novel Adjectives', *Brain and Language*, 84 (2003), 16–37.
Grice, H.P., 'Logic and Conversation' in *Studies in the Ways of Words* (Cambridge, MA: Harvard University Press, 1989), pp. 22–40. (Reprinted from H.P. Grice, 'Logic and Conversation', in P. Cole and J. Morgan, eds, *Syntax and Semantics 3: Speech Acts* (New York: Academic Press, 1975), pp. 41–58.)
Groefsema, M., 'Can, May, Would and Should: A Relevance-Theoretic Account', *Journal of Linguistics*, 31 (1995), 53–9.
Grossenbacher, P.G. and C.T. Lovelace, 'Mechanisms of Synaesthesia: Cognitive and Psychological Constraints', *Trends in Cognitive Sciences*, 5 (2001), 36–41.
Greek–English Lexicon, compiled by H.G. Liddell and R. Scott, (Oxford: Clarendon Press, 1843/1966).
Gruber, J.S., *Studies in Lexical Relations*, Doctoral Dissertation (Bloomington, IN: Indiana University Linguistics Club, 1965).
Harrap's New Standard French and English Dictionary, ed. by J.E. Mansion (London: Harrap, 1972–1980).
Harrap's Standard French and English Dictionary, ed. by J.E. Mansion, revised and edited by D.M. Ledesert and R.P.L. Ledesert (London: Harrap, 1980).
Hardin, C.L., 'Van Brakel and the Not-So-Naked Emperor', *British Journal for the Philosophy of Science*, 44 (1993), 137–50.
Harrison, J. and S. Baron-Cohen, 'Acquired and Inherited Forms of Cross-Modal Correspondence', *Neurocase*, 2 (1996), 245–9.
Haskell, R.E., ed., *Cognition and Symbolic Structures: the Psychology of Metaphoric Transformation* (Norwood, NJ: Ablex, 1987).

Hayakawa, S.I., *Language in Thought and Action*, 3rd edn (London: Allen and Unwin, 1974).
Hering, E., *Outline of a Theory of the Light-Sense* (Cambridge: Harvard University Press, 1920).
Heyman, G.D. and S.A. Gelman, 'Young Children Use Motive Information in Making Trait Inferences', *Developmental Psychology*, 34 (1998), 310–21.
Heyman, G.D. and S.A. Gelman, 'The Use of Trait Labels in Making Psychological Inferences', *Child Development*, 70 (1999), 604–19.
Heywood, C.A. and R.W. Kentridge, 'Affective Blindsight?', *Trends in Cognitive Sciences*, 4 (2000), 125–6.
Hintikka, J. and G. Sandu, 'Metaphor and Other Kinds of Nonliteral Meaning', in J. Hintikka, ed., *Aspects of Metaphor* (Dordrecht: Kluwer, 1994), pp. 151–87.
Honeck, R.P., 'Women, Fire and Dangerous Things. George Lakoff' (Book Review), *Metaphor and Symbolic Activity*, 4 (1989), 279–84.
Hoorn, J., 'Demonstration: RT While Processing Metaphors', Paper Presented at RAAM III Conference (Tilburg, The Netherlands, 1999).
Hubbard, T.L., 'Synesthesia-Like Mappings of Lightness, Pitch, and Melodic Interval', *American Journal of Psychology*, 109 (1996), 219–38.
Humphrey, N.K., 'The Social Function of Intellect', in P.P.G. Bateson and R.A. Hinde, eds, *Growing Points in Ethology* (Cambridge: Cambridge University Press, 1976), pp. 303–17.
Humphreys, G., 'Synesthesia: a Union of the Senses. Richard E. Cytowic' (Book Review), *Nature*, 343 (1990), 30.
Hurford, J.R. and S. Kirby, 'Neural Preconditions for Proto-Language', *Behavioral and Brain Sciences*, 18 (1995), 193–4.
Indurkhya, B., *Metaphor and Cognition: an Interactionist Approach* (Dordrecht: Kluwer, 1992).
Indurkhya, B., 'The Thesis that All Knowledge is Metaphorical and Meanings of Metaphor', *Metaphor and Symbolic Activity*, 9 (1994), 61–73.
Jackendoff, R., *Languages of the Mind: Essays on Mental Representation* (Cambridge, MA: MIT Press, 1992).
Jackendoff, R., *The Architecture of the Language Faculty* (Cambridge, MA: MIT Press, 1998a).
Jackendoff, R., 'Why a Conceptualist View of Reference? A Reply to Abbot', *Linguistics and Philosophy*, 21 (1998b), 211–9.
Jackendoff, R. and D. Aaron, 'Review of *More Than Cool Reason: A Field Guide to Poetic Metaphor*, by G. Lakoff and M. Taylor', *Language*, 67 (1991), 320–38.
Jacobs, B. and J.M. Horner, 'Language as a Multimodal Sensory Enhancement System', *Behavioral and Brain Sciences*, 18 (1995), 194–5.
Jakobson, R., *Child Language, Aphasia, and Phonological Universals* (Paris: Mouton, 1968).
Johnson, C., 'Metaphor vs. Conflation in the Acquisition of Polysemy: The Case of SEE', in M.K. Hiraga, C. Sinha and S. Wilcox, eds, *Cultural, Topological and Psychological Issues in Cognitive Linguistics*, Current Issues in Cognitive Linguistics Theory 152 (Amsterdam: John Benjamins, 1997a), pp. 155–69.
Johnson, C., 'Learnability in the Acquisition of Multiple Senses: SOURCE Reconsidered', in J. Moxley, J. Juge and M. Juge, eds, *Proceedings of the Twenty-Second Meeting of the Berkeley Linguistics Society* (Berkeley, CA: Berkeley Linguistics Society 1997b), pp. 469–80.

Johnson, M., *The Body in the Mind: The Bodily Basis of Meaning, Imagination, and Reason* (Chicago, IL: University of Chicago Press, 1987).
Johnson, M., 'Some Constraints on Embodied Analogical Reasoning', in D.H. Helman, ed., *Analogical Reasoning – Perspectives of Artificial Intelligence, Cognitive Science, and Philosophy* (Dordrecht: Kluwer, 1988), pp. 25–40.
Johnson, M. and G. Lakoff, 'Why Cognitive Linguistics Requires Embodied Realism', *Cognitive Linguistics*, 13 (2002), 245–63.
Julius, D. and A.I. Basbaum, 'Molecular Mechanisms of Nociception', *Nature*, 413 (2001), 203–10.
Kamp, J.A.W., 'Two Theories about Adjectives', in E.L. Keenan, ed., *Formal Semantics of Natural Language* (Cambridge: Cambridge University Press, 1975), pp. 123–55.
Katz, J.J., *Propositional Structure and Illocutionary Force* (New York: Crowell, 1977).
Kay, P. and C.K. McDaniel, 'The Linguistic Significance of the Meanings of Basic Colour Terms', *Language*, 54 (1978), 610–46.
Keil, F.C., *Concepts, Kinds, and Cognitive Development* (Cambridge, MA: MIT Press, 1989).
Kelso, J.A.S., *Dynamic Patterns* (Cambridge, MA: MIT Press, 1995).
Kilgarriff, A., 'I Don't Believe in Word Senses', *Computers and the Humanities*, 31 (1997), 91–113.
Kittay, E.F., *Metaphor: Its Cognitive Force and Linguistic Structure* (Oxford: Clarendon Press, 1987).
Klein, D.E. and G.L. Murphy, 'The Representation of Polysemous Words,' *Journal of Memory and Language*, 45 (2001), 259–82.
Klein, D.E. and G.L. Murphy, 'Paper Has Been My Ruin: Conceptual Relations of Polysemous Senses', *Journal of Memory and Language*, 47 (2002), 548–70.
Klepousniotou, E., 'The Processing of Lexical Ambiguity: Homonymy and Polysemy in the Mental Lexicon', *Brain and Language*, 81 (2002), 205–23.
Korb, K.B., 'Synesthesia and Method', *Psyche*, 2 (1995), http://psyche.cs.monash.edu.au/v2/psyche-2-24-korb.html.
Kripke, S., 'Naming and Necessity', in D. Davidson and G. Harman, eds, *Semantics of Natural Language* (Dordrecht: D. Reidel, 1972), pp. 253–355.
Kripke, S., *Naming and Necessity* (Oxford: Blackwell, 1980).
Kronfeld, C., 'Novel and Conventional Metaphors: A Matter of Methodology', *Poetics Today*, 2 (1980/81), 13–24.
Kuraev, G.A., T.V. Aleinikova, V.N. Dumbaj and G.L. Feldman, *Fisiologia Centralnoj Nervnoj Sistemy* [Physiology of the Central Nervous System] (Rostov-na-Donu: Fenix, 2000).
Lakoff, G., *Women, Fire, and Dangerous Things: What Categories Reveal about the Mind* (Chicago, IL: The University of Chicago Press, 1987).
Lakoff, G., 'Cognitive Semantics', in U. Eco, M. Santambrogio and P. Violi, eds, *Meaning and Mental Representations* (Bloomington and Indianapolis, IN: Indiana University Press, 1988), pp. 119–54.
Lakoff, G., 'The Invariance Hypothesis: Is Abstract Reason Based on Image-Schemas?', *Cognitive Linguistics*, 1 (1990), 39–74.
Lakoff, G., 'The Contemporary Theory of Metaphor', in A. Ortony, ed., *Metaphor and Thought*, 2nd edn (Cambridge: Cambridge University Press, 1993), pp. 202–51.
Lakoff, G. and M. Johnson, *Metaphors We Live By* (Chicago, IL: University of Chicago Press, 1980).

Lakoff, G. and M. Turner, *More Than Cool Reason: a Field Guide to Poetic Metaphor* (Chicago, IL: University of Chicago Press, 1989).

Lakoff, G. and M. Johnson, *Philosophy in the Flesh: The Embodied Mind and its Challenge to Western Thought* (New York: Basic Books, 1999).

LaMotte, R.H. and J.N. Campbell, 'Comparison of Responses of Warm and Nociceptive C-Fiber Afferents in Monkey with Human Judgements of Thermal Pain', *Journal of Neurophysiology*, 41 (1978), 509–28.

Landau, B., 'Object Shape, Object Name, and Object Kind: Representation and Development', in D.L. Medin, ed., *Psychology of Learning and Motivation, Vol. 31* (New York: Academic Press, 1994), pp. 253–304.

Langacker, R.W., *Foundations of Cognitive Grammar, Vol. 1: Theoretical Prerequisites* (Stanford, CA: Stanford University Press, 1987).

Langacker, R.W., *Concept, Image and Symbol: the Cognitive Basis of Language* (Berlin: Mouton de Gruyter, 1990).

Langer, J., 'Comparative Mental Development', *Journal of Adult Development*, 7 (2000), 23–30.

Lass, R., *Historical Linguistics and Language Change* (Cambridge: Cambridge University Press, 1997).

Laurence, S. and E. Margolis, 'Radical Concept Nativism', *Cognition*, 86 (2002), 25–55.

Lehrer, A., *Semantic Fields and Lexical Structure* (Amsterdam: North-Holland, 1974).

Lehrer, A. and E.F. Kittay, eds, *Frames, Fields, and Contrasts: New Essays in Semantic and Lexical Organization* (Hove: Lawrence Erlbaum, 1992).

Le Robert Quotidien, ed. by J. Rey-Debove (Paris: Robert, 1996).

Levin, S., *The Semantics of Metaphor* (Baltimore, MD: Johns Hopkins University Press, 1977).

Lewis, D., 'Scorekeeping in a Language Game', *Journal of Philosophical Language*, 8 (1979), 339–59.

Lewkowicz, D.J. and G. Turkewitz, 'Cross-Modal Equivalence in Early Infancy: Auditory-Visual Intensity Matching', *Developmental Psychology*, 16 (1980), 597–607.

Li, Y.F., 'An Optimized Universal Grammar and Biological Redundancies', *Linguistic Inquiry*, 28 (1997), 170–8.

Liotti, M., H.S. Mayberg, S.K. Brannan, *et al.*, 'Differential Limbic-Cortical Correlates of Sadness and Anxiety in Healthy Subjects: Implications for Affective Disorders', *Biological Psychiatry*, 48 (2000), 30–42.

Liu, L., A. Szallasi, and S.A. Simon, 'A Non-Pungent Resiniferatoxin Analogue, Phorbol 12-Phenylacetate 13 Acetate 20-Homovanillate, Reveals Vanilloid Receptor Subtypes on Rat Trigeminal Ganglion Neurons', *Neuroscience*, 84 (1998), 569–81.

Lowenthal, F., 'Can Handicapped Subjects Use Perceptual Symbol Systems?', *Behavioral and Brain Sciences*, 22 (1999), 625–6.

Lucas, M., 'Context Effects in Lexical Access: a Meta-Analysis', *Memory and Cognition*, 27 (1999), 385–98.

Ludlow, P., 'Implicit Comparison Classes', *Linguistics and Philosophy*, 12 (1989), 521–33.

Ludlow, P., 'Book Review of *Metaphor: Its Cognitive Force and Linguistic Structure* by Eva Kittay', *The Journal of Philosophy*, 88 (1991), 324–30.

Luria, A.R., *Higher Cortical Functions in Man* (New York: Basic Books, 1966).

Luria, A.R., *The Mind of a Mnemonist* (New York: Basic Books, 1968).

Lyons, J., *Introduction to Theoretical Linguistics* (Cambridge: Cambridge University Press, 1968).
Lyons, J., *Semantics, Vol. 2* (Cambridge: Cambridge University Press, 1977).
Ma, Q.-P., 'Expression of Capsaicin Receptor (VR1) by Myelinated Primary Afferent Neurons in Rats', *Neuroscience Letters*, 319 (2002), 87–90.
Mac Cormac, E.R., *A Cognitive Theory of Metaphor* (Cambridge, MA: MIT Press, 1985).
Malt, B.C., 'Water is not H_2O', *Cognitive Psychology*, 27 (1994), 41–70.
Mandler, J.M., 'How to Build a Baby: On the Development of an Accessible Representation System', *Cognitive Development*, 3 (1988), 113–36.
Mandler, J.M., 'The Foundations of Conceptual Thought in Infancy', *Cognitive Development*, 7 (1992a), 273–85.
Mandler, J.M., 'How to Build a Baby II: Conceptual Primitives', *Psychological Review*, 99 (1992b), 587–604.
Mandler, J.M., 'Precursors of Linguistic Knowledge', *Philosophical Transactions of the Royal Society of London*, 346 (1994), 63–9.
Maratsos, M., 'Metaphors of Language: Metaphors of the Mind? (Book Review of Lakoff 1987)', *Contemporary Psychology*, 34 (1989), 5–7.
Marconi, D., *Lexical Competence* (Cambridge, MA: MIT Press, 1997).
Margalit, A. and N. Goldblum, 'Metaphors in an Open-Class Test', in J. Hintikka, ed., *Aspects of Metaphor* (Dordrecht: Kluwer, 1994), pp. 219–41.
Markman, E.M., 'Constraints on Word Meaning in Early Language Acquisition', in L. Gleitman and B. Landau, eds, *The Acquisition of the Lexicon* (Cambridge, MA: MIT Press, 1995), pp. 199–227.
Marks, L.E., 'On Associations of Light and Sound: the Mediation of Brightness, Pitch and Loudness', *American Journal of Psychology*, 87 (1974), 173–88.
Marks, L.E., 'On Colored-Hearing Synesthesia: Cross-Modal Translations of Sensory Dimensions', *Psychological Bulletin*, 82 (1975), 303–31.
Marks, L.E., *The Unity of the Senses: Interrelations among the Modalities* (New York: Academic Press, 1978).
Marks, L.E., 'Bright Sneezes and Dark Coughs, Loud Sunlight and Soft Moonlight', *Journal of Experimental Psychology: Human Perception and Performance*, 8 (1982a), 177–93.
Marks, L.E., 'Synesthetic Perception and Poetic Metaphor', *Journal of Experimental Psychology: Human Perception and Performance*, 8 (1982b), 15–23.
Marks, L.E., R.J. Hammeal, and M.H. Bornstein, *Perceiving Similarity and Comprehending Metaphor* (Chicago, IL: University of Chicago Press, 1987).
Marks, L.E. and M.H. Bornstein, 'Sensory Similarities: Classes, Characteristics, and Cognitive Consequences', in R.E. Haskell, ed., *Cognition and Symbolic Structures: the Psychology of Metaphoric Transformation* (Norwood, NJ: Ablex, 1987), pp. 49–65.
Martin, A., J.V. Haxby, F.M. Lalonde, *et al.*, 'Discrete Cortical Regions Associated with Knowledge of Color and Knowledge of Action', *Science*, 270 (1995), 102–5.
Martin, A., C.L. Wiggs, L.G. Ungerleider and J.V. Haxby, 'Neural Correlates of Category-Specific Knowledge', *Nature*, 379 (1996), 649–52.
Martino, G. and L.E. Marks, 'Perceptual and Linguistic Interactions in Speeded Classification: Tests of the Semantic Coding Hypothesis', *Perception*, 28 (1999), 903–23.
Martino, G. and L.E. Marks, 'Cross-Modal Interaction Between Vision and Touch: the Role of Synesthetic Correspondence', *Perception*, 29 (2000), 745–54.

Martino, G. and L.E. Marks, 'Synesthesia: Strong and Weak', *Current Directions in Psychological Science*, 10 (2001), 61–5.
Maryanski, A., 'The Hominid Tool-Language Connection: Some Missing Evolutionary Links?', *Behavioral and Brain Sciences*, 18 (1995), 199–200.
Mattingley, J.B., A.N. Rich, G. Yelland, and J.L. Bradshaw, 'Unconscious Priming Eliminates Automatic Binding of Colour and Alphanumeric Form in Synaesthesia', *Nature*, 410 (2001), 580–2.
Maurer, D., 'Neonatal Synaesthesia: Implications for the Processing of Speech and Faces', in S. Baron-Cohen and J. Harrison, eds, *Synaesthesia: Classic and Contemporary Readings* (Oxford: Blackwell, 1997), pp. 224–42.
McCleskey, E.W. and M.S. Gold, 'Ion Channels of Nociception', *Annual Review of Physiology*, 61 (1999), 835–56.
McDonald, J.J., W.A. Teder-Sälejärvi and S.A. Hillyard, 'Involuntary Orienting to Sound Improves Visual Perception', *Nature*, 407 (2000), 906–8.
McKenny, D.D., W.M. Neuhausser and D. Julius, 'Identification of a Cold Receptor Reveals a General Role for TRP Channels in Thermosensation', *Nature*, 416 (2002), 52–8.
Medin, D. and A. Ortony, 'Psychological Essentialism', in S. Vosniadou and A. Ortony, eds, *Similarity and Analogical Reasoning* (Cambridge: Cambridge University Press, 1989), pp. 179–95.
Medin, D.L., R.L. Goldstone and D. Gentner, 'Respects for Similarity', *Psychological Review*, 100 (1993), 254–78.
Melara, R.D., 'Dimensional Interactions between Color and Pitch', *Journal of Experimental Psychology: Human Perception and Performance*, 15 (1989), 69–79.
Melara, R.D. and L.E. Marks, 'Processes Underlying Dimensional Interactions: Correspondences Between Linguistic and Nonlinguistic Dimensions', *Memory and Cognition*, 18 (1990), 477–95.
Meltzoff, A.N. and R.W. Borden, 'Intermodal Matching by Human Neonates', *Nature*, 282 (1979), 403–4.
Mezey, E., Z.E. Toth, D.N. Cortright, *et al.*, 'Distribution of mRNA for Vanilloid Receptor Subtype 1 (VR1), and VR1-Like Immunoreactivity, in the Central Nervous System of the Rat and Human', *Proceedings of the National Academy of Sciences of the United States of America*, 97 (2000), 3655–60.
Middle English Dictionary, ed. by H. Kurath, S.M. Kuhn, J. Reidy and R.E. Lewis (Ann Arbor, MI: University of Michigan Press, 1952).
Miller, G.A. and P.N. Johnson-Laird, *Language and Perception* (Cambridge: Cambridge University Press, 1976).
Miller, R.B., 'A Purely Causal Solution to One of the Qua Problems', *Australasian Journal of Philosophy*, 70 (1992), 425–34.
Mills, C.B., E.H. Boteler, and G.K. Oliver, 'Digit Synaesthesia: A Case Study Using a Stroop-Type Test', *Cognitive Neuropsychology*, 16 (1999), 181–91.
Milner, A.D. and M.A. Goodale, *The Visual Brain in Action* (Oxford: Oxford University Press, 1995).
Mitchell, R.W. and H.L. Miles, 'Apes and Language: Human Uniqueness Again?', *Behavioral and Brain Sciences*, 18 (1995), 200–1.
Modern English–Russian Dictionary, 2nd edn, ed. by V.K. Muller (Moskva: Russkij Jasyk, 1995).
Moon, R.E., *Fixed Expressions and Idioms in English: a Corpus-Based Approach* (Oxford: Clarendon Press, 1998).

Morgan, J.L., 'Observations on the Pragmatics of Metaphor', in A. Ortony, ed. *Metaphor and Thought*, 2nd edn (Cambridge: Cambridge University Press, 1993), pp. 124–34.
Morris, J.S., A. Ohman, and R.J. Dolan, 'A Subcortical Pathway to the Right Amygdala Mediating "Unseen" Fear', *Proceedings of the National Academy of Sciences of the United States of America*, 96 (1999), 1680–85.
Morton, J.B. and S.E. Trehub, 'Children's Understanding of Emotion in Speech', *Child Development*, 72 (2001), 834–43.
Murphy, G.L., 'On Metaphoric Representation', *Cognition*, 60 (1996), 173–204.
Murphy, G.L., 'Reasons to Doubt the Present Evidence for Metaphoric Representation', *Cognition*, 62 (1997), 99–108.
Nagy, I. and H.P. Rang, 'Similarities and Differences Between the Responses of Rat Sensory Neurons to Noxious Heat and Capsaicin', *Journal of Neuroscience*, 19 (1999), 10647–55.
Narayanan, S., 'Talking the Talk is Like Walking the Walk: a Computational Model of Verbal Aspect', in M.G. Shafto and P. Langley, eds, *Proceedings of the Nineteenth Annual Conference of the Cognitive Science Society* (Mahwah, NJ: Erlbaum, 1997), pp. 548–53.
Neirlich, B. and D.D. Clarke, 'Ambiguities We Live By: Towards a Pragmatics of Polysemy', *Journal of Pragmatics*, 33 (2001), 1–20.
Nersessian, N.J., 'How do Scientists Think? Capturing the Dynamics of Conceptual Change in Science', in R.N. Giere, ed., *Cognitive Models of Science. Minnesota Studies in the Philosophy of Science, XV* (Minneapolis, MN: University of Minnesota Press, 1992), pp. 3–44.
Newmeyer, F.J., 'Conceptual Structure and Syntax', *Behavioral and Brain Sciences*, 18 (1995), 202.
Nunberg, G., 'The Non-Uniqueness of Semantic Solutions: Polysemy', *Linguistics and Philosophy*, 3 (1979), 143–84.
Odgaard, E.C., J.H. Flowers and H.L. Bradman, 'An Investigation of the Cognitive and Perceptual Dynamics of a Colour-Digit Synaesthete', *Perception*, 28 (1999), 651–64.
Origgi, G. and D. Sperber, 'Evolution, Communication and the Proper Function of Language', in P. Carruthers and A. Chamberlain, eds, *Evolution and the Human Mind: Modularity, Language and Meta-Cognition* (Cambridge: Cambridge University Press), pp. 140–69.
Ortony, A., 'Are Emotion Metaphors Conceptual or Lexical?', *Cognition and Emotion*, 2 (1998), 95–103.
Osgood, C.E., G.J. Suci, and P.H. Tannenbaum, *The Measurement of Meaning* (Urbana, IL: University of Illinois Press, 1957).
Oxford English Dictionary, The, ed. by J.A.H. Murray (London: Oxford University Press, 1933).
Oxford Latin Dictionary, ed. by P.G.W. Glare (Oxford: Clarendon Press, 1982).
Oxford Russian Dictionary, The, ed. by P. Falla, M. Wheeler and B. Unbegaun (Oxford: Oxford University Press, 1984).
Palmer, F.R., *Semantics: A New Outline* (Cambridge: Cambridge University Press, 1976).
Paradis, M., 'The Other Side of Language: Pragmatic Competence', *Journal of Neurolinguistics*, 11 (1998), 1–10.
Pavio, A. and M. Walsh, 'Psychological Processes in Metaphor Comprehension and Memory', in A. Ortony, ed., *Metaphor and Thought*, 2nd edn (Cambridge: Cambridge University Press, 1993), pp. 307–28.

Peacocke, C., *A Study of Concepts* (Cambridge MA: MIT Press, 1992).
Perner, J., *Understanding the Representational Mind* (Cambridge, MA: MIT Press, 1991).
Piaget, J., *The Psychology of Intelligence*, trans. M. Piercy and D.E. Berlyne (London: Routledge, 1950).
Piaget, J., *The Origins of Intelligence in Children* (New York: International Universities Press, 1952).
Piaget, J., *The Mechanisms of Perception* (London: Routledge & Kegan Paul, 1961/1969).
Piaget, J., 'Schemes of Action and Language Learning', in M. Piatelli-Palmarini, ed., *Language and Learning: the Debate between Jean Piaget and Noam Chomsky* (London: Routledge & Kegan Paul, 1980), pp. 163-83.
Piatelli-Palmarini, M., ed., *Language and Learning: the Debate between Jean Piaget and Noam Chomsky* (London: Routledge & Kegan Paul, 1980).
Pickering, M. and S. Frisson, 'Processing of Verbs: Evidence from Eye Movements', *Journal of Experimental Psychology: Learning, Memory, and Cognition*, 27 (2001), 556-73.
Pinkal, M., 'Towards a Semantics of Precization', in T.T. Ballmer and M. Pinkal, eds, *Approaching Vagueness* (Amsterdam: North Holland, 1983), pp. 13-57.
Pinker, S., *The Language Instinct* (New York: W. Morrow and Co, 1994).
Pinker, S., *How the Mind Works* (New York: W.W. Norton, 1997).
Plotkin, H., *Evolution in Mind* (London: Alan Lane, 1997).
Pustejovsky, J., *The Generative Lexicon* (Cambridge, MA: MIT Press, 1995).
Pustejovsky, J. and B. Boguraev, eds, *Lexical Semantics: The Problem of Polysemy* (Oxford Clarendon Press, 1996).
Pustejovsky, J., 'Generativity and Explanation in Semantics: A Reply to Fodor and Lepore', *Linguistic Inquiry*, 29 (1998), 289-311.
Pustejovsky, J., 'Type Construction and the Logic of Concepts', in P. Bouillon and F. Busa, eds, *The Language of Word Meaning* (Cambridge: Cambridge University Press, 2001), pp. 91-123.
Putnam, H., *Mind, Language and Reality* (Cambridge: Cambridge University Press, 1975).
Putnam, H., 'Replies', *Philosophical Topics*, 20 (1992), 347-408.
Pylyshyn, Z.W., 'The Imagery Debate: Analogue Media vs. Tacit Knowledge', *Psychological Review*, 88 (1981), 16-45.
Pylyshyn, Z.W., 'Metaphorical Imprecision and the "Top-Down" Research Strategy', in A. Ortony, ed., *Metaphor and Thought*, 2nd edn (Cambridge: Cambridge University Press, 1993), pp. 543-58.
Pynte, J., M. Besson, F.-H. Robinchon and J. Poli, 'The Time-Course of Metaphor Comprehension: An Event-Related Potential Study', *Brain and Language*, 35 (1996), 293-316.
Quartz, S.R, 'The Constructivist Brain', *Trends in Cognitive Sciences*, 3 (1999), 48-57.
Quartz, S.R. and T.J. Sejnowski, 'The Neural Basis of Cognitive Development: a Constructivist Manifesto', *Behavioral and Brain Sciences*, 20 (1997), 537-96.
Quartz, S.R. and T.J. Sejnowski, 'Constraining Constructivism: Cortical and Sub-Cortical Constraints on Learning in Development', *Behavioral and Brain Sciences*, 23 (2000), 785-92.
Quine, W.V., 'A Postscript on Metaphor', in S. Sacks, ed., *On Metaphor* (Chicago, IL: University of Chicago Press, 1979), pp. 159-60.

Rakova, M., 'The Philosophy of Embodied Realism: a High Price to Pay?', *Cognitive Linguistics*, 13 (2002), 215–44.
Rakova, M., 'Metaphor and Analogy in Science: the Case of Scientific Discovery', in H. Zagal and A. Herrera Ibáñez, eds, *Metáfora* (México: UNAM, Instituto de Investigaciones Filosóficas, forthcoming).
Ramachandran, V.S. and E.M. Hubbard, 'Psychophysical Investigation Into the Neural Basis of Synaesthesia', *Proceedings of the Royal Society of London. Series B – Biological Sciences*, 268 (2001a), 979–83.
Ramachandran, V.S. and E.M. Hubbard, 'Synaesthesia – a Window Into Perception, Thought and Language', *Journal of Consciousness Studies*, 8 (2001b), 3–34.
Récanati, F., *Direct Reference: From Language to Thought* (Oxford: Blackwell, 1993).
Récanati, F., 'What is Said', *Synthese*, 128 (2001), 75–91.
Récanati, F., 'Unarticulated Constituents', *Linguistics and Philosophy*, 25 (2002), 299–345.
Rey, G., 'Concepts', in S. Guttenplan, ed., *Companion to the Philosophy of Mind* (Oxford: Blackwell, 1994), pp. 185–93.
Richards, I.A., *The Philosophy of Rhetoric* (London: Oxford University Press, 1936).
Ricoeur, P., *La Métaphore Vive* (Paris: Editions du Seuil, 1975).
Ringkamp, M., Y.B. Peng, G. Wu, *et al.*, 'Capsaicin Responses in Heat-Sensitive and Heat-Insensitive A-Fiber Nociceptors', *Journal of Neuroscience*, 21 (2001), 4460–68.
Rorty, R., 'Unfamiliar Noises I: Hesse and Davidson on Metaphor', *Proceedings of the Aristotelian Society*, S61 (1987), 283–96.
Rosch, E., 'Linguistic Relativity', in A. Silverstein, ed., *Human Communication: Theoretical Explorations* (New York: Halsted Press, 1974).
Rosch, E., 'Principles of Categorization', in E. Rosch and B. Lloyds, eds, *Cognition and Categorization* (Hillsdale, NJ: Lawrence Erlbaum, 1978).
Rosch Heider, E., 'Universals in Color Naming and Memory', *Journal of Experimental Psychology*, 93 (1972), 10–20.
Rosch Heider, E., 'Natural Categories', *Cognitive Psychology*, 4 (1973), 328–50.
Rosch Heider, E. and D.C. Olivier, 'The Structure of the Color Space in Naming and Memory for Two Languages', *Cognitive Psychology*, 3 (1972), 337–54.
Rose, S.A., 'Cross-Modal Transfer in Human Infants: What is Being Transferred?', *Annals of the New York Academy of Sciences*, 608 (1990), 38–50.
Rose, S.A., A. Gottfried and W. Bridger, 'Effects of Visual, Haptic, and Manipulatory Experiences on Infants' Visual Recognition Memory of Objects', *Developmental Psychology*, 17 (1978), 90–8.
Rousset, F., 'How to "See" the Mind', Paper Presented at the *Braiding the Multiple Threads of Interdisciplinary Research on Metaphor* Workshop at the Japanese Cognitive Science Society's Annual Meeting (Hamamatsu, Japan: Shizuoka Art and Culture University, 30 June–2 July 2000).
Ruhl, C., *Monosemy: A Study in Linguistic Semantics* (Albany, NY: State University of New York Press, 1989).
Sadock, J.M., 'Figurative Speech and Linguistics', in A. Ortony, ed., *Metaphor and Thought*, 2nd edn (Cambridge: Cambridge University Press, 1993), pp. 42–57.
Sann, H., 'Chemosensitivity of Nociceptive, Mechanosensitive Afferent Nerve Fibres in the Guinea-Pig Ureter', *European Journal of Neuroscience*, 10 (1998), 1300–11.
Sansoni-Harrap Standard Italian and English Dictionary, ed. by V. Macchi (London: Harrap, 1970–76).

Saunders, B.A.C. and J. van Brakel, 'Are there Nontrivial Constraints on Colour Categorization?', *Behavioral and Brain Sciences*, 20 (1997), 167–228.

Schumacher, M.A., I. Moff, S.P. Sudanagunta and J.D. Levine, 'Molecular Cloning of an N-Terminal Splice Variant of the Capsaicin Receptor – Loss of N-Terminal Domain Suggests Functional Divergence Among Capsaicin Receptor Subtypes', *Journal of Biological Chemistry*, 275 (2000), 2756–62.

Searle, J.R., *Intentionality* (Cambridge: Cambridge University Press, 1983).

Searle, J.R., 'Metaphor', in A. Ortony, ed., *Metaphor and Thought*, 2nd edn (Cambridge: Cambridge University Press, 1993), pp. 83–111.

Seidenberg, M.S., M.T. Tanenhaus, J.M. Leiman and M. Bienkowski, 'Automatic Access of the Meanings of Ambiguous Words in Context: Some Limitations of Knowledge-Based Processing', *Cognitive Psychology*, 14 (1982), 489–537.

Shams, L., Y. Kamitani and S. Shimojo, 'What You See is What You Hear', *Nature*, 408 (2000), 788.

Shen, Y., 'Cognitive Aspects of Metaphor Comprehension – an Introduction', *Poetics Today*, 13 (1992), 567–74.

Shen, Y., 'Cognitive Constraints on Poetic Figures', *Cognitive Linguistics*, 8 (1997), 33–71.

Shimojo, S. and L. Shams, 'Sensory Modalities are not Separate Modalities: Plasticity and Interactions', *Current Opinion in Neurobiology*, 11 (2001), 505–9.

Simpson, G.B., 'Context and the Processing of Ambiguous Words', in M.A. Gernsbacher, ed., *Handbook of Psycholinguistics* (San Diego, CA: Academic Press, 1994), pp. 359–74.

Simpson, G.B. and C. Burgess, 'Activation and Selection Processes in the Recognition of Ambiguous Words', *Journal of Experimental Psychology: Human Perception and Performance*, 11 (1985), 28–39.

Simpson, G.B. and H. Kang, 'Inhibitory Processes in the Recognition of Homograph Meanings', in D. Dagenbach and T.H. Carr, eds, *Inhibitory Processes in Attention, Memory and Language* (San Diego, CA: Academic Press, 1994).

Smaller English–Latin Dictionary, ed. by Sir W. Smith (London: J. Murray, 1961).

Smilek, D. and M.J. Dixon, 'Towards a Synergistic Understanding of Synaesthesia: Combining Current Experimental Findings with Synaesthetes' Subjective Descriptions', *Psyche*, 8 (2002), http://psyche.cs.monash.edu.au/v8/psyche-8-01-smilek.html.

Smith, L.B., 'Commentary. Perceptual Relations and Perceptual Language', in L.E. Marks, R.J. Hammeal and M.H. Bornstein, eds, *Perceiving Similarity and Comprehending Metaphor* (Chicago, IL: University of Chicago Press, 1987), pp. 94–100.

Smith, L.B., E. Thelen, R. Titzer and D. McLin, 'Knowing in the Context of Acting: the Task Dynamics of the A-Not-B Error', *Psychological Review*, 106 (1999), 235–60.

Soames, S., *Beyond Rigidity: the Unfinished Semantic Agenda of Naming and Necessity* (Oxford: Oxford University Press, 2002).

Spalding, J.M.K. and O. Zangwill, 'Disturbance of Number-Form in a Case of Brain Injury', *Journal of Neurology, Neurosurgery, and Psychiatry*, 12 (1950), 24–9.

Spelke, E.S., 'The Development of Intermodal Perception', in P. Salapatek and L. Cohen, eds, *Handbook of Infant Perception*, Vol. 2 (New York: Academic Press, 1987), pp. 233–73.

Sperber, D., 'Understanding Verbal Understanding', in J. Khalfa, ed., *What is Intelligence?* (Cambridge: Cambridge University Press, 1994), pp. 179–98.
Sperber, D. and D. Wilson, *Relevance: Communication and Cognition* (Oxford: Blackwell, 1986).
Sperber, D. and D. Wilson, 'The Mapping Between the Public and the Private Lexicon', in P. Carruthers and J. Boucher, eds, *Language and Thought: Interdisciplinary Themes* (Cambridge: Cambridge University Press, 1998), pp. 184–200.
Sperber, D. and D. Wilson, 'Pragmatics, Modularity and Mind-reading', *Mind and Language*, 17 (2002), 3–23.
Stanley, J., 'Context and Logical Form', *Linguistics and Philosophy*, 23 (2000), 391–434.
Stanley, J., 'Making it Articulated', *Mind and Language*, 17 (2002), 149–68.
Stanley, J. and Z.G. Szabó, 'On Quantifier Domain Restriction', *Mind and Language*, 15 (2000), 219–61.
Steen, G., *Understanding Metaphor in Literature* (London: Longman Group 1994).
Steen, G. and R.W. Gibbs, 'Introduction' in G. Steen and R.W. Gibbs, eds, *Metaphor in Cognitive Linguistics* (Amsterdam: John Benjamins, 1999), pp. 1–8.
Stein, B.E. and A.M. Meredith, *The Merging of the Senses* (Cambridge, MA: MIT Press, 1993).
Stern, J., *Metaphor in Context* (Cambridge, MA: MIT Press, 2000).
Stuss, D.T. and B. Levine, 'Adult Clinical Neuropsychology: Lessons from Studies of the Frontal Lobes', *Annual Review of Psychology*, 53 (2002), 401–33.
Sutherland, P., *Cognitive Development Today. Piaget and his Critics* (London: Paul Chapman, 1992).
Sweetser, E., *From Etymology to Pragmatics: Metaphorical and Cultural Aspects of Semantic Structure* (Cambridge: Cambridge University Press, 1990).
Szabó, Z.G., 'Adjectives in Context', in R.M. Harnish and I. Kenesei, eds, *Prospectives on Semantics, Pragmatics and Discourse: a Festschrift for Ferenc Kiefer* (Amsterdam: John Benjamins, 2001), pp. 119–46.
Tabossi, P., L. Colombo and R. Job, 'Accessing Lexical Ambiguity: Effects of Context and Dominance', *Psychological Research*, 49 (1987), 161–72.
Tabossi, P. and F. Zardon, 'Processing Ambiguous Words in Context', *Journal of Memory and Language*, 32 (1993), 359–72.
Tompkins, C.A., 'Knowledge and Strategies for Processing Lexical Metaphor After Right or Left Hemisphere Brain Damage', *Journal of Speech and Hearing Research*, 33 (1990), 307–16.
Torebjork, H.E. and R.G. Hallin, 'Perceptual Changes Accompanying Controlled Referential Blocking of A and C Fibre Responses in Intact Human Skin Nerves', *Experimental Brain Research*, 16 (1973), 321–32.
Tranel, D. and A.R. Damasio, 'The Neurobiology of Knowledge Retrieval', *Behavioral and Brain Sciences*, 22 (1999), 303.
Traugott, E.C. and B. Heine, 'Introduction', in E.C. Traugott and B. Heine, eds, *Approaches to Grammaticalization, Vol. 1* (Cambridge: Cambridge University Press, 1991), pp. 1–14.
Traugott, E.C. and E. König, 'The Semantics-Pragmatics of Grammaticalization Revisited', in E.C. Traugott and B. Heine, eds, *Approaches to Grammaticalization, Vol. 1* (Cambridge: Cambridge University Press, 1991), pp. 189–218.

Turkewitz, G. and R.C. Mellon, 'Dynamic Organization of Intersensory Function', *Canadian Journal of Psychology*, 43 (1989), 286–307.

Ulbaek, I., 'The Origin of Language and Cognition', in J.R. Hurford, M. Studdert-Kennedy and C. Knight, eds, *Approaches to the Evolution of Language* (Cambridge: Cambridge University Press, 1998), pp. 30–43.

Ullmann, S., *Language and Style* (Oxford: Blackwell, 1964).

Van Brakel, J., 'The Plasticity of Categories: The Case of Colour', *British Journal for the Philosophy of Science*, 44 (1993), 103–35.

Vandervert, L.R.I., 'The Evolution of Mandler's Conceptual Primitives (Image-Schemas) as Neural Mechanisms for Space-Time Simulation Structures', *New Ideas in Psychology*, 15 (1997), 105–123.

Vosniadou, S., A. Ortony, R.E. Reynolds and P.T. Wilson, 'Sources of Difficulty in Children's Comprehension of Metaphorical Language', *Child Development*, 55 (1984), 1588–606.

Wagner, S., E. Winner, D. Cicchetti, and H. Gardner, 'Metaphorical Mapping in Human Infants', *Child Development*, 52 (1981), 728–31.

Warrington, E.K. and T. Shallice, 'Category Specific Semantic Impairments', *Brain*, 107 (1984), 829–54.

Wellman, H.M., *The Child's Theory of Mind* (Cambridge, MA: MIT Press, 1990).

Wellman, H.M. and S.A. Gelman, 'Knowledge Acquisition in Functional Domains', in D. Kuhn and R.S. Siegler, eds, *Handbook of Child Psychology: Vol. 2, Cognition, Perception, and Language*, 5th edn (New York: Wiley, 1998), pp. 523–73.

Wierzbicka, A., 'What's in a Noun? (Or: How do Nouns Differ in Meaning from Adjectives?)', *Studies in Language*, 10 (1986), 353–89.

Wilkins, W.K. and J. Wakefield, 'Brain Evolution and Neurolinguistic Preconditions', *Behavioral and Brain Sciences*, 18 (1995), 161–226.

Wilks, Y., 'The "Fodor" – FODOR Fallacy Bites Back', in P. Bouillon and F. Busa, eds, *The Language of Word Meaning* (Cambridge: Cambridge University Press, 2001), pp. 75–85.

Williams, J.M., 'Synaesthetic Adjectives: A Possible Law of Semantic Change', *Language*, 52 (1976), 461–78.

Williams, J.N., 'Processing Polysemous Words in Context: Evidence for Interrelated Meanings', *Journal of Psycholinguistic Research*, 3 (1992), 193–218.

Wilson, D. and D. Sperber, 'Truthfulness and Relevance', *UCL Working Papers in Linguistics*, 12 (2000), 215–57.

Wilson, D. and D. Sperber, 'Relevance Theory', in G. Ward and L. Horn, eds, *Handbook of Pragmatics* (Oxford: Blackwell, forthcoming).

Winer, G.A., J.E. Cottrell, T. Mott, *et al.*, 'Are Children More Accurate than Adults? Spontaneous Use of Metaphor by Children and Adults', *Journal of Psycholinguistic Research*, 30 (2001), 485–96.

Winner, E., A. Rosenstiel, and H. Gardner, 'The Development of Metaphoric Understanding', *Developmental Psychology*, 12 (1976), 289–97.

Winner, E. and H. Gardner, 'The Comprehension of Metaphor in Brain-Damaged Patients', *Brain*, 100 (1977), 717–29.

Winner, E. and H. Gardner, 'Metaphor and Irony: Two Levels of Understanding', in A. Ortony, ed., *Metaphor and Thought*, 2nd edn (Cambridge: Cambridge University Press, 1993), pp. 425–43.

Young, J.Z., *Philosophy and the Brain* (Oxford: Oxford University Press, 1987).

Zaidel, E., A. Kasher, N. Soroker, and G. Batori, 'Effects of Right and Left Hemisphere Damage on Performance of the "Right Hemisphere Communication Battery"', *Brain and Language*, 80 (2002), 510–35.

Zuker, C.S., 'A Cool Ion Channel', *Nature*, 416 (2002), 27–8.

Index

Aaron, D., 24, 27, 175n. 6
adjectives, 127, 132, 151–2, 163–5
  polysemous adjectives, 2–3, 12, 14, 28, 32–3, 98, 107–8, 115–16, 127–33, 143, 165
  see also double-function adjectives; synaesthetic adjectives
ambiguity, 7, 14–15, 103, 120, 124, 129–30, 132–3, 136–7, 145, 153–4, 169
  see also homonymy; polysemy
Anaki, D., 100, 187n. 10
Apresjan, J., 167, 204n. 36
Asch, S.E., 30, 74–81, 85–6, 88–9, 98, 114

Bach, K., 154
Badecker, B., 106
Bailey, M.E.S., 51
Ballard, D.H., 25
Barkow, J., 69
Baron-Cohen, S., 51, 52–3, 57, 149
Barsalou, L.W., 25, 34, 111, 153, 177nn. 10, 12
Basbaum, A.I., 37, 41, 42, 43
Baynes, K., 106
Beardsley, M., 5–6
Békésy, G., 141
Berlin, B., 35, 36
Bialystok, E., 88
Bickerton, D., 72
Black, M., 5, 167
Blackburn, S., 117
Blasko, D.G., 129
Boguraev, B., 130
Borden, R.W., 57
Bornstein, M.H., 48–51, 56, 58–63, 67
Boynton, R.M., 36
Bower, T.G.R., 56
Braak, H., 31
Brown, A.L., 87
Brownell, H.H., 101–2

Burgess, C., 97, 98, 187n. 10
Bush, G., 31
Byrne, R., 149

Campbell, J.N., 41
Caplan, D., 31, 106
capsaicin, 34, 36–8, 45
  see also VR1
Caramazza, A., 106, 168
Carey, S., 138
Carston, R., 154–6, 159–60, 163, 170
Cassirer, E., 4
catachresis, 5
Caterina, M.J., 34, 38, 42, 45
causal theory of reference, 143–8
Chiarello, C., 98, 187n. 10
Chobor, K.L., 102–3
Chomsky, N., 176n. 9
Churchland, P.M., 24
Clapham, D.E., 36, 38, 146
Clark, A., 25
Clarke, D.D., 169
co-composition, 131–2
cognitive linguistics/semantics, 12, 18–33, 43, 79, 109–17, 139, 141, 168, 190–1n. 3, 204n. 33
cognitive science, 24–5
Cohen, J., 8
Cohen, T., 5
collocation, 46
compositionality, 13, 60, 127, 130–1, 137–8, 165
concepts, 31–2, 34, 44–5, 72, 105–8, 111, 118, 123–4, 127, 131, 135, 138, 142–3, 145–6, 150, 151, 163–5, 167, 169, 170
  abstract, 20–1, 22, 26–7, 141
  basic-level, 19–20
  colour, 28, 35–6
  of containment, 20, 25–6
  directly meaningful, 19–20, 26–7

concepts (*continued*)
  psychologically primitive, 68–9, 72–3, 79, 86, 96, 107, 139, 142–3, 148, 149–50, 152, 157, 165, 167, 168
  supramodal, 108, 142, 151, 183n. 21
conceptual atomism, 82–5, 122, 135–8
conceptual metaphor, 18, 21, 22, 27, 28, 31, 109, 176–7n. 10
conceptual primacy, 14, 19, 23, 33, 43, 67–8, 116, 139
conceptual structure/organization, 18, 23, 26, 31, 34–5, 44, 59–61, 67–8, 71–3, 84–5, 93, 96–7, 111, 115–17, 118–24, 129, 138, 140–1, 150, 165–7
Connine, C.M., 129
context
  independence, 11–12
  individuation, 201n. 24
  invariance, 136–8
  minimal, 158–9, 161
  modulation by, 119–20, 123, 151
  and pragmatic enrichment, 156–8
  and sense generation, 126–8, 132
  and sentence understanding, 153
Cooper, D., 9, 15
Costall, A., 72
Cramer, P., 88
cross-modal associations, 48–51, 54–70, 72
  neural basis of, 55–6
  innate character of, 56–8
Curtis, M., 88
Cytowic, R.E., 51–4, 69–70

Dahl, O., 24, 27
Dailey, A., 52
Damasio, A.R., 106, 111, 149
Dann, K.T., 52
Davidson, D., 9–11, 12, 14–15, 166
Davis, J.B., 42
dead metaphors, 8, 11, 15
de Gelder, B., 149
denotation, 6, 82, 131, 158, 162, 166–7
developmental psychology, 56–7
Dingwall, W.O., 71

Dixon, M.J., 52
Dixon, R.M.W., 73, 151
double-function adjectives, 3, 15, 74–82, 85–9, 90–104, 109–10, 114–16, 131, 135, 138, 139–140, 147–8, 167, 169, 200n. 18
Dretske, F., 84
Dummett, M., 82
Durkin, K., 168

Edelman, G.M., 19
Eimas, P., 26
embodiment, 18–20, 24–5, 27, 28, 34, 153, 157
  neural, 28–9
Ettlinger, G., 71, 72
etymology, 13, 110–13, 167
euphemism, 6
evolution, 69, 188n. 1
experience
  sensorimotor, 28–31
  subjective, 28–31
experientialism, 18, 19, 21, 176n. 10
explicature, 154–5, 202n. 26
extension, 6–7, 8, 9, 10–11, 13, 82, 144, 166

Fauconnier, G., 19, 170
Fields, H.L., 40–2
Flavell, J.H., 25, 185n. 9
Fodor, J.A., 53, 60, 82, 105, 119–20, 122–4, 127, 131–8, 151, 158, 169, 190n. 10, 196n. 1, 199n. 15, 203n. 32
Fodor, J.D., 120
Fogelin, R., 9
Frazier, L., 168
Frisson, S., 168
Frith, C.D., 70
Fuster, J.M., 70

Gardner, H., 86–9, 98–100, 102, 116
Garrett, M.F., 106
Gazzaniga, M.S., 106
generative lexicon, 124–38
Geschwind, N., 70–1
Gibbs, R.W., 15, 19, 23, 24, 27, 87, 97, 115, 129, 166, 168, 170, 171, 176–7n. 10, 182n. 14

Gibson, J.J., 56
Gilbert, A.N., 55
Giora, R., 97, 102, 166, 169
Glenberg, A.M., 19
Glucksberg, S., 129, 170, 177n. 11, 200n. 18
Goatly, A., 22, 174n. 2 to Ch. 2
Gold, M.S., 42
Goldstein, K., 103
Goodale, M.A., 22
Goodman, N., 6–7, 11, 13, 14
Goswami, U., 87
Grady, J.E., 29
Grice, H.P., 153, 158
Grober, E., 168
Grossenbacher, P.G., 52, 53, 181n. 7
Gruber, J.S., 121

Hallin, R.G., 41
Harrison, J., 57
Haskell, R.E., 61
Hayakawa, S.I., 169
hemispheric differences in language processing, 98–104
Hering, E., 36
Heywood, C.A., 149
Hintikka, J., 83
homonymy, 88, 91, 103, 125, 135–7, 140, 167–9, 175n. 4
Honeck, R.P., 27
Horner, J.M., 215
Hubbard, E.M., 51–3, 57, 70, 149, 182n. 18
Hubbard, T.L., 55
Humphreys, G., 70
Hurford, J.R., 72

image schemas, 20, 25–7, 29
implicature (conversational), 153–4
Indurkhya, B., 24, 27, 32
ion channels, 37
Iven, C., 106

Jackendoff, R., 24, 27, 119–24, 127–30, 175n. 6, 176n. 9, 195n. 20
Jacobs, B., 71
Johnson, C., 28
Johnson, K.J., 51

Johnson, M., 18–31, 109, 117, 168, 188n. 2
Johnson-Laird, P.N., 118–19
Julius, D., 34, 36–8, 41–3

Kamp, J.A.W., 153
Kang, H., 97
Katz, J.J., 158
Kay, P., 35, 36
Kelso, J.A.S., 25
Kentridge, R.W., 149
Keysar, B., 170
Kilgariff, A., 94, 97
Kirby, S., 72
Kittay, E.F., 7, 13, 22, 82, 168
Klepousniotou, E., 138, 170
Korb, K.B., 70
Kripke, S., 143–4
Kuraev, G.A., 113

Lakoff, G., 18–31, 34, 109, 117, 168, 176n. 9, 188n. 2
LaMotte, R.H., 41
Landau, B., 26
Langacker, R.W., 19
Langer, J., 73
languages
  Burmese, 81
  Chinese, 75–6, 79–80
  Dutch, 39–40
  English, 39–40, 46, 75–6, 79–80, 196n. 1, 198n. 9
  French, 39–40
  German, 39–40
  Greek (ancient), 39–40, 75, 80, 190n. 1
  Hausa, 75–6, 79, 81
  Hebrew, 75–6, 79–80
  Italian, 39–40
  Latin, 39–40
  Malayalam, 75–6, 79
  Russian, 39–40, 46–7, 80–1, 192n. 8, 197n. 1, 198n. 9
  Shilha, 76
  Spanish, 39–40, 198n. 9
  Thai, 75–6, 79–81
Lass, R., 111
Laurence, S., 26
Lehrer, A., 82

Lepore, E., 82, 127, 131–8, 169
Levin, S., 8
Lewkowicz, D.J., 57
lexical acquisition, 87
lexical semantics, 118–38, 140
Lewis, D., 165
Li, Y.F., 75, 107
limbic system, 31, 70
Liotti, M., 31
literal–meaning, 2, 11–12, 15, 68–9, 97, 144–7, 161–2, 165, 166–7
  as basic or primary, 7, 11, 12, 15, 111, 130, 138, 139, 164–5
literal–metaphorical distinction, 3, 8, 13, 22–3, 33, 82, 91, 141, 148, 166
literally or properly (speaking), 2, 11, 12, 59, 67, 113, 142–3
Lovelace, C.T., 52, 53, 181n. 7
Lowenthal, F., 31
Lucas, M., 97
Ludlow, P., 83, 199n. 17
Luria, A.R., 51, 53, 103
Lyons, J., 112, 168

Ma, Q.-P., 42
Mac Cormac, E.R., 22
Mandler, J.M., 26
Manning, J., 168
Maratsos, M., 24, 27, 32
Marconi, D., 13, 28, 177n. 10
Margolis, E., 26
Markman, E.M., 87
Marks, L.E., 48–51, 54–6, 58–68, 113, 143
Martino, G., 54–5, 64–6, 68
Maryanski, A., 71
Mattingley, J.B., 52
Maurer, D., 57
McCleskey, E.W., 42
McDaniel, C.K., 36
McDonald, J.J., 55
meaning, 8, 27–8, 105, 125, 127, 131, 136, 142, 144–6, 148, 150, 152–3, 164, 165–8
  see also literal meaning; metaphoric meaning
meaning atomism, 82–3, 131, 135–7
meaning holism, 60, 82–3

meaning representation, 93–4, 96–7, 101, 115–16, 120, 125–9, 137–8
Melara, R.D., 64, 65
Mellon, R.C., 56
Meltzoff, A.N., 57
mental lexicon, 90–2, 94, 130–1, 136
mental representation, 105, 117, 118–22, 131
  see also concepts; conceptual structure/organization
Meredith, A.M., 55–7, 70
metaphor, 3, 4, 67, 130, 163, 166–71, 200n. 18
  and development, 28–31, 49–50, 58–62, 64–5, 77–9, 85–9
  and imagery, 14–15
  paraphrasability of, 5, 10
  primary, 29–32, 44, 181–2n. 14
  and propositional content, 10, 170
  and reality, 174n. 3
  tension in, 5
  theories of, 4–11, 139
  and unidirectionality, 29, 111
metaphor understanding, 98–104, 115, 166
  see also metaphor and development
metaphoric meaning, 2, 141, 143, 146–8, 167, 169–70
metaphoric representation, 24, 28, 32
metaphorical projection, 20, 22, 26, 44, 113–16
metaphorical use, 4, 13, 110, 164, 167
metaphysics, 202–3n. 27
Mezey, E., 43
Miles, H.L., 71
Miller, G., 118–19
Mills, C.B., 52
Milner, A.D., 22
Mitchell, R.W., 71
modularity, 52–3
monosemy, 168
Morgan, J., 83
Morris, J.S., 149
Morton, J.B., 88
multisensory integration, 55, 65, 113
Murphy, G.L., 24, 27, 32, 115, 175n. 2, 189nn. 4, 8, 205n. 36

Nagy, I., 42
Narayanan, S., 29
natural kind terms, 144–8
Neirlich, B., 169
Nerlove, H., 77–8, 85–6, 88–9
Newmeyer, F.J., 72
no-polysemy view, 67–9, 79, 82–3, 86–7, 89, 90–1, 94, 96–7, 98, 108, 119, 139–53, 165–71
nociceptors, 37–8, 40–1
Nunberg, G., 195n. 20

Odgaard, E.C., 52
Olson, C.X., 36
Origgi, G., 155
Ortony, A., 30
Osgood, C.E., 51

Paradis, M., 98, 100
Paulesu, E., 70
Perner, J., 25
Piaget, J., 25, 56, 175–6n. 9
Pickering, M., 168
Pinkal, M., 166
Pinker, S., 69, 106
Plotkin, H., 69
polysemy, 22, 28–9, 32, 45, 75, 87–8, 91–4, 118–26, 131–8, 165–6, 167–9
  logical, 125–6, 130, 134–5, 167
  see also adjectives, polysemous adjectives
pragmatic processes, 153–8, 161, 163
properties
  and literal meaning, 5–6, 11, 141–6, 149–50, 166
prototypes, 60
psycholinguistics, 90–4, 101–3
Pustejovsky, J., 125–38
Putnam, H., 143
Pylyshyn, Z.W., 15, 167

qualia structure, 125–35
Quartz, S.R., 178n. 13
Quine, W.V., 167

Ramachandran, V.S., 51–3, 57, 70, 149, 182n. 18
Rang, H.P., 42

Rayner, K., 168
Récanati, F., 154, 156, 161, 201–2n. 24, 203n. 27
relevance
  theory, 154–61
  principle of, 154, 159, 161, 163
Rey, G., 105
Richards, I.A., 4–5, 12, 200n. 18
Ricoeur, P., 4
Ringkamp, M., 42
Rorty, R., 9
Rosch, E., 35
Rose, S.A., 57
Rousset, F., 15
Ruhl, C., 168, 186n. 6

Sadock, J.M., 9
Sandu, G., 83
Schumacher, M.A., 42
Schweiger, A., 102–3
Searle, J.R., 9, 74–5, 161–2
Seidenberg, M.S., 97
Sejnowsky, T.J., 178n. 13
selective binding, 127
semantic change, 109–13
semantic decomposition, 119–24
semantic fields, 120–4
semantic fields theory, 7, 82–3
semantic generalizations, 120–2
semantic knowledge, 153
semantic mediation (in metaphor), 44, 51, 64–6, 140–1
semantic normativity, 13, 14, 28
semantic primitives, 119–21, 127
semantic representation (level of), 151–3, 165, 169
  see also meaning representation
semantics, 118–19, 138, 169
sense
  in context, 126–7
  enumeration, 125, 127, 141
  relations, 82, 119
sentence meaning, 153
Shen, Y., 113–14, 174n. 2 to Ch. 2
similarity
  in metaphor, 3, 67, 78, 87, 169, 200n. 18
  perceptual, 44, 49, 142
  types of, 48–9, 87

Simpson, G.B., 97
Smilek, D., 52
Smith, L.B., 25, 182n. 15
Spalding, J.M.K., 53
Spelke, E.S., 57
Sperber, D., 154–5, 159–65, 170, 196n.1
standard assumption, 3, 5, 7, 8, 23, 32–3, 43, 66–7, 82, 90, 98, 139–43, 203n. 32
Stanley, J., 151, 155, 199–200n. 17
Stein, B.E., 55–7, 70
Stern, J., 7–8, 9, 15, 171, 177n. 11, 188n. 2
Sutherland, P., 25
Sweetser, E., 61, 109–17, 174n. 2 to Ch. 2
synaesthesia, 48, 51–4, 57–8, 64–6, 69–70
adaptive character of, 52–4
synaesthetic adjectives, 2, 15, 48–50, 56, 58–69, 72–3, 99–100, 109, 113–14, 116, 131, 135, 138, 139–44, 146–8, 150, 152–3, 167, 169
synaesthetic metaphors, see synaesthetic adjectives
Szabó, Z.G., 151, 155, 199–200n. 17

Tabossi, P., 91, 97
thematic relations hypothesis, 121–2
Tompkins, C.A., 101

Torebjork, H.E., 41
Tranel, D., 106
Trehub, S.E., 88
true complement coercion, 133–4
Turkewitz, G., 56–7
Turner, M., 19, 170, 177n. 11

Vandervert, L.R.I., 26
Vosniadou, S., 89
VR1 (vanilloid receptor subtype 1 or 'capsaicin receptor'), 36–8, 42, 145–7

Wagner, S., 57
Wakefield, J., 71–3
Wellman, H.M., 25
what is said, 153–4
Wierzbicka, A., 151
Wilkins, W.K., 71–3
Williams, J.M., 111
Williams, J.N., 91–7, 115
Wilson, D., 154–5, 159–65, 170, 196n. 1
Wilson, W.A., 72
Winer, G.A., 140
Winner, E., 86–7, 98–100, 102, 116

Young, J.Z., 178n. 13

Zaidel, E., 102
Zangwill, O., 53
Zardon, F., 97

西方语言学原版影印系列丛书

06884/H·0963　语义学与语用学：语言与话语中的意义　K.Jaszczolt
06878/H·0957　字面意义的疆域：隐喻、一词多义以及概念概论　M.Rakova
06883/H·0962　英语语篇：系统和结构　J.R.Martin
06877/H·0956　作为语篇的语言：对语言教学的启示　M.McCarthy 等
06887/H·0966　布拉格学派，1945–1990　Luelsdorf 等
06881/H·0960　认知语法基础1　R.W.Langacker
07694/H·1090　认知语法基础2　R.W.Langacker
06686/H·0965　论自然和语言　N.Chomsky
06880/H·0959　语料库语言学的多因素分析　S.T.Gries
06882/H·0961　美国社会语言学：理论学家与理论团队　S.O.Murray
06879/H·0958　英语教学中的教材和方法——教师手册　J.Mcdonough 等
07592/H·1055　英语语言文化史　G.Knowles
06885/H·0964　分析散文　R.A.Lanham
07596/H·1059　语法化　P.J.Hopper
08727/H·1451　古英语入门　B.Mitchell 等
07594/H·1057　美国英语入门　G.Tottie
07593/H·1056　英语语言史：社会语言学研究　B.A.Fennell
07595/H·1058　语言学入门纲要　G.Hudson
08673/H·1422　语言的结构与运用　E.Finegan
08738/H·1454　语言艺术的学与教　D.Strickland

北京大学出版社

邮购部电话：010-62534449　　联系人：孙万娟
市场营销部电话：010-62750672
外语编辑部电话：010-62767315　62767347

出 版 说 明

  "西方语言学原版影印系列丛书"旨在推介国外语言学领域经典的和新近的英文原版优秀著作和文献,使我国读者能够接触到原汁原味的第一手资料。

  需要申明的是,对于作者的一些观点和结论尚需商榷,有些甚至是不可取的。这些观点不代表出版社观点,也提请读者加以甄别。

北京大学出版社
2004 年 8 月